The Beginning of Broadcast Regulation
in the Twentieth Century

The Beginning of Broadcast Regulation in the Twentieth Century

by MARVIN R. BENSMAN

McFarland & Company, Inc., Publishers
Jefferson, North Carolina, and London

Library of Congress Cataloguing-in-Publication Data

Bensman, Marvin R., 1937–
    The beginning of broadcast regulation in the twentieth century /
by Marvin R. Bensman.
        p.   cm.
    Includes bibliographical references and index.
    ISBN 0-7864-0737-9 (softcover : 50# alkaline paper) ∞
    1. Broadcasting—Law and legislation—United States—History.
I. Title.
KF2814.B46   2000
343.7309'94—dc21
                                                    99-56536

British Library Cataloguing-in-Publication data are available

Manufactured in the United States of America

McFarland & Company, Inc., Publishers
    Box 611, Jefferson, North Carolina 28640
    www.mcfarlandpub.com

ACKNOWLEDGMENTS

Appreciation and gratitude are expressed to many individuals who assisted me with this project.

I wish to acknowledge my dear friend, the late Armand Schneider for his encouragement and his time and skill in assisting in the editing of this work.

Acknowledgment goes to the librarians at the Herbert Hoover Presidential Library in West Branch, Iowa; the National Archives; and the Smithsonian Institution's Division of Electricity, which provided me with their time and expert knowledge.

But most of all, this work is dedicated to my family, whose patience, understanding and forbearance are without measure—my wife Harriet, my children David and Saiko and Lauren and John and, of course, my grandchild, Berret—and who supply the love that makes work a joy.

Marvin R. Bensman
Professor
University of Memphis

CONTENTS

PREFACE

The current electronic media are the inheritors of a tradition where problems of regulation have been long debated and thrashed out. Broadcasting quickly became an important element in the political and social structure, and this importance was acknowledged by the government's determination to impose regulations. The electronic media are so vital to the security and well-being of the people that their work cannot be carried on effectively without some government regulation. The question of how much regulation is necessary has yet to be completely resolved.

The mushrooming growth of radio broadcasting led to problems such as technical interference and "chaos in the ether," wavelength piracy, hucksterism, censorship and monopoly. Most of the earliest regulatory activity was devoted to preventing interference among stations. However, the Commerce Department began to regulate content when it determined in 1923 that stations using live, local programming would get preferential treatment in power and frequency. When Congress passed the first legislation to deal with "radio," the Radio Act of 1927, the Department of Commerce had already been regulating the infant broadcast industry for six years.

The issues that dominate today's discussions of media control have their antecedents during those crucial early years. It is these issues which this book attempts to address. Always the central question remains: What is the function of government in regulating the broadcast media?

I began my research for this book while a student at the University of Wisconsin–Madison. Research has continued through a career in teaching at the University of Vermont and the University of Memphis. The result you have in your hands is a distillation of how our unique regulatory system developed. It discusses the primary technological, economic and social factors

which led to the American system of broadcasting, combining private enterprise and limited government regulation.

The development of government regulation of broadcasting is a story of
America's struggle to achieve maximum benefits from a new technology under
a system of democratic, free enterprise as a product of particular needs and
values. That struggle was a long evolutionary process, yet the basic features
are much the same today as they were at the beginning.

Knowing how America dealt with the crucial issues facing the regulators and the regulated during the 20th century is fundamental to an understanding of broadcast regulations today. Future development and insight come
from knowing how "the past is prologue."

Marvin R. Bensman
Winter 2000

Chapter I

THE DEVELOPMENT
OF RADIO REGULATION

Radio technology and its regulation began in the first decades of the 20th century. Social, political and technological implications paved the way to regulation of broadcasting by the federal government. Without some knowledge of the developmental and historical factors, one cannot understand the present or predict the future. We are at a crossroads of fundamental policy decisions that will determine the future of communications access and control for the next century.

The history of congressional action in the field of communications reaches well back into the 19th century with the Post Roads Act of 1866, in which Congress sought "to aid in the construction of telegraph lines and to secure to the Government the use of the same for postal, military, and other purposes."[1]

Scotch physicist James Clerk Maxwell laid the foundation for radio transmission experimentation in an 1873 paper describing the nature of electromagnetic energy. His theories were tested by a German, Heinrich Hertz, the first person actually to generate and detect radio waves in a laboratory. A paper written by Hertz in 1888 describing his experiments was read by Guglielmo Marconi, who actively applied what was being developed by others.

With commercial application in mind, Marconi moved radio transmission outside the confines of the laboratory in 1895 by sending a signal a mile through space. Patriotically, he offered his wireless system to his own Italian government, which refused to consider the invention, saying it was "not serious enough to deserve official consideration."[2] Marconi received a friendlier reception in England as he began his struggle to achieve more distance. His efforts reached a triumphant climax in 1901 when he claimed to have transmitted a radio signal 2,000 miles across the Atlantic Ocean.[3] Marconi established his first company in the U.K. and then others throughout the world.

A newly combined U.S. Department of Commerce and Labor came into being on February 14, 1903. With 13 subdivisions, the combined department was one of the largest and most complicated branches of the federal government and would assume responsibility for the oversight of electronic transmissions which were still in their embryonic stages.[4]

The increase in experimental activity between 1903 and 1916 led to attempts to specifically regulate wireless transmission. Between 1902 and 1912 some 28 bills were introduced in Congress to deal with the increasing problem of interference between wireless transmissions. Most of the proposed legislation did not take into account the fact that electromagnetic energy does not recognize boundaries or state lines.[5]

The Wireless Telegraph Act of Great Britain was passed in 1903, which placed wireless under the British Post Office. Wireless was clearly such a potential saver of lives and property in peril at sea that other types of transmission, which caused interference, had to be overcome. That same year Germany called the First International Convention on wireless, stemming partly from the refusal of the Marconi Company to relay signals from a yacht belonging to a German prince on a visit to North America. The eight nations represented at the conference issued a protocol calling for cooperation between all wireless systems. Each country would have to pass enabling laws to encourage, yet control, this phenomenon within its borders. Plans were to reconvene the following year.[6]

The United States took its first steps to regulate wireless regulation on July 12, 1904, when President Theodore Roosevelt formed an interdepartmental board consisting of the Departments of Commerce and Labor, Navy, War and Agriculture.[7] The Department of Commerce and Labor's interest in radio had begun that year when Dr. Louis W. Austin, an assistant professor in physics at the University of Wisconsin, joined the staff of the Bureau of Standards, a division of the Department.[8] Dr. Austin came to the Bureau as a guest worker to investigate the practical applications of wireless telegraphy as they applied to Navy problems.[9] The Interdepartmental Board's recommendations constitute the first well-defined radio policy of the United States government.

In brief, these were:

> a) The Navy be designated to provide efficient coastwise [ship to shore] radio communications for the United States Government and when not in competition with commercial stations to receive and transmit all radio messages to and from ships at sea.
>
> b) The Army be authorized to erect such stations as deemed necessary provided they do not interfere with the coastwise radio system of the Government under the control of the Navy Department.

c) Legislation to prevent the control of radio telegraphy by monopolies or trusts should place supervision in the Department of Commerce and Labor.[10]

A few months later the subject of wireless legislation became a topic of discussion in the Navy Department and the Department of Commerce and Labor. In January 1905 the Secretary of the Navy sent to the Department of Commerce and Labor a memorandum by Admiral Manney containing a proposed draft for wireless legislation. This was referred to a committee which had been appointed to consider the recommendations of the Interdepartmental Board and the positions the United States should take at the Second International Wireless Telegraph Conference. Manney's proposed legislation was opposed by Marconi's company and others, but some wireless companies believed it would be beneficial alike to both governmental and private interests.

Two men were instrumental in developing the devices which turned electromagnetic waves into a vehicle for speech and sound during the early 1900s. One was Reginald A. Fessenden, a professor of electrical engineering at the University of Pittsburgh who had worked in Edison's lab. In 1906 he succeeded in impressing sound on an electromagnetic carrier wave. He broadcast to Navy radio operators who were astonished to hear sound and music in earphones that previously had only brought them dots and dashes. The second was Lee de Forest (Ph.D. Yale–1899) who in 1907 invented the audion tube, which became one of the basic elements in modern transmitting and receiving equipment. This tube made it possible to: 1) amplify radio energy without distortion, and 2) generate the high-frequency radio wave needed to carry speech and music. However, de Forest initially only considered his invention as a detector of radio energy rather than a more advanced generator and or amplifier as well.

The German government called the Second International Wireless Telegraph Conference in 1906 after it had been postponed for various reasons. This conference, attended by 27 nations, provided for the use of two wavelengths for public correspondence in the maritime services: 200 (999.4 kHz) and 600 (499.7 kHz) meters. Wavelengths over 1600 (187.4 kHz) meters were, under certain conditions, to be used for long distance communication with coastal stations. Six hundred to 1600 meters were reserved for use by military and naval stations.[11] The international distress call was also changed from CQD (roughly, "calling all stations, disaster") to an arbitrary three dots, three dashes, and three dots, the famous SOS (Save Our Ship). These agreements were to take effect on July 1, 1908, but there were many delays and complications. Countries with Marconi company contracts asked for time to work out modifications of their agreements. Other factors helped to sway public opinion in the direction of some governmental control of wireless.

There were business scandals involving de Forest in the United States and Marconi stock in the United Kingdom. The most technologically developed countries were militantly nationalistic, and each rallied around and supported its own radio equipment manufacturers with standards based on political policy rather than technology alone. There was confusion over rates, equipment standards and interconnection procedures.[12]

Congress initially refused to ratify the Berlin Convention agreement, accepting the testimony of American wireless manufacturing firms that the agreements would stifle the development of wireless and place it under international rather than national control.[13] The Senate's failure to ratify caused all government departments concerned with radio to intensify their efforts to obtain legislation for federal supervision of wireless. The Navy Department led these efforts. Commercial wireless companies and amateur interests were opposed to any legislation which would affect their interests.[14]

Public opinion overcame the reluctance of the second ("lameduck") session of the 60th Congress to regulate wireless. There were no early resolutions involving wireless introduced to replace those which had died at the adjournment of the first session of 1908, and there is no indication that any would have been introduced had not the public's attention been attracted by a marine disaster.

On January 23, 1908, the liner *Republic*, with 440 passengers, collided with the Italian S.S. *Florida*, crowded with 830 immigrants. The *Republic's* sole wireless operator was able to signal for assistance. Six people were lost, but all the rest were saved by ships which arrived in response to the wireless message. Within days there was considerable editorial comment on the role wireless had played in limiting the loss of life. Like life preservers, wireless became a shipboard necessity. President Theodore Roosevelt sent a special message to Congress on February 8, 1908, recommending the immediate passage of legislation requiring, within reasonable limits, ocean-going vessels to be fitted with efficient wireless equipment.[15]

This bill was supported by commercial interests because it did not specifically regulate their activities and, if it became law, would actually enhance their business. The Commissioner of Navigation of the Department of Commerce, Eugene T. Chamberlain, urged an amendment requiring all companies to exchange messages in time of distress or emergency, which had been recommended by the First International Wireless Conference to prevent the monopoly developing from Marconi patent control. The controversy surrounding this issue prevented the amendment from being added to the legislation.[16] It was not until the planners of a Third International Wireless Conference, to be held in London in 1912, quietly withdrew the invitation to the United States for lack of compliance with their earlier protocols that Congress would pass the first wireless law in the U.S., the Wireless Ship Act of 1910.[17]

Wireless Ship Act of 1910. The Wireless Ship Act of 1910, passed after several attempts, contained in one page nearly all the requirements called for in the 1906 Berlin protocol: ocean-going vessels with 50 or more passengers traveling between ports 200 or more miles apart had to carry wireless apparatus capable of reaching 100 miles day or night and an operator to run it. It met the demands of the 1903 and 1906 conferences indirectly, calling for "an efficient apparatus for radio-communication" and then defining "efficient" by stating that "apparatus for radio-communication shall not be deemed to be efficient unless the company installing it shall contract in writing to exchange, and shall, in fact, exchange ... messages with shore or ship stations using other systems of radio-communication." This provision, together with similar laws passed in other countries (one in the United Kingdom as early as 1904 called for trained wireless operators), solved the problem of compliance with the international agreements.

The 1910 act was not cited as the logical precedent it was when television was faced with the problem of sets that could not pick up UHF stations in the late 1950s and early 1960s. Congress then required manufacturers to make sets that could receive all channels.[18]

Enforcement of the first U.S. radio law was placed under the jurisdiction of the Department of Commerce and Labor. Since the United States was still not bound to the Convention of 1906, there was no compulsion in the Act of 1910 for stations to use the wavelengths of 300 and 600 meters prescribed for maritime use. However, many ships involved in international trade adhered to the Convention regulations.[19]

The first step under the new law was the creation of a radio inspection service headed by Eugene T. Chamberlain, commissioner of navigation for the Department of Commerce from 1908 to 1921.[20]

In 1911 the Bureau of Standards of the Department of Commerce entered the wireless field when an engineer for one of the new commercial electric signaling companies sent in a frequency meter for calibration. The problem of setting up a standard for this instrument was given to J. Howard Dellinger, a physics instructor working on his doctorate from Western Reserve University. Dellinger soon headed the new radio measurements section of the electrical division.[21]

Earlier in 1911 Professor A. G. Webster of Clark University had submitted his draft of proposed regulations on the use of wireless as a safety aid in navigation. Dellinger reviewed the paper and suggested that the word "wireless" be changed to "radio" everywhere in the text, in keeping with its connotation of radiation.[22] Thus, "radio" rather than "wireless" became the accepted term in this country.

On the night of April 14, 1912, two months before the Third International Wireless Conference in London, the liner *Titanic*, on its maiden voyage, struck an iceberg 800 miles off the coast of Nova Scotia. The disaster disclosed how unreliable maritime wireless telegraphy was at that time. Ships' wireless were often in the hands of inexperienced operators who found signals hard to understand and who were hampered by the necessity of having to relay and send repeats of messages—most of them for passengers beguiled by the novelty of wireless. Most ships had only one operator.

Four ships were within 60 miles of the *Titanic* when it sent out its first call for help. All, at various times that day, had warned the ship of the ice fields in the vicinity. One, the *Californian*, was less than ten miles away when the CQD went out.[23]

Of the other ships in the vicinity of the *Titanic*, only the Cunard liner *Carpathia*, 58 miles away, dared to chance the ice field in which the *Titanic* was sinking. When it arrived, a bare handful of lifeboats and rafts drifted in the area where the *Titanic* had sunk more than an hour before.[24]

The *Titanic* disaster was the compelling reason behind the passage of an amendment to the Act of 1910, which provided that two operators be available for continuous duty on ships carrying more than 50 passengers.

The *Titanic* is also often cited inaccurately as the reason for drawing up the Radio Act of 1912. The subcommittee of the Senate Commerce Committee had actually completed its work on this bill and the bill had been reported out prior to the *Titanic* disaster.[25] It had become apparent that the United States would have to ratify the 1906 Berlin Convention in order to be invited to the forthcoming London Conference.[26] The Senate Committee on Foreign Relations hastily removed the treaty from its tabled status and quickly reported it out, where it was passed by Congress.[27]

With ratification of the treaty it was necessary to pass a new radio law to ensure compliance with the Berlin Convention provisions. This became the Radio Act of 1912. The *Titanic* disaster had awakened Congress to the necessity for such legislation and ensured its final enactment.

Radio Act of 1912. The Radio Act of August 13, 1912, passed shortly after the London Convention, was a new piece of legislation to provide for the licensing of radio operators and transmitting stations. For nearly 15 years radio operators and radio stations were licensed under this law, which remained in effect until 1927.

The law was designed to serve two purposes:

> First, to promote safety of life and property at sea and to promote commerce by facilitating the dispatch of ships.
> Second, to secure by Federal regulation the fullest use of radio communication made necessary by the fact that in the present state of the art unregulated interference would impair or prevent almost all use.[28]

Congress provided for licensing and entrusted the administration of the system to the Department of Commerce's Bureau of Navigation. The bureau had inspected ships leaving United States harbors for proper wireless apparatus under the Wireless Ship Act of 1910.

The Senate Committee, in its report on the bill, said:

> The term "radio communication" instead of "radio telegraphy" is used throughout the bill so that its provisions will cover the possibility of the commercial development of radio telephony (Sec. 6, p. 14). Experiments have been made here and abroad for some years in carrying the human voice on hertzian waves, but with only limited and occasional results. Radio telephony involves the application of the same principles as are involved in inventions to enable apparatus to select and record accurately one message on a given wavelength out of a mass of messages on various lengths. When this latter result has been obtained—an unfulfilled promise of some years' standing—radio telephony will quickly follow. The bill is framed to be adjustable to that improvement when it comes, but in the meantime it deals with the art as it exists today.[29]

A deficiency of the Radio Act of 1912, which had far-reaching consequences, was that 19 very specific regulations were embodied in the law but no power to establish and enforce further regulations was given to the Secretary of Commerce.

The accompanying report of the Senate Committee on Commerce stated:

> The former bills delegated to the President of the United States in the first instance and subsequently to the Secretary of Commerce and Labor the power to make regulations governing radio communication which would have the force of law. That amounted practically, at least in the judgment of some members of this committee, to the surrender by Congress of its powers and the bestowal of legislative power to all intents and purposes upon administrative officers.[30]

Thus, the committee, which understood that radio telephony (voice transmission) might someday be possible, decided the political issue of delegation of powers to make it difficult to regulate radio broadcasting with the Act of 1912. There was little recognition that there could not be direct congressional control of spectrum allocation. The new medium of communication was too complex and involved for the individual senator or representative to understand. Without such expertise, Congress would not be able to respond quickly to changed circumstances with constantly updated legislation.

Opinion of the Attorney General. The Committee on Merchant Marine and Fisheries in its report to the House said:

> The first section of the bill defines its scope within the commerce clause of the Constitution, and requires all wireless stations, ship and shore, public and private, to be licensed by the Secretary of Commerce and Labor. This section does not give the head of that department discre-

> tionary power over the issue of the licenses, but in fact provides for ...
> the same as that in use for the documenting of ... merchant vessels.[31]

Soon after the act was passed the question was raised as to whether the Secretary of Commerce could exercise any discretion in the issuing of licenses, or whether he was under the mandatory duty to grant them to any and all applicants.

This question first arose when the Secretary of Commerce attempted to deny a license to a station which was a subsidiary of certain German interests. Germany did not allow American-owned or controlled stations to operate in their country and the Secretary wanted to apply pressure until a reciprocal arrangement could be arranged with Germany.

The Secretary of Commerce asked for an opinion from the U.S. Attorney General concerning the scope of his licensing power. The Attorney General stated on November 22, 1912, that:

> The language of the act, the nature of the subject matter regulated, as well as the general scope of the statute, negate the idea that Congress intended to repose any such discretion in you in the matter of licenses. It is apparent from the act as a whole that Congress determined thereby to put the subject of radio communication under Federal supervision so far as it was interstate or foreign in its nature. It is also apparent there from that supervision and control is taken by Congress upon itself, and that the Secretary of Commerce and Labor is only authorized to deal with the matter as provided in the act, and is given no general regulative power in respect thereto. The act prescribes the conditions under which the licenses shall operate, containing a set of regulations, with penalties for their violation.[32]

Fifteen years later, in 1927, Attorney General William Donovan gave a similar opinion to Secretary Herbert Hoover. Although the 1912 opinion clearly restricted the Secretary of Commerce to the 19 regulations specifically embodied in the Act of 1912, the Department of Commerce used as a lever a clause that directed him to license for the "least possible interference." However, in reality Congress had given no one the authority or power to meet any new problems which might arise with the rapid development of radiotelephony. The Secretary of Commerce and Labor could not assign wavelengths for commercial use within the band of 600 to 1600 meters (499.7 kHz to 187.4 kHz) reserved for the government. The fact that a "normal" wavelength might be written on the face of the license did not give the Department of Commerce actual power of wavelength assignment, only nebulous control. Nevertheless, the controls which did exist were a step forward and no serious problems arose for some eight years until the explosive growth of regular commercial broadcasting.[33] When the Wilson administration took office in 1913 the Department of Commerce and Labor was separated into two departments.

The primary impetus for radio research and development during this early period was the Navy. Equipment utilizing the de Forest three-element vacuum tube was being developed and refined. However, the tubes were expensive, short-lived, and lacked uniformity due to de Forest's persistent belief that some residual gas should be left in the tube. By the end of 1913 Dr. H. E. Arnold of the American Telephone and Telegraph Company and Dr. Irving Langmuir of the General Electric Company arrived at the same conclusion: that the instability of de Forest's tubes "was caused by gas ionization, that this defect could be removed by increasing the vacuum."[34]

Edwin H. Armstrong had patented what was to become an important device, the regenerative, or "feedback" circuit.[35] The de Forest experimental radiophone station at High Bridge, New York, broadcast election bulletins to a limited audience in 1916. These were heard by amateur operators within a radius of 200 miles.[36]

World War I. The First World War reduced the activities of the Bureau of Navigation of the Department of Commerce considerably; however, the Bureau of Standards increased its radio research activities.

The Bureau of Standards radio laboratories, under Dr. J. Howard Dellinger and Frederick A. Kolster, as well as labs operated by the Navy and the Signal Corps, were relatively small units and for the most part were more concerned with basic radio phenomena than with their practical applications.

How far behind the United States was in utilization of the vacuum tube became known in 1917 when a French scientific mission left some of its scientific apparatus with the Bureau. Included was a great variety of radio equipment which had been developed around the electron tube.[37]

Although the electron or vacuum tube amplifier was the invention of Fessenden and de Forest in this country, its use by the military was only experimental. They still used damped wave apparatus that limited them to code telegraphy. A decade of patent litigation centering around the vacuum tube had blunted the growth of radio in the United States. The French, on the other hand, with government control of rights to the vacuum tube, used it in all their radio apparatus, in wire telephony, and in their radio telephone.[38]

Bureau of Standards Director Samuel Wesley Stratton, who had founded the Bureau in 1901 and remained its director for 21 years, reported to Congress in 1918: "It is time we should be working out the new things in radio communication instead of depending on foreign countries for scientific developments."[39] But even the Bureau had been unable to function with freedom because the experimental and commercial exploitation of the vacuum tube remained locked in the courts.

The patent impasse in the United States was broken on April 7, 1917, when by presidential proclamation all commercial radio, which comprised some 60 stations serving maritime commerce, were handed over to the Navy and all other stations were closed down for the duration of the war. The only exception, apparently, was the University of Wisconsin station, WHA, which served as a navigational aid in the Great Lakes area.[40]

The Navy, long anxious to secure better equipment for its ships, its coastal stations and the radio chain it operated over the Pacific, immediately pressed for better technology and equipment. Small companies sprang up overnight to manufacture radio equipment because the government assumed all liability for patent infringements. The big three, General Electric, Westinghouse and Western Electric dominated the field over the smaller and newer companies.[41]

The President's proclamation, the French contribution of apparatus, and the needs of the Army and Navy provided the major stimuli for the attack on the nation's wartime radio problems: the training of technicians, civilian and military, in a complex and rapidly changing subject; the establishment of low-powered radio equipment for battlefield communication; radio means for locating radio stations, airplanes, submarines when submerged; and portable radio apparatus.[42]

Dr. Louis Austin, who had begun work in the Navy laboratory at the Bureau of Standards to try to strengthen signals from the upper layer of the atmosphere, now took up the development of new radio apparatus.

In the Bureau of Standards laboratories the immediate consideration was the training of thousands of men in radio communication for the Signal Corps to meet battlefield needs.

The Bureau and the military services were bombarded with ideas for using radio as a weapon of war. Most notable perhaps was Thomas Edison's proposal to establish a transmitting station near Ostend, in British-held Flanders, to interfere with radio communication between German submarines and their bases. The Bureau told him that a single station probably would not be sufficient. And even if it were, interfering signals sent out from that one station in Flanders might well spread along the whole of the Western Front and confuse all radio communication in the area.[43]

A more practical approach to the U-boat menace at the beginning of the war seemed to be the further development of an experimental radio direction finder by Frederick Kolster of the Bureau of Standards radio lab. With the incorporation of a French electron tube amplifier and a new coil antenna replacing the former aerial, a more compact unit with greater range was achieved. It was seen not only as an aid to air and sea navigation but as a potential means of locating enemy radio-sending apparatus and the enemy himself. Experiments with the radio direction finder as an aid to aviation began in 1918, soon after the Post Office Department started a daily airmail service between New York and Washington.[44]

The Bureau of Standards was drawn into these and other projects as the organization best able to handle such problems for other governmental agencies. One of the prime functions of the bureau was the solution of problems relating to measurement, and this, in turn, led to a number of patentable materials, processes and products.

The Bureau of Standards' mission of providing and maintaining basic measurements in radio research was invaluable for its careful and constant reassessments of standards of inductance and capacitance on which regulatory standards of radio-frequency or wavelength were based. The Bureau's work on the new electron tube was also a major contribution to the industry.

With patent litigation suspended, radio manufacturers turned out large numbers and varieties of vacuum tubes as generators, detectors, amplifiers and modulators of radio waves and other electrical currents. The Bureau measured the characteristics of experimental and production tubes, devised test methods and apparatus, standardized certain types of tubes and conducted studies of tube behavior in a number of different circuits.[45]

Of special importance in the Bureau's work with vacuum tubes were its studies of such phenomena as the effects of diurnal fluctuations, solar activity and atmospheric electricity on radio communication.

Wartime research on the electron tube helped develop reliable long-distance wire telephony as well as wireless speech communication between ground stations and airplanes. Incorporating the vacuum tube in the directional finder made it a convenient and portable device that was to later prove as useful in detecting transmitting stations violating radio laws as it was in guiding planes and ships though fog. As an amplifier, the vacuum tube permitted very small antennas and, by greatly extending the range of radio communications, ushered in radio's coming of age.[46]

Radio Development After the War. The radio age did not leap forward with the armistice. The development of radio broadcasting was delayed first by the threat of government ownership and then by renewal of the patent wars of the radio industry. Under the widely held assumption that radio was essentially an instrument of navigation and of national defense, and therefore should be under government control as it was in Europe, bills to that effect were introduced to Congress. These bills were proposed on behalf of the Navy Department and presented in January 1917, and again in 1918. On both occasions Congress was reluctant to establish outright governmental control and tabled the proposals.[47] Secretary of Commerce William C. Redfield and Dr. Samuel W. Stratton both favored government control of radio, either by the Navy Department or Department of Commerce.

Unable to convince Congress to keep total control within the government, but still concerned with the development of its radio system, the Navy urged General Electric, largest of the radio manufacturers, to buy out the British-backed Marconi Company. The Marconi commercial radio system had been taken over by the Navy in 1917 and was to be returned at the end of the war. General Electric's acceptance of the Navy's suggestion resulted in the formation in October 1919 of the Radio Corporation of America. In this country RCA became owner of practically all the commercial high-power wireless telegraph facilities.[48]

Because no one had an important infringement-free patent, and the moratorium over patent disputes had been lifted, the expectations of commercial radio were stalled for a short time. Except for laboratory experimentation, the wartime work on vacuum tubes, radio circuits and transmission apparatus remained tantalizingly out of reach.

Until the legal problems could be overcome in 1920-21, no radio manufacturer could make anything but simple crystal sets for the public. The Bureau of Standards continued its basic research while the Bureau of Navigation Radio Service took up its inspection and licensing work.

The use of wireless at sea increased rapidly after 1914. On June 30, 1915, there were only 585 American ships equipped with wireless; on June 30, 1920, the number was 2,808. The use of wireless communications by armies during the war led to its use on land for purposes of communication between points difficult to reach with wire.

In 1920 the Bureau of Navigation licensed 272 land radio stations and 6,103 amateur radio operators as the domestic operation of radio stations was returned to civilian status by the President. The phenomenal growth of radio had begun.

As 1920 began, it became increasingly apparent that the future of radio lay in the development of voice radio. Until then, practically all communications had taken place via the spark or arc-alternator devices of wireless telegraphy. All the allocations of wavelengths were still based upon the London Convention of 1912, and domestically, the radio act of the same year.

After World War I the de Forest High Bridge station again operated, but apparently due to naval and commercial station complaints about interference, New York radio inspector Arthur Batcheller closed the station under a technical license violation. He stated that "interference with commercial communication could not be tolerated," and that "there is no room in the ether for entertainment."[49]

David Sarnoff, as commercial manager of the recently formed Radio Corporation of America, wrote a memorandum, "Subject: Report on prospective radio business" on January 31, 1920, to the President of GE, Owen D. Young. This report proposed that GE and RCA get into the business of broadcasting. The myth that Sarnoff had written a remarkable memo in 1915 predicting broadcasting became common currency among historians. This supposedly separate memo, Sarnoff claimed, was sent in September 1916 to E. J. Nally, Vice President and General Manager of the Marconi Company. Had this prognostication actually been made in 1915 then David Sarnoff deserved the prophetic reputation he affected and cherished. We now know that a section of the 1920 report to Young is practically word for word the purported 1915 memo about the manufacture of "radio music boxes."[50] Some ten months later broadcasting became a tangible reality to the general public.

H. P. Davis, a vice president of the Westinghouse Company, was one of the other people who immediately recognized radio's potential. He had been aware of a Westinghouse experimental station under the direction of Dr. Frank Conrad. To test the transmitting equipment, Dr. Conrad played phonograph records over licensed 8XK. Westinghouse's Davis discovered that people were purchasing radio sets from a local Pittsburgh department store because they wanted to listen to music. Davis realized that radio might find its most important role not as a means of point-to-point confidential communication but as a means of instantaneous collective communication. He recommended establishing a station to broadcast programs to the public and the Westinghouse Company would profit by selling radio sets to people who wanted to hear the programs. KDKA went on the air in Pittsburgh on November 2, 1920, with a report of the Harding-Cox election returns.[51] Other stations began broadcasting at about the same time and there is some dispute over KDKA's "earliest" claim. However, what is important is that broadcasting had begun and regulation of these stations became necessary.

The importance of amateurs fascinated with radio has not been given the credit it deserves in the furtherance of broadcasting. Amateur enthusiasts played a fundamental role in experimenting with reception and transmission and they evolved their own unique culture.[52] Most of the few people who listened to early radio had built their own sets. "The advent of the crystal detector ... had brought radio within the reach of almost everybody."[53]

In order to learn about radio transmitting at first hand, the Bureau of Standards itself became one of the first broadcasters, antedating KDKA by several months, when, in 1920, at the request of the Bureau of Markets in the Department of Agriculture, it pioneered an experimental radio market and crop report service. Even prior to these broadcasts the Bureau had successfully transmitted music and speech for short distances over its station. Voice transmission was so novel that to ensure reliability the Bureau resorted to Morse telegraph code for the market reports.[54] After operating the service for four months, the Bureau turned it over to the Post Office Department, whose stations already served the air mail service.[55]

The long patent war in radio was finally resolved with the cross-licensing agreements of General Electric, Western Electric and Westinghouse in 1920-21, involving some 1,200 radio patents. For the first time since its discovery in 1907, the three-element vacuum tube was free from danger of infringement and could be manufactured by the three companies and sold to the general public. Radio was not going to become a government monopoly, so there were no taxes on receiving sets to support the broadcasting system as there was in Europe. The privatized boom of commercial radio was beginning.

Organization of the Department of Commerce: Administration and Staff Personnel 1921–1928. The United States had emerged from its participation in the First World War as the world's richest and most powerful nation. A nationalistic America set about building self-sufficiency and plenty on a broad industrial base with the techniques of mass production it had achieved during the war.

The technology and facilities to create and manufacture consumer products were far in advance of demand. In the city and suburb, industries stood ready to provide the automobile, radio, telephone, in-door bathroom plumbing and kitchen appliances which quickly became the essentials of the good life. Wages rose steadily, but not fast enough to provide the buying power to match the pace of mass production. Advertising and installment buying became giant adjuncts of industry to achieve mass consumption. At the heels of a short boom period came a brief but severe depression in 1920-21.[56]

President Wilson's War Industries Board and other emergency regulatory agencies were dissolved at the conclusion of the war, ending nationwide government control of the economy. For a time business boomed, but as prices rose, demand fell and production and employment declined. Thousands of new companies suffered. Soon there was widespread criticism of the high cost of living, which had seen the 1916 dollar reduced in purchasing power to 45 cents; the new income tax and surtax were seriously felt for the first time since they began in 1913; and there were charges of inefficiency, extravagance and overdevelopment against the government.

The early years of President Wilson's administration had seen a continuation of federal efforts begun under Theodore Roosevelt and William Howard Taft to curb corporate monopolies and give a measure of control back to the people. The reform impulse died with the advent of the war, and the disillusionment of the postwar period, climaxed by the short severe depression, led to a massive rejection of political experimentation that swept Wilson and his policies off the scene.

The period of Republican ascendance that followed contributed to the deliberate pursuit by government of policies favorable to large business concerns. The trusts of the early century were to rise again in the mergers of the twenties, and the soaring wealth of the nation reflected the artificial rise of values as often as it did new capital investment. The consolidation of industries and utilities exercised measurable control over price and production, so that the cost of living, after a steady decline from its peak in 1920, held steady to the end of decade. The farmer, professional man and the laborer, unless he was in the automobile or radio industry, had small shares in the new wealth.

Economies in government spending, a balanced budget, lower taxes, a high protective tariff and an able and energetic Department of Commerce all acted to accelerate the development of commerce and industry.[57]

When Herbert Hoover accepted the post of Secretary of Commerce on March 4, 1921, it was with reluctance and only on his terms. His friend, Oscar Straus, Commerce and Labor Secretary from 1907 to 1909 under Theodore Roosevelt, once told him that the office required only a couple of hours of work a day and "had no other qualifications than to be able to put the fish to bed at night and turn on the lights around the coast."[58] Hoover thought otherwise.

He was quoted as saying that the Department, composed of uncorrelated scientific and semi-scientific bureaus, had too long "been a Department of Commerce in name only." With Harding's support, he intended to expand foreign commerce through organized cooperation with industry, aiming at lower production costs, and to assist domestic commerce in improving its industrial processes, abolishing waste, establishing better labor relations and better business methods. The *New York Times* editorialized that Hoover, with his knowledge, experience and driving power, seemed destined to make his office in the Cabinet "second only to that of the Secretary of State."[59]

The Department of Commerce in 1921 consisted of the Bureaus of Fisheries, Census, Standards, Foreign and Domestic Commerce, Lighthouses, Navigation, the Coast and Geodetic Survey and the Steamboat Inspection Service. They all had been established prior to the creation of the Department of Commerce itself. Each was an inbred bureaucracy of its own. There was, according to Mr. Hoover, little departmental spirit and "some of the bureaus even placed their own names on their letterheads without mentioning the Department of which they were a part."[60] In 1922 Congress was to add a Building and Housing Division to Commerce and, in 1925, Hoover secured by executive order the transfer of the Bureau of Mines and the Patent Office from the Department of the Interior.[61] In 1926 a congressional act added the Aeronautics Division, and in 1927 the Radio Service of the Bureau of Navigation became the Radio Division within the Department of Commerce.[62]

On taking over the Department, Hoover seemed to reflect the times as he declared: "This is no time to ask for appropriations to undertake new work. It is the time to search for economy and reorganization, for effective expenditure on essentials, the reduction of less essentials, and the elimination of duplications."[63]

He held the same prescription for the general economy. Recalling the scene of widespread unrest and unemployment as he took office, he was to say: "There was no special outstanding industrial revolution in sight. We had to make one."[64] His remedy for the recovery of industry from its war deterioration was through "elimination of waste and increasing the efficiency of our commercial and industrial system all along the line."[65]

To do this, Hoover, after removing the political appointees who were running the bureaus, divided the direction of his bureaus between two special assistants, both paid out of his own pocket. One was Christian A. Herter, who had been secretary of the U.S. Peace Commission in Paris in 1918-19, where he had impressed everyone with his ability.[66] The other was Paul Kruesi. It was noted, even by critic Oswald Villard, that Secretary Hoover "picked able lieutenants."[67] Hoover, however, retained direct control of "Foreign and Domestic Commerce and Standards, which I took under my own wing."[68] The latter two bureaus represented the instruments for jogging a lagging economy and putting industry back on its productive road. The "wing" Hoover spoke of proved to be Assistant Secretary J. Walter Drake, brought to Washington from the Detroit automobile industry.

Secretary Hoover gave all his bureaus his wholehearted support and most original documents examined in the files in research for this book contain his handwritten initials.

He determined:

> that the practical approach ... by the Department of Commerce was to take up some area where progress was manifestly possible, thoroughly to investigate its technology, and then to convene a preliminary meeting of representatives of that particular segment of industry, business and labor. If that preliminary meeting developed a program, a committee was appointed to cooperate with us in its advancement. There was no dictation or force of law. During my term as Secretary of Commerce more than three-thousand such conferences or committees were brought into action....[69]

These meetings were to accomplish three primary reforms:

> First to group together all agencies having the same predominant major purpose, under the same administrative supervision; second, to separate the semi-judicial and the semi-legislative and advisory functions from the administrative functions, placing the former under joint minds, the latter under single responsibility; and third, we should relieve the President of a vast amount of direct administrative labor.[70]

As Secretary of Commerce, Hoover was the greatest influence in the development of the radio communication regulatory agencies. He was deemed the most capable man to have come in with the Harding administration and was considered to have the potential for the presidency. With his efficient handling of wartime Food Administration and of Belgian Relief, Hoover had made his name a household word. His engineering background and knowledge of industry were needed as the nation slid into the postwar recession.

Hoover entered the commerce office determined to rescue the nation from its wartime overproduction, consequent depletion of resources and the general economic demoralization into which it had plunged.

Hoover's plan for recovery, in order to boost employment, was to stimulate building and housing, lend direct assistance to both new and established industries and to minister to the new aviation and radio industries.

Hoover's basic belief was "self-government in industry." Hoover preferred "conferences and cooperation to legislative compulsion—the government, he thinks, too often becomes the 'persecutor instead of regulator.'" Therefore, he sought to change the attitude of government toward business from interference toward cooperation. He felt that "it is possible to devise, out of the conscience and organization of business itself, those restraints which will cure abuse." He saw in the process of development the whole organization of economic life. "We are passing from a period of extremely individualistic action into a period of associational activities."[71]

Hoover's views were very consistent. Theodore Joslin, who examined closely all the utterances and writings of Hoover over a 10-year period, says:

> In all of those million-odd words, dealing with every important subject, the number of times he reversed himself or modified an important position could be counted on the fingers of one hand.[72]

The principles Hoover held so consistently were not simply conservative in nature, as has so often been erroneously assumed. When he began his political career as Secretary of Commerce, he was the darling of the progressives who had clustered around Wilson. College and university faculties were calling upon him to run for president that year—on either ticket. Indeed, his silence as to which party he belonged to, for a time, caused his name to figure prominently in Democratic as well as Republican presidential primaries in 1920.[73]

Hoover's principles were distinctly progressive for their time. In 1920, he defended the concepts of collective bargaining and the right to strike, which were very unpopular issues then. While Secretary of Commerce he opposed the sweeping federal injunction against railroad strikers and worked with Harding to have the steel industry abandon the 12-hour day. In his book of guiding principles, *American Individualism*, which was published in 1922, he was careful to distinguish between his views and laissez-faire capitalism. "The American way," he insisted, "is not capitalism, or socialism, or syndicalism, nor a cross breed of them."[74] It did include, though, government regulation in order to preserve equality of opportunity and individual rights. He wrote: "Progress of the nation is the sum of progress of its individuals. Acts that lead to progress are born out of the womb of the individual mind, not out of the mind of the crowd."[75]

American individualism, according to Hoover, differed from other concepts:

> because it embraces these great ideals: that while we build our society upon the attainment of the individual, we shall safeguard to every

individual an equality of opportunity to take that position in the community to which his intelligence, character, ability, and ambition enti-
tle him; that we keep the social solution free from frozen strata of classes;
that we shall stimulate effects of each individual to achievement; that
through an enlarging sense of responsibility and understanding we shall
assist him to his attainment; while he in turn must stand up to the emery
wheel of competition.[76]

Hoover believed that "the primary duty of organized society is to enlarge
the lives and increase the standards of all people."[77]

In short, though he served both the Harding and Coolidge administrations, Herbert Hoover was not of their political philosophies. As he wrote
in his memoirs, "Mr. Coolidge was a real conservative, probably the equal of
Benjamin Harrison.... He was a fundamentalist in religion, in the economic
and social order, and in fishing."[78] (The last because Coolidge, the fishing
beginner, used worms for bait.)

Hoover was an activist within a rigid framework of ideology. As such,
he placed great reliance upon the expectations of businessmen. The remedies
he offered were designed to maintain and secure agreement among business
leaders and to foster in them a sense of confidence in their own abilities to
deal with their problems. He made most of the positions he held nonparti-
san as much as possible. As a successful mining engineer he could afford to
work for little, donating most of his salary to charity.[79]

The basis for his actions as Secretary of Commerce, in leading the Bureau
of Navigation and Bureau of Standards in their broadcast involvement, reside
in his application of the concept of individualism in society:

> Our mass of regulation of public utilities and our legislation against
> restraint of trade is the monument to our intent to preserve an equality
> of opportunity. This regulation is itself proof that we have gone a long
> way toward the abandonment of the "capitalism" of Adam Smith.[80]

His public speech, like his writing, was formal, stiff, and sometimes bor-
dered on the pedantic. He appeared shy in public, although impassive might
be more accurate.[81] He insisted on writing all of his own speeches. His method
of writing was tedious and incredibly time consuming, involving innumerable drafts meticulously rewritten. Yet, even after all this effort, the final draft
was sometimes too dry, too long and ponderous.[82]

Hoover's relations with the press while Secretary of Commerce were
strained, and sometimes painful. Nevertheless, the Department of Commerce
became a superb source of information for the press. Hoover gave many
speeches and the Department's press releases "come like flakes of snow in a
heavy storm, and they do not forget to mention Mr. Hoover."[83] It was reported
that a small-town editor declared he received a daily piece of Hoover publicity, a picture, or a cut, for several years.[84]

His schedule was somewhat rigid and planned. Members of the department were instructed the day Hoover took over the department:

> He is always ready to see you, with the least possible delay, at any hour of the day on matters requiring urgent attention. The suggestion that these matters be taken up between the hours of 9 and 11, when possible, is made to avoid confusion resulting from conflicting appointments.[85]

He set aside time from four to seven P.M. to see callers on business which did not have to do with the department.

Day-to-day regulation was the task of the Bureau of Navigation. The Commissioner of Navigation from 1908 to 1921 was Eugene T. Chamberlain. When the Act of 1910 was passed to regulate wireless on ships, Chamberlain hired two radio inspectors. One was assigned to the Atlantic Coast, the other to the Pacific Coast. Shortly afterward a third man was assigned to the Gulf of Mexico. The first appropriation to meet the expense of the service amounted to $7,000.[86]

When Secretary Hoover took office, he found the staff of the radio service reduced from its previous level.

In December 1920 there were 33 full-time employees in the Bureau of Navigation Radio Service, including clerical staff. With a reduction in appropriations for 1921, 12 men were dropped. "This condition existed despite the fact that the 1920 force was entirely inadequate for the work that year, new instruments were essential, important parts were neglected, and there was in the immediate future the certainty of greatly increased work, while the advance in the development, importance, and use of wireless was a matter of common knowledge."[87]

Because Congress did not appropriate a requested supplementary expenditure, the situation became worse in 1921, "owing to our inability to pay out of reduced appropriations the necessary salaries, the entire force of inspectors with three exceptions has left us and we do not know how long these three will remain."[88]

David B. Carson, the Commissioner of Navigation appointed by Hoover to take over Chamberlain's duties in 1921, was soon to be involved in broadcast regulation, with the assistance of the deputy commissioner, Arthur J. Tyrer. Tyrer was with the Department of Commerce since the Bureau of Navigation's creation in 1903.[89] However, they had to depend on the talents and abilities of the Chief of the Radio Service, William D. Terrell.

Terrell became Chief of the Radio Service in March 1915. Early in his career he was a radio telegraph operator on a hot line between New York and Washington. Terrell entered the new radio service in 1910 after he passed the examination and served as the first radio inspector for the Port of New York for five years. Then he was transferred to Washington and placed in charge of the radio service.[90]

The radio inspectors reported directly to Terrell, or his assistant, William Downey. The Washington staff of 1921 also had two clerks.

As of February 20, 1923, the radio inspectors were C. C. Kolster, Boston; A. Batcheller, New York; R. Y. Cadmus, Baltimore; W. Van Nostrand, Jr., Norfolk; T. G. Deiler, New Orleans; J. F. Dillon, San Francisco; O. R. Redfern, Seattle; S. W. Edwards, Detroit; and E. A. Beane, Chicago.[91]

Charles C. Kolster recommended that the radio inspectors be called Supervisors of Radio, and from 1924 on this was their official title.[92]

The Supervisors of Radio in 1926 were C. C. Kolster, Boston; A. Batcheller, New York; R. Y. Cadmus, Baltimore; J. W. Swanson, Norfolk; T. G. Deiler, New Orleans; J. F. Dillon, San Francisco; O. R. Redfern, Seattle; S. W. Edwards, Detroit; E. A. Beane, Chicago; and W. Van Nostrand, Jr., Atlanta.[93]

In 1921 the lowest salary for radio inspector was $2,000 a year. Pay increased to a top of $4,000 for Batcheller by 1926.[94] Terrell received $5,200; Carson, $7,000; and Tyrer, $5,800 in 1926.[95] The salaries were carefully adjusted by the Department of Commerce Secretary:

> having in mind the importance of the duties in each case. That has been done throughout the department with the understanding that field salaries would be determined on a basis comparable to the classification of employees in the District of Columbia although the classification law does not apply to the field.[96]

It was felt by the inspectors that:

> We had broad delegated authority to carry out our respective duties, although hiring and firing, of course, was the responsibility of Washington. We made out monthly and annual reports; sent in records of inspections, examinations, and investigations, but the inspector in charge of the respective field offices had a lot of authority to do the job as was needed to be done.[97]

Kolster noted:

> Changes in regulations and frequency allocations came from Mr. Hoover's staff of administrative assistants, radio inspectors and division heads.
>
> Mr. Hoover had final say as to the acceptance of all recommendations as far as the Department was concerned.[98]

George Turner, an early radio inspector, stated:

> There was not a whole lot of centralization of authority in Washington—they couldn't have undertaken such responsibility because of their small staff.
>
> They were involved in ... matters affecting the field, but ... Mr. Terrell was engaged in attending conferences at the Washington level with other top staff of other organizational groups....

The field, on the other hand, was autonomous in a lot of areas and knew their jobs and went ahead and did what they had to do. We initiated investigations.[99]

The duties of the radio inspectors, described in a Bureau of Navigation Service Bulletin, were:

Primarily to inspect the radio apparatus on steamships, to insure its compliance with the law, and to inspect shore stations. The inspectors may also be called upon to examine radio operations. The duties of radio inspectors require some office experience....

The duties of the assistant radio inspectors will be primarily the assisting of radio inspectors. [This also] involves the carrying of 30 to 40 pounds of test and measuring equipment.[100]

Applicants were required to have a college degree from a recognized school and knowledge of radio, or at least a high school education and two years of experience in special radio work. All the applicants had to be wireless telegraph operators.[101]

George Turner, who joined as an assistant radio inspector in 1923, recalled:

When I first reported for duty at the Chicago office, Mr. Beane ... took me by the arm and walked me around and introduced me to the very limited staff—I guess there were two or three other assistant inspectors plus about an equal amount of clerks.

There was just one fairly large room with a cubbyhole glassed off in the back which was the inspector-in-charge's private office. The rest of us were clustered in the general office. On these desks were stacked high papers, on top of papers.

Mr. Beane told me that my first job would be to sit down and grade these and check applications and examination papers.[102]

To license operators, the inspector "goes on the inspection trip which he has prearranged, taking in, perhaps, a dozen different cities, and he notifies the applicants in the locality surrounding each city that he will hold an examination at that place, and the applicants collect there and take examinations, just as they do in the case of a civil service examination."[103] These trips were by train or other public transportation because automobiles were not provided the inspectors by the Department.

Turner became familiar with the type of paper work that was required and was given the task of making ship inspections. He noted, "Mr. Hoover was our big boss in Washington and I looked to him as a person that was very high in authority and sort of untouchable.... But those young inspectors in the field looked upon Mr. Terrell, as chief inspector, as that kind of gentleman. We had a great respect for authority in those days."[104]

Another radio inspector, Arthur J. Batcheller, who was assigned to New

York, joined the Department's radio service on November 20, 1917. He had been interested in radio since 1909 when he had his own amateur radio station in Revere, Massachusetts. "I had a small telephone spot transmitting station at the time, and I did some telephone work and broadcasting [of] phonograph records, although the broadcast was not thought of in those days." Batcheller then taught radio in a school he founded, and in 1917 joined the radio service. After two years as a radio inspector in Boston, Mr. Batcheller was transferred to the New York office.[105]

Other than the licensing of radio operators, the radio inspectors examined ship stations. "This is the most important work that we do under this law—that is the inspection of ship stations.... The inspection of those ships is a fundamental duty of the service."[106]

Chief Inspector Terrell felt the position of radio inspector assisted the public as they:

> Saw to the careful adjustment of the transmitters to their assigned wavelengths and constant observation to insure their remaining so adjusted....
>
> Investigation of complaints of interference by electrical devices other than radio transmitters ... cities they visit concerning the problems....
> To the amateurs the radio inspector gives protection in explaining or demonstrating that much of the interference experienced by listeners-in believed to be caused by amateurs is in fact caused in some other way.[107]

Appropriations for the Bureau of Navigation. The Bureau received an ever-increasing budget to perform its duties as the industry grew.[108]

Year	Appropriation	Year	Appropriation
1919	$ 45,000	1924	$139,000
1920	65,000	1925	180,000
1921	60,000	1926	220,000
1922	80,000	1927	335,000
1923	130,000		

The increase in funds from 1922 to 1923 of $50,000 was directly related to the growth of broadcasting. On March 3, 1922, Secretary Hoover requested from the Budget Bureau a supplemental appropriation.

> The most [of increase] was not included in the regular estimates of the bureau for the year [1923] ... for the reason that within the past 60 days there has been a tremendous development in the radio field throughout the United States of the system known as "radio broadcasting" and the employment of radio telephones in connection with the distribution to the public of government reports, including weather forecasts, crop and market estimates, etc.; and in addition to these, concerts, news, lectures

on educational, health and other subjects of public interest, religious services and general broadcasting by amateurs. This service is extending with great rapidity to every part of the country and it is estimated that there are at least 600,000 listening in stations now in operation to get the benefit of this broadcasting. This number is still increasing so rapidly that the manufacturers of instruments are unable to meet the demand.

The interference caused by these broadcasting stations with each other and with the regular use of radio communication both in connection with safety to life at sea and for commercial purposes, has been followed by demands from all sections of the country that immediate steps be taken to remedy a condition which is rendering this popular and important use of wireless impossible. Our present force is entirely insufficient to cope with this emergency.[109]

In April of 1921 the Department requested 12 new positions be filled in the radio service to replace those refused by Congress in 1920.[110]

About a year later an additional 22 employees were requested.[111] By 1925 the Bureau employed 34 people, which included radio inspectors, clerks and secretarial help.[112] Further requests were made for four more inspectors and 17 assistant inspectors. Of 34 already employed by the Bureau, 20 were located in the Washington office. The other 14 were radio inspectors in field offices.

The only year during the rise of broadcasting in which a requested increase in staff was refused by Congress was 1925.

It was proposed to set up additional field offices in 1926 with an assistant inspector and one clerk in areas not covered by the Bureau. These sub-offices would have been located "at the present centers of sending stations, at strategic points."[113] They were to be in Dallas, Memphis, Los Angeles, Portland (Oregon), Pittsburgh, Buffalo, Denver, St. Louis, Minneapolis and Omaha. The Department also asked to increase each of the existing nine major field offices with another assistant inspector who would handle night duty, with Detroit getting two men.[114] Before this plan could be approved, the Federal Radio Commission took over the duties of the Bureau of Navigation.

The Bureau of Standards began research into the physics of radio in the early 1900s. By 1918 the Bureau had expanded its Radio Measurements Division into the Radio Communications Section under the direction of J. Howard Dellinger. Research was conducted on vacuum tubes, measurements, design and development.[115]

By 1923 the Bureau's staff and plant was the largest physical laboratory in the world. The Bureau published letter circulars on all aspects of radio, from how-to-do-it diagrams of radio sets, to measurements of frequencies.[116]

Members of the radio section of the Bureau of Standards participated as technical advisors at all of the early radio conferences. Usually the advisors were Dr. Howard Dellinger and Dr. Charles B. Joliffe.[117]

The Bureau set up a standard of frequency and sent out signals to allow stations to adjust their own emissions. The Bureau's piezo-oscillator, which used a quartz plate vibrating at a radio frequency much like a tuning fork, furnished an extraordinarily selective, precise, and portable frequency standard both for radio inspectors and stations by 1923.[118]

Studies were made of the ionosphere and its effect on radio signal fading, and the industry worked closely with the Bureau's technicians to solve radio reception and transmission problems.

Dr. Burgess urged support for the Bureau of Standards' radio activities:

> The work we are doing, first, is concerning the underlying principles regarding broadcasting. There are a good many technical questions involved.... Second, there is the actual determination of the improvements in and accuracy of the frequency measurements, which has to be more and more precisely done, because there is more and more demand of interested parties to get in on these various wavelengths.[119]

The Bureau calibrated the instruments used by the radio inspectors of the Bureau of Navigation and assisted with any technical problems.

Appropriations for the Bureau of Standards. Dr. George K. Burgess found he could not negotiate with Congress for funds as had his predecessor, Dr. Stratton. This was primarily caused by the Bureau of the Budget created as a buffer between the government agencies and the Congress. However, Dr. Burgess impressed both Congress and the budget bureau by compiling records of the Bureau of Standards' operations which often ran 100 pages or more, much of it in fine print.[120] This was in spite of a wave of economy which hit the nation and the Bureau in 1923. Reports in the third year of Secretary Hoover's tenure were reduced in size.[121]

As private industry began to realize the potential of broadcasting and started its own extensive research and development to provide material and instruments for the public, the Bureau of Standards found less need to continue its research. Thus, the following table of appropriations which the Bureau received tells the story of increasingly viable and vigorous private broadcast industry programs of research and development.[122]

Year	Appropriation	Year	Appropriation
1919	$106,000	1923	$ 46,000
1920	60,000	1924	45,000
1921	57,000	1925	45,680
1922	65,000	1926	44,800

The figures include all the funds used for radio research and standardization, not merely the direct appropriations. Some funds used by the Bureau were transferred from other departments, e.g., from the military for special projects. The years 1925 and 1926, however, contain no such special or transferred funds.

The Radio Service of the Bureau of Navigation was discontinued following the passage of the Radio Act of 1927 which created the Federal Radio Commission.

The decade of the 1920s is perhaps the most significant in broadcast regulation history. There are three major periods of regulation: 1921 through 1924; 1925 through 1926; and 1927 to the beginning of 1928. What follows is the story of that regulation and its impact upon the 20th century.

Chapter II

BROADCAST REGULATION
AND POLICY FROM 1921 TO 1924

The period from 1921 to 1924 was the beginning of the radio broadcasting era. What came to be called broadcasting is generally dated from November 2, 1920, when station KDKA (Pittsburgh) achieved nationwide publicity with its reports on election returns. This event and other similar "broadcasts" attracted public attention. This led to an increase in the number of people and companies requesting licenses, which in turn led to problems for the Department of Commerce.

The Department of Commerce's Bureau of Navigation Radio Service began to license broadcast stations as "limited commercial stations" on September 15, 1921.[1] No special license was required prior to that time for stations experimenting with broadcasting. The stations which were required to be licensed as "limited commercial stations" were authorized to operate on only one frequency, 360 meters (832.8 kHz), which was utilized for "news, lectures, entertainment, etc."[2] This was not far from the international distress and calling frequency of 600 meters (500 kHz), a range familiar to experimenters and amateurs. Six hundred meters was selected partly because it was the longest wavelength possible from an antenna which could be strung between the masts of the typical ship.

In December 1921, before the number of broadcast stations began to increase rapidly, a second wavelength was added. The wavelength of 485 meters (618.6 kHz) was allocated to any stations that wished to periodically transmit government reports such as weather and crop information. A station could switch easily from 360 meters up to 485 meters because early transmitters were tuned much like a radio receiver.

The growth of stations can best be illustrated as follows:[3]

Date	New Stations	Total Stations
December 1, 1921	3	23
January 1, 1922	6	28
February 1, 1922	8	36
March 1, 1922	29	65
April 1, 1922	68	133
May 1, 1922	84	217
June 1, 1922	97	314
July 1, 1922	64	378
August 1, 1922	63	441
September 1, 1922	55	496
October 1, 1922	43	539
November 1, 1922	15	554
December 1, 1922	16	570

Most of the stations were non-profit, with a large number affiliated with colleges and universities who were experimenting with the physics of this new phenomenon. The majority of the other fledgling radio stations were owned and operated by newspapers, department stores, power companies and other private concerns. They were operated primarily to generate favorable publicity for the owner's primary business.[4] There was general agreement that not-for-profit broadcasting would play a significant and perhaps even a dominant role in the U.S. system, and commercial advertising was viewed with skepticism as to its contributions to the public.[5]

At the end of 1922 there were anywhere from 500,000 to 1,000,000 radio receivers in the country. As the number of broadcasting stations increased, interference increased proportionately with the density of stations in a particular area. In locations along the seacoasts the Navy's older high-powered arc-transmitters disrupted reception of stations as their signals spread out over a number of frequencies. Similarly, broadcasting stations increased the difficulties of Navy reception.[6] The Department of Commerce, the agency given the power by Congress to regulate "wireless" transmission, became the only means of controlling and regulating this phenomenon. With its limited resources the Department of Commerce found itself with the task of controlling the growth of broadcasting, improving reception and planning for the future development of this service to the public.

There were extraordinary developments in radio technology and sales in the 1921 to 1924 period. The radio and automobile industries were the bellwethers of this decade, paying the highest wages and leading the way in mass production and mass consumption techniques. Salaries and the standard of living inched up, goods and groceries were plentiful and relatively cheap, and boom followed boom, real or inflated, in industry, in consumer services, in real estate and utilities.

By 1923 the greatest year for the increase of interest in radio by the public, sales exceeded all expectations. Radio-related sales reported by 290 retail outlets to the Commerce Department reflected that huge increase:[7]

Loudspeakers:	Number	623,146
	Value	$5,608,330
Headsets:	Number	1,781,783
	Value	$5,345,380
Receiving sets (tube type):	Number	190,374
	Value	$23,326,116
Receiving sets (crystal type):	Number	223,303
	Value	$669,906
Transmitting sets:	Number	1,082
	Value	$919,930
Transformers:	Number	1,571,817
	Value	$3,929,581
Rheostats:	Number	1,085,171
	Value	$955,396
Lightning Arrestors:	Number	1,758,723
	Value	$422,036
Radio tubes:	Number	4,687,400
	Value	$9,824,172
Miscellaneous parts:	Value	$12,999,623
	Total Value	$54,000,470

Herbert C. Hoover took the oath of office as Secretary of Commerce on March 4, 1921, several months after the first "limited" commercial broadcasting license was issued.[8]

Hoover stated, upon taking his oath, that the Department of Commerce "is fundamentally a department of service ... Its functions are not to control or regulate. They are constructive."[9]

His son, Herbert Hoover, Jr., who at the age of 12 had become avidly interested in wireless, had some influence upon his father:

> I owned and operated a ham station ... and participated ... in the first exciting days of tube transmitters, super-hets, and short waves.
> My father, being an engineer [mining], followed all this with much interest though he did not actually participate himself. But it undoubtedly gave him something of a technical background for his later responsibilities as Secretary of Commerce.[10]

Broadcasting was not as much a technical development as it was a shift in emphasis. The type and interests of the audience being reached was different from earlier days and the type of material presented was rapidly changing too.

Secretary Hoover was quickly introduced to the problems facing the Department of Commerce in briefings with William D. Terrell, the chief radio inspector. They discussed: 1) wireless telegraphic communication with China; 2) the Intercity Radio Company's request for continuation of its telegraphic license; and 3) the need for further legislation.[11]

Terrell informed the Secretary, "I have mentioned to you the desirability of legislation to give the Secretary of Commerce some discretionary power about issuing licenses, now it is purely ministerial; we are rapidly moving in wireless along the lines cable development proceeded for years when the government had little to say about cable landings in the United States."[12]

With appropriations reductions for the Bureau of Navigation, the entire force of inspectors, with the exceptions of Dillon, Kolster, and Batcheller, had left the service at the beginning of 1921. The Bureau had endeavored to fill the positions through civil service appointments, but only three eligible applicants passed a special exam. Two of them refused appointments because of the low pay of about $2,000 a year.

Commissioner of Navigation Eugene T. Chamberlain noted:

> The work of inspecting stations for license has practically been abandoned, which leaves the bureau without knowledge as to the nature of the stations, the wavelengths they are using, or to what extent they may be causing interference....[13]

Congress made a special appropriation of $20,000 for the radio inspection service. However, most of these funds were used primarily for inspecting ship stations. Broadcasting did not begin to explode until 1922. "It is expected that the work of the service may be brought up to date having special reference to the inspection of ship stations for licenses."[14]

The 1921 through 1924 period was rocky for the Department, first with the preparation for legislation, followed by the failure of legislative efforts. With the failure of legislation the Department of Commerce was required to develop alternative means to regulate broadcasting. The importance of the Bureau of Standards intensified during this period.

I. Preparation for Legislation

After only a month in office, Secretary Hoover began to organize the Department for its quest for legislation. He wrote:

One of the misfortunes of our present Government structure, and one which needs constructive thought, is that we have no bureau or central organized authority for dealing with the communications question. The problem of cable, radio, and telegraphic service in their expansion and conduct are now disintegrated over several departments in Washington with no one in authority, and none of them in a position for constructive study or action. It would seem desirable that this whole question be studied by the commercial community.[15]

Six bills were introduced in the Senate during the 67th Congress (1921-1923), most of them titled, "To regulate the operation of and to foster the development of radio communication in the United States." (Bills which are preceded by the letter "S." are Senate bills). The House of Representatives displayed the same interest, with Representative Wallace H. White (later Senator) leading the agitation for an amendment of the Radio Act of 1912. Fourteen separate amendments were introduced in the house. (House bills number designations are preceded by the letters "H. R."). None of the 20 attempts was to pass *both* the House or Senate.

Radio Bills Introduced in 1921. As of September 1921, there were three bills pending before Congress.

Bill S. 31, introduced by Congressman Poindexter, was referred to the Committee on Naval Affairs. This bill was supported by the Navy Department and met with considerable opposition by commercial and private interests. It was based on the Roosevelt Report of 1904, which stated in part, "in radio the interests of the Navy are paramount."[16]

Bill S. 1627, introduced by Senator Kellogg, was referred to the Committee on Interstate Commerce. It was similar to Poindexter's bill, except that the duties of a National Radio Commission were to be delegated to the Secretary of Commerce.

Sen. Kellogg notified Hoover on April 9, 1921, that hearings would resume on the radio question during the early part of the next session of Congress. He requested "you, or some one of your department prepare to give the subcommittee the benefit of your views, or the views of your department on this question." Sen. Kellogg also asked for suggestions on "the form which legislation for the purpose of protection of radio communication should take."[17] Hoover appointed Commissioner of Navigation Eugene T. Chamberlain and Director of the Bureau of Standards Dr. Samuel Wesley Stratton to represent the Commerce viewpoint at any hearings.[18]

Secretary Hoover also notified Sen. Kellogg that "we have in the last few days set up an inter-departmental committee, merely for the purpose of getting the views of the various departments on this subject in order that they might be put in some systematic order for your use."[19] However, the Inter-departmental Radio Advisory Committee did not formally meet until 1922.

The Department of Commerce's Proposed Bill. Bill S. 1628, later introduced by Sen. Kellogg, was similar to his S. 1627 bill which had actually been written by the Department of Commerce's Commissioner of Navigation Chamberlain in 1915-16. An informal committee from several departments concerned with radio communication had prepared a substitute bill for S. 1627. No action was taken on that measure, but its provisions were then incorporated into S. 1628. The Department of Commerce was very "much interested in giving attention to such hearings and other considerations as may be given to it."[20]

This proposed bill made one radical change in the underlying principle of the Act of 1912. The 1912 law had 19 mainly technical regulations which the Secretary of Commerce was to enforce. The draft eliminated the 19 specific regulations but gave the Secretary of Commerce general powers to make regulations for four purposes; "to prevent or minimize interference with radio-communication, to further the communication of distress and safety signals by sea, land and air, to promote the use of radio-communication supplementary to other methods of communication, and generally to facilitate radio-communication and foster its development."[21]

The strengthening of the Commerce Department power was felt necessary because the situation had changed so swiftly. Regulations governing radio communication, it was felt, "follow closely scientific discovery and invention in the principles, methods and instruments of radio communication, all of which are subject to rapid change."[22] It was noted that the Secretary of Commerce, by being in close touch with scientific progress through the Bureau of Standards, would be in a better position than Congress to react and to change or create new regulations. As new international agreements were reached, it would be far simpler to allow the Secretary to change regulations to adapt to them than to require a new law from Congress after each round of negotiations.

The Department of Commerce's proposed bill differed further from the Act of 1912 by providing for an advisory committee on radio communication. Though the Act of 1912 narrowly limited the discretion of the Secretary of Commerce on statutory regulations especially regarding allocations, "it was found desirable to create an informal committee of representatives of the departments concerned to consider technical and other matters." This concept was to be applied by Secretary Hoover through the Interdepartmental Radio Advisory Committee.

Chamberlain believed that it was necessary to include an advisory committee in the bill. The reasoning, as he wrote to Hoover:

> First, to secure the best available technical advice, which involves the addition of men in civil life of recognized attainments in radio-communication to a staff of Government experts.
>
> Second, to secure the cooperation of those branches of government especially concerned with radio-communication.[23]

The suggested bill also differed from the Act of 1912 because it provided for licenses for receiving stations in special instances. One example, "a high-powered foreign radio transmitting station could transmit messages to a receiving station in the United States, which in effect would be a terminal, and under present law no license for the receiving station or its operator is required."[24] This bill would require a license for receiving stations as in earlier telegraphic cable legislation. It also required that all licensed radio operators should be American citizens.

Secretary Hoover submitted this draft bill to Sen. Kellogg on April 23, 1921, along with his comments:

> A certain number of wavelengths have been assigned to the United States under the international convention. The question arises in my mind as to whether the ultimate assignment of all these different wavelengths will not create a situation where vested interest has been created; a sort of national resource will have been parted with which will come to have ultimately a commercial and monopolistic value.[25]

This issue is still alive today with the government auctioning off spectrum to commercial companies for large sums and the extension of license terms. This concern with a wavelength being a national resource and the uneasiness over the possibility of monopoly is Hoover's first hint of the need for radio broadcast licensing.

> The second point is that it seems to me that the provision in the Poindexter Bill [which the Kellogg committee was considering] dealing with the issuance of licenses before construction, [construction permits] has some merits as I do not believe any great expansion of the wireless facilities would arise unless there was assurance of the license. On the other hand, there appears to be a great deal of protection about people securing licenses to any particular wavelength and holding it out of use, or even benefiting by monopoly value.[26]

Hoover's concerns, as expressed early in 1921; the potential for monopoly of a frequency and the acceptance of the principle of construction permits reservations on how rights provided by permits could be limited were some of the basic issues which broadcast regulation had to solve, and which were addressed in the S. 1628 bill.

Congressman Wallace H. White's Proposed Bill. Richard S. Emmet, a personal secretary on Hoover's staff, forwarded to Chamberlain and Dr. Stratton a draft of a bill received from Congressman White on April 11, 1921. He asked that they "go over this as quickly as possible and give him [White] your views on it, as Mr. White wishes to introduce it as quickly as possible."[27]

Just a day later Chamberlain submitted a memorandum on the White bill to Hoover, who forwarded it to both White and Kellogg. This bill eventually became a proposed bill introduced by the Radio Conference Committee as the White-Kellogg Bill on June 9, 1922.

The memorandum reported that "Mr. White's bill will serve as the groundwork for legislation to regulate radio-communication though rather elaborate, but later it would be simplified."[28] A number of changes were suggested, such as deleting the required licensing of *all* receiving sets. "This is going too far, as the license of only *commercial receiving* stations can be justified."[29] Chamberlain and Dr. Stratton were referring to stations which received payment for receipt of messages, such as Western Union.

Certain sections of the proposed bill gave the Secretary of Commerce power over some commercial aspects of wireless telegraphy.

Chamberlain suggested that "Mr. White's bill would be strengthened by adding the Advisory Committee provision we have drawn for the bill [S. 1628] Dr. Stratton and I are preparing at your [Hoover's] request."[30]

White submitted his first draft of this bill to the House in April of 1921. It included a provision for an advisory committee of seven. Five would be government officials, and two would be experts on radio communication.[31] This was modified in a later bill, H. R. 11964, introduced in the 1922-23 House session, by increasing the advisory committee to 12 members, six of whom would be civilian (public) representatives.

White commented at hearings on H. R. 11964, "I was never in favor of including it [the Advisory Committee] in the bill at all. It was recommended by the radio conference [held in 1922] that it go in."[32]

Apparently, White had forgotten that the suggestion had been made many years before by the Department of Commerce in 1915-16. He had accepted it when his first regulatory effort was introduced in the House in 1921.

Consideration of Turning Control Over to the Post Office. Hoover wrote in a letter early in June 1921, that "we have been giving a great deal of consideration to this entire communications problem and I hope will be able to evolve some constructive national policy."[33] What this constructive national policy might be was indicated by Christian A. Herter, an assistant to Hoover, who wrote:

> I might add for your very confidential information that there is some possibility of the whole question of radio being centralized under the Post Office Department as a communications matter, in which case, of course, it would not be a matter of primary concern to Mr. Hoover. This point, has not, however, as yet been determined.[34]

A number of reports were prepared for Hoover by individuals in the Department of Commerce on the radio "question." In response to one of these reports, David B. Carson, the new Commissioner of Navigation, wrote:

> throughout the statement there runs an argument in favor of retention in this Department of the administration of the radio laws.

As you are aware the question whether such administration should be transferred to the Post Office Department is under consideration and it is understood that this Department is not adverse to such transfer and it therefore would appear inopportune for this Department at this time to put out a statement of the policy which it proposes to pursue in co-operating with the wireless interests in the advancement of this work.[35]

These proposals did not go much further because events and the regulatory problems faced by the Department of Commerce soon led to the First National Radio Telephony Conference. The Post Office Department presented a resolution to Congress in May 1922 asking that it be given "exclusive jurisdiction over all government radio broadcasting, including radio telegraph and telephone."[36] The resolution also requested that the Postmaster General be given the power to perform the work of broadcasting for all *government* departments, prescribe all the necessary regulations "not inconsistent with general rules which the Secretary of Commerce may be authorized by law to prescribe."[37]

Hoover endorsed this resolution with the comment, "The enclosed draft [of the resolution] is perfectly all right as far as this Department is concerned."[38]

However, the Interdepartmental Radio Advisory Committee began to effectively perform the suggested functions following the First National Radio Telephony Conference, so the Post Office's proposal was not seriously considered by Congress.

Department Public Radio Policy. Six days after the first "limited" commercial radio station license was issued on September 21, 1921, the Department of Commerce began to search for a position it could maintain as an unbiased agency serving civic, commercial and governmental radio interests.

Bureau of Standards head Dr. Stratton had his assistant director, F. C. Brown, send a policy memorandum to Hoover, noting that the Bureau felt that the Department of Commerce was the government representative of the commercial radio telegraph companies, the amateur operators and those interested in the technical development of radio communication.

It must also keep in view the needs of the shipping interests and the general public, which is dependent upon radio communication....

Among the most rapidly growing uses are: aids to navigation and aviation, radio broadcasting, and radio telegraphy....

It should be pointed out that the Navy Department has shown it keeps its own interests uppermost, while the Department of Commerce is depended upon by the civic and commercial radio agencies of the country to cooperate with them in the non-military uses of radio communication. The private companies, however, desire that the Department of Commerce not operate stations in competition with them, but simply deal with licensing and ... giving them statistical and technical information.[39]

Recommendations were offered by the Bureau of Standards staff on the duties to be continued by various bureaus of the Department of Commerce.

> 1) Obtain information leading to the enlargement of business possibilities in radio. This was considered the duty of the Bureau of Foreign and Domestic Commerce.
>
> 2) Clarify government policy. This was the duty of the Bureau of Navigation, through its *Radio Service Bulletin* and radio inspectors.
>
> 3) Regulate, through the Radio Inspection Service.
>
> 4) Publish information, through the Public Relations Division.
>
> 5) Radio research, through the Bureau of Standards.

It was then suggested that the Department of Commerce hold an informal conference of representatives of both commercial and civic radio interests to discuss the radio work of the department. It was hoped that such a conference would permit the Department to "learn their views regarding the service which the Government should render to them." Hoover's personal interest is shown in his note in the margin of Brown's document: "being arranged as suggested by Huston."[40]

Chief radio inspector Terrell seconded the Bureau of Standards memorandum calling for a radio conference to arrive at a public policy. He stated: "It has been recognized for some time that because of the rapid progress being made in radio, new legislation is necessary and it is the belief of this office that Bill S. 1628, which was prepared by Chamberlain, best meets the present requirements."[41]

Interallied Provisional Technical Committee on Radio. From June 21 to August 22, 1921, delegates representing the United States, Great Britain, France, Italy and Japan met in Paris to discuss technical questions about radio, and to formulate a common stand to be considered at the next International Communications Conference scheduled for 1923. Department of Commerce delegates were Dr. A. E. Kennelly of Harvard University and Dr. Dellinger of the Bureau of Standards. The various countries made so many revisions to the proposals that the International Communications Conference did not take place until 1927, almost 4 years later than planned.

It was reported to Hoover that "General [George O.] Squier [head of the American delegation] is enthusiastic about the showing which the American delegation has made."[42] The decision to delay allocation of wavelengths among the different countries "was substantially the viewpoint of the American delegation, viz., the formation of sound and general scientific-principles, leaving the administrative and political aspects of the question to a subsequent and generally international conference."[43] Drs. Kennelly and Dellinger noted:

> We regret that the preponderating influence of military control in European countries stood in the way of securing all that the commercial

interests in the United States desired, especially in regard to the ... distribution of waves among the four services; mobile, fixed, military and special.[44]

Commercial broadcasting, still in the early stage of development, was not among those services considered seriously at this preliminary conference in 1921.

Hoover wrote in his annual report for that year: "For obvious reasons the basic regulation of radio communication must be international, and for this and other reasons the Department has not urged consideration of a bill submitted to Congress early in the summer [1921] to bring the Act of 1912 to regulate radio communication more into accord with present requirements."[45]

Interference Problem. In the same Commerce Department Annual Report, Hoover wrote:

> The only justification for Federal regulation of radio communication lies in the fact that no such communication at all would be possible unless some authority determined the power and wavelengths to be employed by different stations and classes of stations in order to prevent mutual interference with the transmission and reception of messages. Invention has already done much to reduce such interference and will doubtless do more, but interference is still the important factor to be considered from the point of view of the practical use to-day of this indispensable means of communication.[46]

The department felt that a major cause of interference stemmed from amateur radio operations. Letters were being received at the Department of Commerce from individuals around the country with such comments as: "It has been noted that several amateur radio operators cause a great deal of interference with the reception of signals [from KDKA and WBZ]."[47] The reply to this complaint on November 17, 1921, was sent very quickly, because the complainant was the Chief Signal Officer of the War Department.

S. W. Edwards, radio inspector for the Eighth Radio District (Detroit) replied that the stations involved were technical and training school stations. "This is to advise the Bureau that this interference is known to exist, and I have already taken the necessary steps to see that it is eliminated immediately."[48] Edwards also made the suggestion that to avoid further interference with broadcasting, "it will be necessary to place a time restriction on all stations of special class operating on wave lengths in excess of 200 meters [1499 kHz and lower]."[49]

President Hiram Percy Maxim of the American Radio Relay League (ARRL) focused attention on the interference issue in a speech to amateur radio operators:

> Let us discourage interference with it [broadcasting] for what would a thousand listeners to a great speech or a great discussion or a great musicale program do if one single amateur transmitter, in idle amusement, created an interference which spoiled the listening of the thousand! The one would be promptly sacrificed for the good of the many.[50]

Secretary Hoover felt a close relationship to the amateur radio operator. His son had received license 6XH, at Stanford University in 1921.[51] Six months after taking office, Hoover had instructed Terrell to see Maxim personally at the first ARRL convention in Chicago, August 30 through September 3, 1921. Hoover also sent a telegram:

> The Department of Commerce is by the authority of Congress, the legal Patron Saint of the amateur wireless operators. Outside of its coldly legal relations the Department wishes to be helpful in encouraging this very important movement.[52]

The Department of Commerce initiated a rather drastic solution to temporarily solve the interference problem which they blamed on amateur radio operations. If the president of the largest amateur organization felt that the amateurs were interfering with broadcasting then "the great body of the public which maintains receiving stations solely for the reception of broadcasting can be expected to be as much more emphatic in their opinion."[53] The department issued an order on January 1, 1922, forbidding amateur radio sending stations from transmitting until some solution could be devised.

> Because of the rapid development of radio broadcasting during the last three months, the value of such service to the public, and the limitation of wavelengths which can be assigned to this service, it has been necessary to take precautions to protect the broadcasting service from interference. The privilege of amateur broadcasting was temporarily withdrawn pending the adoption of a plan....[54]

It was estimated that there were more than 14,000 amateur radio sending stations operating in the United States at that time.

However, the so-called interference by amateur radio operators was exaggerated then and has been overstated since. The real common problem of early radio reception was that stations could not always adhere to a wavelength with any degree of accuracy and receivers also experienced drift. The highest permissible assignment to amateurs under the Act of 1912, 200 meters (1500 kHz), was occasionally exceeded until the Department of Commerce took measures to further enforce that regulation.

During the 1922 Radio Telephony Conference, H. F. Breckel, representing the Precision Equipment Company of Cincinnati, added further to the interference issue:

We are not troubled with amateur transmission except where the listening station happens to be located fairly close to an amateur station of high power in which case the amateur's transmission may "force in" regardless of how selective the receiving set being used by the listener might be.[55]

Interference was not the only reason for suspending amateur licenses temporarily, although that was the public stance of the Department of Commerce. Carson reported:

A number of amateur stations and other stations were beginning to broadcast phonograph records which had no real value as entertainment or instruction and which threatened to so seriously interfere with the higher classes of service that it was considered necessary to stop broadcasting by amateur stations until some plan can be arranged which will allow amateurs to do work of this kind, if it can be shown to be of value, on a wavelength just below or just above 200 meters.[56]

The radio inspectors, ARRL officials and other interested individuals were asked to recommend regulations they considered desirable, "which will give protection to the amateurs and allow them to conduct their operations in a manner which will not disturb other services."[57]

One of the plans suggested placing the amateur stations using spark and continuous wave apparatus on 1710 kHz when they first received a license, reserving 1499 kHz for telephone and broadcasting. After two years of experience, 1220 kHz and 1199 kHz would be assigned to amateurs who qualified.[58]

The "temporary" restriction on amateur radio operations raised the ire of many amateurs who complained to the Department. Hoover, with his personal interest in amateur stations, asked his staff for a statement he could use to justify the action. Commissioner of Navigation Carson provided Hoover such a raison d'être:

In the recent restriction placed upon amateur broadcasting this office did not lose sight of the recognized value of the amateur radio operator. The action was taken for the purpose of preventing interference and to stop broadcasting by amateurs of phonograph records, which are not enjoyed by the public but at time became annoying.[59]

The Bureau of Navigation in January provided a definition of "broadcasting" by authorizing the insertion of the following on all general and restricted amateur radio station licenses:

This station is not licensed to broadcast weather reports, market reports, music, concerts, speeches, news or similar information or entertainment.[60]

Ever since, such programming to the general public has been limited to the standard broadcasting station, and constitutes the definition of "broadcasting." This policy meant that the Department of Commerce had instituted a class of stations solely transmitting such material and no longer permitted other classes to transmit those categories of programming. With the restriction of amateurs, station classification by programming began in January 1922.

About a year later, *Radio News* owner-editor Hugo Gernsback proposed that amateur radio stations be allowed to rebroadcast broadcasting stations. His article noted that over one-half of the population was being deprived of radio entertainment because "the farming and agricultural districts as a rule are out of range and are not in a position to invest, for many reasons, in expensive vacuum tube outfits."[61] He suggested that amateurs be allowed to rebroadcast stations to solve this difficulty. This would require amateurs to purchase a tube receiver and then rent crystal receivers to the population at two dollars a month, providing through rebroadcasting a strengthened signal which would be easily picked up by the rented crystal sets.

Prior to World War I, Gernsback launched a device he called "America's first home radio set." Amateur enthusiasts could use his $7.50 transmitter kit to ring a bell on a receiver about a mile away. It was a hot item, selling at Macy's, Gimbel's and Marshall Field's. When the U.S. government banned all amateur radio transmissions at the start of the war, Gernsback was stuck with more than $100,000 worth of parts. He then repackaged the parts as electrical experiment sets for boys. After the war, Gernsback sold through mail order low-end products such as crystal sets. Thus, he had an economic interest he was promoting.[62]

Gernsback noted: "We have received several thousand letters from amateurs all over the country who wish to thus re-broadcast music and it would seem a pity if the country were deprived of hearing broadcasts if the amateurs were not permitted to do this work."[63]

Carson quickly responded:

> It seems to be the general impression that there are at present [December 1922] more broadcasting transmitting stations in many parts of the country than necessary to furnish the public satisfactory service.
>
> Practically all of the reliable information reaching this office indicates that the farmers and others in rural districts appreciate good service and are willing to pay for good receiving sets in order to get it satisfactorily.
>
> There are at present time between 16,000 and 17,000 licensed amateur stations in the United States operating on the wavelength of 200 meters and it is not reasonable to expect that a broadcasting service on the same wavelength would be very successful.[64]

Gernsback claimed to have statistics "showing that in the average small town of below 5,000 inhabitants: ... as a rule, do not go in for vacuum tube sets, which, anyway, they do not know how to handle."[65]

Deputy Commissioner of Navigation Arthur J. Tyrer also wrote Gernsback that a new radio law was being worked on, which "will make possible a reallocation of wavelengths and when this is accomplished it may be possible to provide a plan which will permit the amateurs to carry on broadcasting to limited extent."[66] This never came about.

Interference was actually coming from many sources besides amateur transmissions. Henry B. Joy, president of Packard Automobile Company, wrote:

> Much of the time [listening] was wasted due to interference by U.S. Naval Stations. The stations NRQ and NRH sending on improperly broad tuning from Detroit and Cleveland destroyed much of the evening's effort.
>
> I know this problem is one to which you are giving much study, but sometimes I feel that it is perhaps impossible for you to get as close to the very bad Naval Station conditions as do we who are giving especial study to the matter. Other interferences exist but when the chief offender is the Government itself against its own regulations and the international conventions, how can we well expect that others will confirm.[67]

Secretary Hoover personally replied:

> It is to be regretted that radio communication has not yet reached the stage where all interference can be avoided, but in our investigations we find that the commercial organizations are complained of as serious offenders more often than the Navy and other branches of governmental radio service.... I may add, however, that under the present law it is very difficult to provide wavelengths for all stations that will permit transmission from all stations at the same time, but as new legislation is inevitable, that defect will, no doubt be remedied.[68]

Detroit radio inspector S. W. Edwards complained with some frustration about dealing with the problem of interference. "This office has repeatedly taken this matter up with Great Lakes and the local stations but nothing has apparently been done by the Navy ... I do not even receive replies to official letters on the subject."[69]

Henry Joy felt that radio should be de-militarized so it would become even more popular and perform a greater benefit to both business and pleasure. He wrote:

> I wish I could present to you the picture of the rapidity with which radio is expanding. I can hardly get into a radio equipment store on account of the crowd.[70]

The amateur operators and the Navy's broad-band transmitters were not the sole or the major problem. The major interference problem was because all stations were transmitting on the one frequency of 360 meters unless they broadcast special government information, at which time they were permitted to switch to 485 meters. With stations of varying powers on the same frequency operating at the same time, overlapping and commingling of signals could not be avoided and interference was impossible to overcome.

New York radio inspector Arthur J. Batcheller suggested that WGY ([G]eneral Electric, Schenectad[Y]) be allowed to operate on 400 meters (749.6 kHz) while station WHAZ broadcast on 360 meters (832.8 kHz). It was hoped that a 40 meter separation would allow both stations to operate simultaneously without interference. An experiment was conducted in December 1922, and it was determined that with properly designed receiving sets it was possible to separate the stations. However, most sets then in existence were incapable of discrimination and unable to tune out either station when both were in operation.[71]

Intercity Radio Company Case: Regulatory Control Tested. The Intercity Radio Company had opened a wireless telegraphy station on December 1, 1920, in New York City. The *New York Times* had begun operating a receiving station 11 months earlier for transatlantic wireless messages sent from Europe. The stations' antennas were located within 1,200 feet of each other. The *New York Times*, U.S. Navy and other interests complained to the Department of Commerce about interference from the Intercity station. The *New York Times* noted:

> [Previously] … there was no time during the day or night when the *Times* could not pick up wireless messages…. Since the coming of the Intercity Radio Co. into the field of wireless communication, the *Times* has not been able to receive any of its trans–Atlantic messages except upon the sufferance of the operators of the Intercity Radio Co. office.[72]

The Intercity Company station had a 30-year contract with the German Telefunken Company obtained through the influence of William Randolph Hearst. Hearst wished communication between the United States and Germany to be free of propagandistic interpretation from British and French sources.[73]

The interference caused by the Intercity Company transmitter also affected the Navy station in New York, and Admiral William Hannah Grubb Bullard, Chief of Naval Communication, was consulted on the problem. He "agreed the radio communication act must be brought up to date" to handle such a problem. (Bullard later became the first chairman of the Federal Radio Commission when it was formed in 1927.)

On May 12, 1921, Claudius H. Huston, a personal secretary of Hoover's who was Acting Secretary while Hoover was absent, revoked the Intercity license on the grounds that it was interfering with ship-to-shore traffic of commercial and government stations. He noted that Intercity was simply communicating with inland stations in Detroit, Cleveland and Chicago which were already well served by land-line telegraph.

The revocation was re-confirmed by Secretary Hoover and counsel for Intercity started proceedings to enjoin the department from revoking their license.

United States Attorney Earl Barnes stated, "the methods of the company were not satisfactory to the Government and its operators interfered with radio messages."[74]

Judge A. N. Hand found for the Intercity Company. The Intercity attorney grounded his case "upon the assumption that so long as the New York corporation has on file with you [Department of Commerce] an application for a license it is entitled to operate."[75] The basis for this belief was Departmental Regulation 86, published in the *Radio Laws and Regulations of the United States*, August 15, 1919, which ruled:

> When applications and forms have been properly submitted, ship and amateur stations may be operated in accordance with the laws and regulations governing the class of station for which application for license has been made.[76]

The government argued that an amendment to that regulation, published in the *Radio Service Bulletin*, number 36, April 1, 1920, page 16, gave them discretion: "until such time as the application can be acted upon unless the applicant is otherwise instructed."[77]

Hoover granted the Intercity Company another hearing on May 23, 1921, to attempt to find a non-interfering frequency, but New York was too congested.

The license of Intercity expired on August 24, 1921, and renewal was denied. Radio experts in the New York area were asked to prepare data to prove interference by the Intercity plant should the case go to court again.[78]

On November 17, 1921, Secretary Hoover was ordered to appear in the District of Columbia State Supreme Court to show why he should not be requested to grant a renewal to the Intercity Company. A statement by the president of Intercity, Emil J. Simon, claimed the court proceedings were "a gentlemen's agreement: between the company and the lawyer for the Commerce Department to test the legal authority of the Secretary to refuse to reissue a license for the trafficking in wireless messages in interstate commerce."[79]

Hoover disagreed with this interpretation of his actions. His refusal to reissue the license "followed the result of a long period of experiment and investigation, during which time that company received all the assistance that could be given by this Department, as well as the assistance of others in the radio field, to remove, if possible, the aggravated interference that in many instances prevented the actual operation of government radio stations while ... Intercity ... was in operation."[80]

Justice Wendell P. Stafford, on November 18, 1921, ordered Secretary Hoover to issue a radio license renewal to the Intercity Company. During the arguments before the court, both Intercity and the Commerce Department agreed that the Act of 1912 was an obsolete statute, but differed on their interpretation of the powers granted by Congress. The court interpreted the statute as containing an omission by Congress to give the Secretary of Commerce discretionary power to refuse to license. Judge William E. Lamb, solicitor for the Department at that time stated that this was the first time since the law was enacted that it was subject to an interpretation by the courts. Lamb's reported statement laid out the government's concern:

> Of course, it has always been more or less of a puzzle. But, as I understand things now—and I am not criticizing Justice Stafford—the hands of the Federal Government are tied. We are unable to control the situation. Not only will the administration of the Government be hindered, but ships at sea which may have occasion to send an SOS call must wait their turn if the Intercity plant is working when a disaster occurs.
>
> Then, too, the inconvenience to ships and ship owners, Government vessels of all sorts, the nuisance to privately owned plants over which the news of the day, urgent private messages of both a business and a personal character are sent, and all ships and shore stations within reach of 3900 meter [76.88 kHz] wavelength of the Intercity plant—Well, you see by what I have just said just what is to be put up with.
>
> I can say this, that the Department has done everything in its power to prevent a contest in court. We have been patient. We have tried every known means to allow the Intercity plant to keep working without interfering with everybody else within its range. We find that it is both physically and mechanically impossible to devise to arrange a wavelength at which this plant can operate....
>
> What will be exceedingly interesting now will be an application from some other person or concern for a license to operate in New York with a plant as powerful or more powerful than the one operated by the Intercity Company....
>
> Unless the Court of Appeals or the United States Supreme Court reverses Justice Stafford's decision, all the department can do is to wait patiently and see what develops. I have contended all along that Mr. Hoover had authority at law to refuse to ... license.[81]

The Department of Commerce did not claim the station had violated any regulations. The Intercity Company's counsel jumped on this omission, contending that the reason no such argument was made was because the Secretary knew he had no authority under the law to enact any regulations governing wireless traffic. "Only such regulations as are contained in the law itself were legal, counsel declared, and the court upheld this contention."[82] It was declared that Hoover had assumed powers which only Congress could exercise and the Intercity Company's counsel introduced the congressional record of the committee report on the Act of 1912 as evidence.[83]

Four days after the court rendered its decision against the Commerce Department on November 22, 1921, Secretary Hoover instructed the Justice Department to appeal the case.[84]

An order was issued by Justice Stafford directing the Secretary to state upon the face of the license a wavelength or wavelengths at which the Intercity Company could operate *without* interference with other stations. The federal attorney protested that it was mechanically, scientifically and physically impossible to comply with this request. "The Department will not issue a license, as we will appeal."[85]

The Court of Appeals affirmed on February 5, 1923, that the Secretary had no authority to refuse to license any station.[86] In this first test case before the courts the Department of Commerce's power to make regulations under the Act of 1912 had been found to be nonexistent.

Hoover requested the Solicitor General to appeal the case to the Supreme Court, but to delay the argument in the case as long as possible. The department officials were certain they would likely lose on any appeal to the Supreme Court, however, delays would at least allow some semblance of control to remain with the Department while other options were pursued.

II. First National Radio Telephony Conference

In some respects the Intercity case contributed to the calling of a conference with leaders in the radio industry. Such a conference had been requested by the Department of Commerce's staff in early September of 1921. Chief radio inspector William D. Terrell wrote to Secretary Hoover on February 1, 1922:

> Broadcasting is growing so rapidly, is of such importance to the public and the difficulty of properly controlling it is so serious, I believe it desirable to have a conference here and invite representatives of the different interests in order that the Bureau may have the benefit of their recommendations and possibly arrange some language agreeable to all parties which will make it possible to carry on a broadcast service which will be for the public good.[87]

Secretary Hoover went before President Harding's cabinet, February 7, 1922, to ask for such a conference just two days after the Court of Appeals decision against the Department on the Intercity case. The press reported:

> The subject was discussed at length in today's Cabinet session, in which the President was told that the use of wireless telephony had suddenly become important. The President was told that through the broadcasting

of news, advertising, music, concerts, and other reports there had arisen the danger of interruption to the use of the wireless telephone for purposes of national defense and commercial purposes.[88]

During the discussion it was suggested that just as agreements had been made with foreign governments on the regulation of wavelengths in wireless telegraphy, so legislation might be enacted to control the use of wireless telephony by wavelengths. When President Harding authorized the conference to consist of Army, Navy and commercial interests, Hoover said, "he would be present as the special representative of the small boy."[89] Herbert Hoover, Jr.'s, amateur radio signals were heard in transatlantic tests being conducted by amateurs in Switzerland at the end of that year.[90]

Two days after the cabinet meeting, Secretary Hoover publicly noted that the question of control of the ether was:

> rapidly becoming as vital a topic as forest preservation and protection of water power rights. Both commercial and amateur use of the wireless telephone has developed to such an extent that the "air is full of chatter." The fact that in ordinary wireless telephonic communication there are but four or five wavelengths has clogged up this medium of communication to such an extent, that ... some form of "ether cops" will have to be established to regulate traffic.[91]

"Ether" was thought of at this time as being the necessary all-pervading, infinitely elastic, massless medium through which radio waves traveled.

Commissioner of Navigation Carson clarified his bureau's viewpoint on the need for regulation when he wrote: "No one has any intention of recommending any new legislation or any new regulations which will retard radio development, but without practical restrictions its full value cannot be realized.[92]

Fifteen representatives—nine government members and six from the radio industry—attended this First Radio Telephony Conference which was chaired by Dr. Stratton of the Bureau of Standards.[93]

Secretary Hoover, in his letters of invitation, suggested that participants' thoughts be directed to three possible solutions:

> First, an ideal solution, assuming suitable changes in the International Radio Convention and the U.S. Radio Law;
> Second, a solution compatible with the present International Convention, assuming that urgently needed changes in the U.S. Law will be made; and,
> Third, an immediate solution which can be effected under the present law.[94]

Because proposed legislation lacked industry backing, it did not pass Congress, so the alternate solution suggested by Hoover had to be implemented.[95]

One of the problems the Department of Commerce faced was the opposition from those "who have accepted literally the term, 'free as the air.'" Several factions were striving to gain control of the recently developed medium but all were in agreement that a definite U.S. radio policy was needed and that federal control was essential to a limited degree.[96]

Secretary Hoover's opening address at the Conference on February 27, 1922, set the tone for this and subsequent conferences. It could be applied today in this age of the Internet. His statement was important in setting forth the concepts he and his staff saw affecting the broadcast regulatory landscape.

> This conference has been called at the request of the President and its purpose is to inquire into the critical situation that has arisen through the astonishing development of the wireless telephone, to advise the Department of Commerce as to the application of its present powers of regulation and to develop the situation generally with a view of some recommendation to Congress, it being necessary, to extend the present powers of regulation. This is one of the few instances that I know of in this country where the public—all of the people—are unanimously for an extension of regulatory powers on the part of the Government. In undertaking the organization of this Conference, we have considered that it was desirable to make up the committee that is to give consideration to the results of the Conference largely from technical men representing the different Government departments and science. We have felt that it would be desirable to undertake the matter by way of a sort of inquiry and that this committee, set up in this fashion, would undertake at once the opening of public hearings in the whole matter with a view to getting the opinion and recommendations of every element in the community....
>
> We have witnessed in the last four or five months one of the most astounding things that has come under my observation of American life. The Department estimates that today over 600,000 (one estimate being 1,000,000) persons possess wireless telephone receiving sets, whereas there were less than fifty thousand such sets a year ago. We are indeed today upon the threshold of a new means of widespread communication of intelligence that has the most profound importance from the point of view of public education and public welfare. The comparative cheapness with which receiving stations can be installed, and the fact that the genius of the American boy is equal to the construction of such stations within the limits of his own savings, bid fair to make the possession of receiving sets almost universal in the American home.
>
> I think that it will be agreed at the outset that the use of the radio telephone for communication between single individuals as in the case of the ordinary telephone is a perfectly hopeless notion. Obviously if ten million telephone subscribers are crying through the air for their mates they will never make a junction; the ether will be filled with frantic chaos, with no communication of any kind possible. In other words,

the wireless telephone has one definite field, and that is for the spread of certain pre-determined material of public interest from central stations. This material must be limited to news, to education, to entertainment, and the communication of such commercial matters as are of importance to large groups of the community at the same time.

It is therefore primarily a question of broadcasting, and it becomes of primary public interest to say who is to do the broadcasting, under what circumstances, and with what type of material. It is inconceivable that we should allow so great a possibility for service, for news, for entertainment, for education, and for vital commercial purposes, to be drowned in advertising chatter, or for commercial purposes that can be quite well served by our other means of communication.

Congress some few years ago authorized the Secretary of Commerce to license radio sending stations, and to impose certain conditions in the licenses designed to prevent interference between the stations and to serve the public good. This legislation was drawn before the development of the telephone was of consequential importance. Until the last four or five months there has been but little difficulty in handling these regulations, because sending purposes have been largely confined to radio telegraph, and to a very small extent to the radio telephone. The extraordinary development of the radio telephone, however, has brought us face to face with an entirely new condition upon which licenses should be issued. It raises questions as to what extension in the powers of the Department should be requested of Congress in order that the maximum public good shall be secured from the developments of this great invention. During the last five months, while this extraordinarily rapid installation has been in progress, I and my colleagues in the Department have felt that we should take a very conservative attitude on the issuance of sending licenses, and I am able to inform you that there are today, outside of government broadcasting stations, and the field authorized to the American boy, but few licenses outstanding—and these are limited to a small proportion of the number of available wavelengths. We have therefore kept the field clear for constructive development. The experience gained indicates that the time has arrived not only when this large mass of subscribers need protection as to the noises which fill their instruments, but also when there must be measures to stop the interferences which have already grown up between even the limited number of sending stations which threaten to destroy them all.

The problem is one of most intensely technical character, but is not one without hope of fairly complete solution. Fortunately, the sending of radio telephone messages can be arranged in wavelengths sufficiently far apart so as not to interfere with each other, and receivers can at their option tune their receiving instruments to the different wave bands. With the improvement in the art and in the delicacy of instruments, the distance between wavelengths may eventually decrease and thus the number of layers of messages increase. Furthermore, it is possible to increase the number of sending stations and thus the variety of material, if the power applied to certain wavelengths is limited so as to circumscribe the area of distribution for a given station. Beyond this again certain times a day may be set aside within certain wavelengths for certain types of information.

With the permutations possible to work out in different wavelengths, in different geographical areas, in different times of day, we should be able to make it possible for the owner of a receiving instrument, by tuning his instrument to different wavelengths, at different times, to possess himself of a great variety of entertainment, information, news, etc., at his own option. Even if we use all the ingenuity possible I do not believe there are enough permutations to allow unlimited numbers of sending stations.

One of the problems that enters into this whole question is that of who is to support the sending stations.... I believe that we ought to allow anyone to put in receiving stations who wishes to do so. But the immediate problem arises of who will do the broadcasting and what will be his purpose. It is at once obvious that our universities, our technical schools, our government bureaus, are all of them willing and anxious to distribute material of extremely valuable order without remuneration. Also judging from the applications we have had, any number of merchants are prepared to distribute entertainment provided they are allowed to interlard discussion as to the approaching remnant sale. Many of the larger newspaper publishers are asking for licenses to install broadcasting sets in which news and entertainment will be distributed, and the commercial companies are requesting licenses for the establishment of systematic distribution of news and entertainment conditional upon their being given permission to undertake commercial broadcasting of one kind or another.

It is my belief that, with the variations that can be given through different wavelengths, through different times of day, and through the staggering of stations of different wavelengths in different parts of the country, it will be possible to accommodate the most proper demands and at the same time protect that precious thing—the American small boy, to whom so much of this rapid expansion of interest is done.

It is, however, a problem of regulation, if we are to get the maximum use. It is one of the few instances that I know of where the whole industry and country is earnestly praying for more regulation. Regulation will need to be policed, if there is not to be great prejudice to the majority, and thus the celestial system—at least the ether part of it—comes with the province of the policeman. Fortunately, the art permits such a policeman by listening in to direct those ether hogs that are endangering the traffic.

There is involved, however, in all of this regulation the necessity to so establish public right over the ether roads that there may be no national regret that we have parted with a great national asset into uncontrolled hands. I believe this conference with the high skill it represents will be able to determine upon a method which should give satisfaction in all directions, and should stimulate the creation of a new addition to our national life.[97]

Programming considerations. The conference backed Hoover's disapproval of direct advertising. Hoover had made the point that commercial interests were not to be placed before public service.

It was recommended that direct advertising be prohibited and any indirect advertising be limited to a statement of the call letters of the station and the name of the concern responsible for the broadcast matter.[98] This format is familiar to us today through its application on National Public Radio and PBS.

The American Telephone and Telegraph Company had announced plans to establish a "toll" station in New York City (WEAF). The Conference considered the possibilities and recommended that commercial stations should be at the end of a priority list for consideration. It also recommended that the degree of *public interest* of a private or toll station (which charged for use and was profit-making) should be considered not only in the granting of licenses, but in the assignments of wavelengths and permissible power.[99]

The order of recommended priorities was:

1. Government Broadcasting
2. Educational and Public Broadcasting
3. Private Broadcasting
4. Toll Broadcasting.

Technical Considerations. As Secretary Hoover noted in his opening address to the Conference: "the problem is one of most intensely technical character, but is not one without hope of fairly complete solution." He suggested different wavelengths, different times of operation, and staggering stations on different wavelengths in different parts of the country to allow the greatest development of broadcasting. During the hearings he stated, "it is hoped we can find enough wavelengths so we can have at least two [stations] in each town and competition may lead to a high class of service."[100] These technical considerations and limitations dominated the Conference meetings and resulted in specific recommendations for regulations to improve reception.

Regulatory Suggestions. Secretary Hoover reiterated his concept that broadcasting and the use of the spectrum was a national resource, a concept he arrived at during his 11 months in office prior to the Conference.

He noted that few licenses were outstanding and the field had been kept clear for future needs. Fifty-five stations had been licensed, and 22 applications were on file with the Commerce Department as of February 1922.[101]

A suggestion was made at the conference by AT&T that 12 stations of one-kilowatt capacity might be adequate for a broadcast service. The fear of early broadcasters concerning so-called "high" power was evident throughout the testimony in various hearings and conferences. Station KDKA, Pittsburgh, used a power of 500 watts which apparently blanketed receivers in the city up to a wavelength of 600 to 700 meters. (KDKA operated on 360 meters as did all other stations. They were blanketing the dial from approximately 832.8 kHz down to 428.3 kHz.) The station also radiated a strong second harmonic signal, as reports indicated reception at 180 meters (166 kHz) as well.[102]

The general agreement of the 1922 Conference called for an amendment to the existing legislation to give the Secretary of Commerce adequate legal authority to prevent such interference.

Further controls were suggested for:

> 1. Transmissions of all stations, except amateur, experimental, and governmental stations, and
> 2. Operations of non-governmental transmitting stations.

Further resolutions decreed radio communication as a *public utility*, which should be regulated as such by the federal government, and determined that radio receivers designed to be more effective in reducing interference should be made readily available to the public.

Proposals for new regulations suggested that each radio telephone broadcasting station be assigned a certain power based on the normal range of the station. The normal range of the station was to be based on the following:

> 1. Government stations, 600 (land) miles
> 2. Public Broadcasting stations, 250 miles
> 3. Private and Toll stations, 50 miles.

Many at the Conference felt it would be unwise to push for legislation unless there were definite rules and control was placed in the hands of a single government body with broad-based powers.[103]

Representatives of commercial radio interests reportedly favored authority vested in the Department of Commerce. "There is said to be opposition to this in Army and Navy circles, but these matters the conference will endeavor to iron out."[104]

Recognizing that radio interference was a major broadcast reception problem, members of the conference suggested studies should be conducted by the Bureau of Standards.[105]

It was suggested that the Secretary of Commerce make a study of the geographical distribution of broadcast stations. This was an early determination that a zonal method was necessary for a nationwide distribution of broadcast stations.

The Secretary was requested to assign suitable hours of operation to existing stations where congestion was evident.

It must be remembered that the First National Radio Telephony Conference had no legal authority. Its purpose was to achieve voluntary cooperation from members of the broadcasting industry. Those present agreed to abide by the decisions of the Secretary of Commerce, whether or not Hoover had legal authority.[106]

Industry Reaction to the First Radio Conference. A number of industry groups submitted alternatives to the Conference recommendations, some of which were adopted in the final report.

One of the more interesting documents was a six-page report submitted by the Radio Corporation of America (RCA) in April for consideration by the conference. The corporation approved of the "broadcast possible statutes." The report strongly recommended the Commerce Department had to have the right to regulate all radio stations, including amateur, experimental and government stations which the conference had not considered.

The report by RCA was heeded by the Department staff which was writing the final draft of the conference proposals.

The recommendation of RCA that the Secretary be allowed to license *all* stations was not accepted because there was difficulty in obtaining cooperation from the military. Secretary Hoover was to press for such power later in his tenure.

The corporation also asked that the following phrase be included in the final report:

> Resolved that it is the sense of the Conference that radio communication is a public utility and as such should be regulated by the Federal Government in the public interest.[107]

This was adopted just as RCA submitted it in the final recommendations of the Conference. It is one of the earlier uses of the term, "public interest" although not exactly in the same sense as it was to be used in the Radio Act of 1927.[108]

The statement that "radio apparatus be freely available to the public which would eliminate interference" be amended by striking "without limitations" was also requested by RCA. The controlling patents which RCA held restricted, in their minds, any concept of totally "free availability" because, of course, nothing patented was "free."

The basic argument of the Radio Corporation was, "the firm conviction of this company, that in times of peace, *all* transmitting stations should be subject to the same general law without discrimination favorable or unfavorable to any particular class or group of stations."[109]

Conference Accomplishments. Years later, in discussing the advances made at the first Conference, Secretary Hoover said in a broadcast on the Columbia Broadcasting System (CBS):

> There were certain principles adopted at that conference which laid the foundations of all our present broadcasting. Summarized they were:
>
> 1. That the broadcasting channels should be public property just as are the navigation channels in our waterways.
>
> 2. That the broadcasting should be conducted as a private enterprise and not governmental broadcasting as had already been started in Britain....

3. There should be no monopoly in broadcasting.

4. There must be regulation of the traffic to prevent interference.

5. There should be no person-to-person use of wavelengths except by the military and licensed amateurs as there was no room for such service.

6. We divided the then known wave band into three parts among the broadcaster, the amateurs, and the military authorities.[110]

III. Failure of Legislation

Introduction of S. 3694. The Department of Commerce began a campaign to gain public support for the bill as proposed by the First Radio Conference. Secretary Hoover sent a news release to the Boston *Evening Transcript* on May 4, 1922, which read:

> One of the first necessities for development is adequate control. There are but a limited number of wavelengths and there must be some traffic direction or the whole road will be blocked. This is the only industry where anybody is asking the Government for regulation and it is hoped that the present Congress will adopt the recommendations of the National Conference on Radio recently called at my request.[111]

Sen. Kellogg had introduced S. 3694 on April 20. It had been prepared by the legal committee of the conference: Sen. Kellogg, Rep. White, Chief radio inspector William Terrell, and Assistant Commissioner of Navigation Arthur Tyrer.

The first draft of a House bill submitted to the legal committee by Rep. White was approved in general principles but a number of changes had to be made.

Kellogg's Senate bill, approved in its entirety, was considered an emergency measure by the legal committee, while work went forward with the revision of White's House bill. Tyrer commented: "It may be possible to avoid the delay which could be occasioned by hearings before the committees [of the Senate and House] inasmuch as the representatives of the Radio Interests throughout the country were here during the conference and approved the bill [S. 3694]."[112]

Hoover asked a personal secretary, Paul Kruesi, "to take particular interest in this subject." Kruesi said the revocation provisions were not strong enough. "Would it not be well to provide for summary action by the Secretary of Commerce, giving him, in case of public need, according to his discretion, authority to suspend operation of any station [except.... Government ...], pending a hearing?"

An analogy was drawn between such a provision and the power of the Interstate Commerce Commission to suspend charges against railroads until hearings were held.[113]

Commissioner Carson replied:

> While undoubtedly, the suggestions which you have made would clar-
> ify the bill, it appears to me that in view of the urgent necessity for
> prompt action and the fact that the bill as drawn has been approved by
> the Conference and further that this is understood to be an emergency
> bill subject to later amendments, we should not offer amendments if
> they can be avoided.[114]

Kruesi made clear:

> I have no desire to suggest superfluous changes that would result in delay
> of the bill.... This does not change my view that an ideal bill would pro-
> vide authority in specific terms for summary action by the Secretary—
> station suspension first—hearing next—revocation or reinstatement
> afterward.[115]

Press comments on the bill were found to be "favorable, as there is growing recognition of the need for better Federal regulation."[116]

Members of the legal committee and the department's solicitor, Judge
Lamb, attended a conference with Kruesi, Commissioner Carson and Chief
Inspector Terrell on June 23. Judge Lamb agreed with Kruesi that the bill
did not give the Department enough power, especially on suspension and
revocation, and suggested changes he described as necessary to "put teeth
into the Bill."[117]

Apparently, in a conflict between Hoover's secretary, Paul Kruesi, and
Commissioner Carson and Inspector Terrell on accepting the bill as proposed
by the Conference, or changing it to strengthen the Department of Commerce's ability to take action against violations, Kruesi won.

Carson then suggested that Hoover ask Judge Lamb to draft a change
which would be suitable for the legal committee.

Hoover asked Congressman White to include provisions to provide
definite power to suspend or revoke station and operator's licenses in his H. R.
11964. "It is essential in the administration of a law of this nature that the
penalty provisions should be entirely clear and I feel that the ... changes are
of sufficient importance to warrant the amendment of the Bill in committee."[118]

Introduction of H. R. 11964. The revision of White's proposed bill was being
carried out during discussions on the Kellogg bill. White conferred often
with Terrell and Tyrer and asked that they "not be backward about criticiz-
ing [the bill]."[119]

By the end of May 1922 Hoover's legal committee had reviewed the
House bill which incorporated the recommendations of the Radio Conference. Terrell felt, "no effort will be made to prepare regulations under the
authority of the proposed bill until it becomes effective." It was hoped that
the proposed new legislation would pass that session of Congress.[120]

White announced that the bill, as finally drafted, was not a general radio law. Those interested in radio believed that interference was the biggest problem, and White remarked that the bill was designed to "enlarge and clarify the power of the Secretary of Commerce so the present interference may be reduced to a minimum."[121]

The proposed bill would give the Secretary the power to classify radio stations and the service each would provide, assign wavelengths to each class, and make regulations concerning power, location, times and methods of operation. The most sweeping change between this bill and the Act of 1912 was the power given to the Secretary of Commerce to make rules and regulations. The power of licensing under this proposed law would be discretionary, not mandatory.

Rep. White introduced H. R. 11964 to the House on June 9, 1922. Tyrer compared the Senate and House bills, and noted "the bill introduced in the Senate by Senator Kellogg ... is identical to the one introduced in the House by Congressman White."[122] The Department staff began calling both efforts the White-Kellogg Bill.

Both bills were so similar because the Department of Commerce staff had advised both men on the proposed legislation, suggesting, guiding and rewriting complete sections of the proposed law.

The hope that hearings would be held before the end of 1922 continued to pervade the correspondence of the various bureaus of the Department of Commerce. But the Committee on Merchant Marine and Fisheries, considering other legislation first, did not hold hearings on the proposed legislation until January 2 and 3, 1923.

Preparation for the Hearings on the White-Kellogg Bills. Secretary Hoover issued a press release stating: "It [the radio bill] looks to procuring for the largest number the benefits to be derived from systematized use of the ether...." He was aware that the military, in particular the Navy "contended vigorously and with justification that their stations ought not to be subjected to civilian control."[123]

Optimistically, the radio inspectors were asked to "go over the new bill carefully in conjunction with the present law and carefully make notations concerning amendments to the present regulations or new regulations which your experience indicates as being necessary."[124]

Industry Opinion on the Proposed Legislation. New York radio inspector Batcheller conducted interviews with the industry leadership. David Sarnoff of the Radio Corporation of America stated that while he was in favor of placing the responsibility for regulation in the hands of the Secretary of Commerce, "He was of the opinion that a question might arise as regards the advisability of placing such complete authority, as would be provided under the White-Kellogg Bill, in the hands of a single head of a Government bureau."[125] Sarnoff admitted that his company had not taken any action for or against the bill because it was not clear in his mind as to what the future had to hold for radio broadcasting.

A. H. Griswold, assistant vice president of American Telephone and Telegraph (AT&T) expressed his opinion that the bill would be satisfactory to his company. He wanted the section on monopoly changed to read "unlawful monopoly," because certain forms of monopoly were allowed by the federal government, including the operation of AT&T itself. The Bureau of Navigation did not object to this proposal.[126]

"Mr. Griswold recognizes the necessity of legislation and more legal power for the Secretary of Commerce, sufficient to enable him to properly administer the radio communication affairs of the United States.... American Telephone and Telegraph has complete confidence [in] Mr. Hoover's regime."[127]

Powel Crosley, Jr., president of the Crosley Manufacturing Company and owner of radio station WLW (Cincinnati), stated "the only objection ... is the fact that it delegates too much power upon the part of the Secretary of Congress [sic]."[128]

W. H. Easton of the publicity department of the Westinghouse Company stated his company was in favor of the bill. Westinghouse had not taken any active action for or against the bill, "because, under the present system of regulation, national and local, his company was well taken care of ... and that peace and harmony prevailed."

George Lewis, secretary of the National Radio Chamber of Commerce, expressed his organization's approval of the bill. Lewis thought that the reason why radio interests had not taken some definite action for or against the White-Kellogg bills was based on the fact that none of the commercial companies was very sure what the future had to offer for radio broadcasting.[129]

Paul Nagle, communications expert for the Bureau of Foreign and Domestic Commerce of the Department, also made a tour of the major companies in New York to learn their feelings toward the proposed legislation. His information agreed with Batcheller's, except on one point:

> The people to whom he [Batcheller] had talked were of the opinion that the attitude of their companies would be to question the giving of such complete power to the Secretary of Commerce. I did not hear any mention of this, and in fact, the companies principally concerned questioned only the clause on monopolies and the composition of the Advisory Committee.[130]

Dr. Alfred N. Goldsmith, secretary of the Institute of Radio Engineers, voiced the views of the Institute toward the radio bills.

1. the Department of Commerce was the logical department to exercise authority;
2. the monopoly clause was not necessary, and
3. the bill in general was quite satisfactory.

Batcheller, who had conferred with Dr. Goldsmith, said: "He questioned somewhat the advisability of granting to the Secretary such complete power as the new bill will provide, unless the Secretary intends to make full use of the powers granted." Batcheller said Dr. Goldsmith used an analogy of the Prohibition Law where ample authority was given the government, but the powers were not fully used.[131]

The Department of Commerce also solicited comments on the White-Kellogg bills from the Navy, which held to the position that the wavelengths between 600 and 1600 meters (499.7 kHz–187.4 kHz) should remain exclusively naval and military. The White-Kellogg bills wished to change the wording to "Government" wherever "Military" appeared. The Navy Department officials wrote Hoover:

> This change of "Naval and Military" to "Government" should not be made. These words were taken from the International Berlin Radio Telegraph Convention and were purposely adopted so as to give the Navy the exclusive wave bands between 600 and 1600 meters.... Other departments of the Government might be assigned wave bands exclusively reserved for military and Naval defenses.... Even if we remove them, the change will not be accepted or binding on other nations.[132]

The Navy justified its authority over their current allocations.

> President Roosevelt, by Executive Order in 1904, directed that the Navy take over and operate all the radio stations on the coast and that the Army take the interior ones, and that these two Departments of the Government would furnish the service for any other Governmental Departments. This executive order has been the growing principle with reference to the operation of radio stations.[133]

The Department of Commerce's position was that the Navy's viewpoint was based "on the order of President Roosevelt made in 1904, when conditions were extremely different than at present and has long been considered obsolete. It is eight years worse off than our present law."[134]

The American Radio Relay League (ARRL) wanted the word "commercial" placed before the term "radio stations" wherever these appeared in the law. This would have cast some doubt on the Department's jurisdiction over amateur, experimental, technical and training schools, and in some instances broadcasting stations that were not considered "commercial."[135] The Department refused to consider such a limitation because all of these types of stations could cause interference.

The ARRL proposed that the advisory committee not include any individual connected with the manufacture, sale, transmission or operation of radio instruments for sale. The Department responded:

> This would destroy the purpose of such a committee as to properly administer laws governing the great commercial interests of the country ... it is essential that the administering office should have the advice and cooperation of such interests. We must have practical administration of the law and not theoretical.[136]

During 1922, radio broadcasting was experiencing explosive growth from 28 stations to 570. Only 67 stations had ceased operations during the year.[137] Interference was the main problem faced by the public:

> It is imperative, if the development of the radio art and its more general use are not to be greatly retarded, that the regulatory powers of the department in connection with "interferences" should be greatly extended.[138]

Hearings on House Bill 11964. Secretary Hoover entered the 1923 hearings on the White-Kellogg bills knowing that the situation was becoming increasingly difficult and which criticisms had been directed at the bill.

He was aware that: 1) some organizations were fearful of the power being vested in the Department of Commerce; 2) objections were being raised on the section concerning monopoly; 3) there was some concern about the make-up of the advisory committee, with some wanting more seats for industry, while others wanted no industry representation; and 4) various governmental departments objected to Department of Commerce control over their particular stations.

The first questions directed to Hoover concerned the Navy's argument against the licensing of Navy stations and operators. Hoover answered, "I do not see how we can set up any systematic control of radio throughout the country, to prevent interference, if the Navy is to be a complete outlaw in the fabric."[139]

Concerning the monopoly provision, Hoover did not see any objection to including the word "unlawful" before "monopoly," as "I do not assume the Secretary of Commerce can dissolve a monopoly that is lawful."[140]

The concern with monopoly stemmed from early 1921 and was generally reflected in Commerce Department files in relation to international communications. British, French, German and RCA interests had met in Paris for two months in 1921 and concluded an agreement for the development of communications in South America. The RCA group contended it was carrying the principle of the Monroe Doctrine into the field of communications in the Western hemisphere. Because it had been founded at the behest of the United States Government in 1919, RCA asserted that it was within their rights to monopolize South American communications development.

Secretary Hoover had then expressed his opinion on monopoly to the Secretary of State:

> We need further consideration of the many elements surrounding international radio communications. We are faced with one of four theories of organization, i.e., competition, regulated monopoly, unregulated monopoly, government ownership. We can generally agree to exclude government ownership.[141]

In international communication Hoover recognized that most European governments had erected monopolies so "we cannot now discuss competition even if we want to."[142] However, the United States could still make this decision within its own borders.

In January 1922 AT&T proposed to the New York radio inspector that they erect 50 stations throughout the U.S. to be used for chain (network) broadcasting. The plan was immediately seen to have elements of a monopoly based solely on patent rights. Commissioner of Navigation Carson was initially supportive of the proposal but soon realized that if any individual or company could ask for a broadcasting license that would have to be given there would not be any appreciable reduction in stations.

The Department of Commerce did not have the right to limit licenses by number or by nature of ownership which contributed to the growth of diversity in the broadcasting industry. Had there been some means to limit the amount or the categories of licenses, it is likely that both the number and type of people entering the field of broadcasting would have been different. Competition in United States broadcasting developed because the Act of 1912 did not give the Secretary of Commerce discretionary powers. We can only speculate what might have developed had the Secretary had the right and duty to restrict licenses to those whom he felt would provide the best service to the listening public.

The question of monopoly had a long history, and was central to the thoughts of the industry when the hearings on the proposed radio bills began. Elwood of AT&T asked Nagle, "How set is the Secretary [of Commerce] on the clause in regard to monopolies?" Nagle thought it best not to discuss the question and called Elwood's attention to the fact that the whole subject matter of the bill had been fully discussed at the First Radio Conference.

Nagle's reply:

> I rather expected that the American Telephone and Telegraph Company and the Radio Corporation would not like that particular clause in the bill but I do not believe that either one of them is in a position to publicly oppose it. If any opposition to it develops it would be through some apparently disinterested person who will present what might be the views of these two companies.[143]

At the hearing Secretary Hoover again stressed the main problem in the proposed legislation.

> I do not think it would be any exaggeration to say we are receiving thousands of protests monthly over questions of interference. We are engaged in endeavoring to compromise and compose the difficulties between broadcasting stations, on a purely voluntary basis, all over the country. Some cities have as high as 20 broadcasting stations, all interfering with each other, and our agents have endeavored at one time and another to get them into voluntary agreements as to the division of the time and other methods of preventing interference; but we are totally without the necessary authority to effect results. And this is not a case of regulation as against the will of the industry, and the wish is that there should be some regulation by which these problems can be disentangled at least to some extent. It is unique in the way of regulatory legislation.[144]

Following the hearings on H. R. 11964, it was brought to the attention of Secretary Hoover, Commissioner Carson and Rep. White that AT&T and RCA wanted to insert in the bill a provision to allow the owners and or operators of a station to appeal to the courts if they were not satisfied with a decision of the Secretary of Commerce. Nagle offered the Department's reaction:

> The recommendation made by the only two concerns in the United States having any large interest in international radio would set up a reverse process, it seems ... and would invoke the aid of the court against the execution of the law rather than to aid in its enforcement....
>
> I have discussed this matter with Mr. Terrell and we are in agreement that this matter should be brought to the attention of Mr. Hoover....[145]

Expectations of Passage. New York radio inspector Arthur Batcheller noted: "As the Bureau is aware, radio represents one of the most important and difficult problems that the Federal Government, commercial representatives and engineers, have had on their hands to solve." He recommended the following for the advisory committee provided for in the proposed bill:

> A. H. Griswold, Asst. Vice President, American Telephone and Telegraph Company;
> George S. Davis, General Manager, Tropical Radio Telegraph Company;
> Dr. Alfred N. Goldsmith, Secretary, Institute of Radio Engineers;
> John V. L. Hogan, consulting engineer;
> Hiram P. Maxim, President, American Radio Relay League; and
> C. B. Cooper, Vice President, Ship Owners' Radio Service, Inc.[146]

Batcheller pointed out the importance networks would have. "It might not be out of order if I should mention at this time that radio broadcasting in the future will be largely accomplished by wire control to distant points, and that the American Telephone and Telegraph Company have a most complete network of wires all over this country."[147]

Carson prepared biographical material for Hoover on each of the men on Batcheller's list, adding the names of Frederick A. Kolster, formerly of the Bureau of Standards, and Frederick G. Simpson, a consulting engineer.[148]

Consideration of the membership of the proposed advisory commission was rather premature because Congressman White had to confer with Secretary Hoover and the Secretary of the Navy in an effort to overcome the objections of the Navy to the bill. A section of the bill relating to the allocation of wavelengths for the Navy was rewritten and this power was assigned to the President of the United States, with the advice and assistance of the Secretary of Commerce.[149]

Increasing optimism was expressed by the members of the Radio Service staff concerning the possibilities of the bill being passed. Early in January of 1923, Commissioner of Navigation Carson reported:

> At the recent hearing ... there was not very much opposition or objection and the indications are that there is a very good prospect of the bill passing at the present session of Congress, possibly within a month.[150]

Just as six months earlier, Carson requested that the field staff be called upon to propose any rules and regulations necessary when the new bill was enacted.

H. R. 11964 Amended Into H. R. 13773. H. R. 11964 was amended and the numerical designation changed to H. R. 13773. Included was a provision for charging nominal fees for licenses, both for operator and station. The Department of Commerce arranged for the collection of fees by the Comptroller General of the United States.

The Comptroller General notified Secretary Hoover that "accounting difficulties in the way of the proposed plan are perhaps not insurmountable, but they do constitute a substantial objection to the plan.[151]

At the end of January 1923 Secretary Hoover stepped up the pressure for radio legislation:

> The present radio telephone situation in the United States is simply intolerable to those who have at heart the full value of radio broadcasting. Yet there is absolutely no adequate solution of the problem open to the Department of Commerce until pending legislation makes available to the public the use of the wave-band, 1600 to 600 meters, which is reserved for governmental purposes....
>
> In the meantime the Radio Division of the Bureau of Navigation has utilized its ingenuity and resourcefulness to the full to make the most of the allocation of such wavelengths outside, but by no means including all outside, the governmental band. Thus, to make the most of the 400-meter [749.6 kHz] wavelength, with an eye to the enjoyment of the

greatest number, a new classification of broadcasting stations, Class B, was set up, with special requirements designed to make each broadcasting station using the 400-meter wavelength of the largest possible service to those having receiving sets.

The passing of the bills now before Congress will not, of course, constitute a panacea that will entirely do away with the necessity, for instance of improving the selecting power of receiving sets in general use. But until the existing law is amended certainly no considerable improvement in the situation can be looked for. Then a re-allocation of wavelengths can be made such as will, at least, make the most of existing potentialities.[152]

The Bureau of Navigation prepared figures to be used in requesting increased appropriations for additional radio inspectors, money for travel, instruments and other items that would be needed when the bill passed.

Secretary Hoover wrote a letter to President Harding, including a draft of a note he hoped the President would send on to the Senate floor leader. The note asked assistance in getting the White-Kellogg Bill pushed through. Hoover said: "I am in hopes that it can be slid in at some apropos moment in the Senate."[153]

However, opposition developed from Sen. Oscar Underwood who was opposed to the so-called RCA monopoly. Walter S. Rogers, of the legal staff of the Department of Commerce, in writing to Sen. Kellogg, felt this opposition could be overcome:

My suggestion is simply this—that the pending radio bill be passed and at the same time a resolution be adopted directing the Federal Trade Commission to conduct an investigation to ascertain what, if any, efforts are being made in any way to monopolize or to restrict the manufacture or sale of radio apparatus....

Certainly the pending radio bill does not confer a monopoly, and Senator Underwood's objection can only go to the question as to whether the bill as it now stands full protects the public against monopoly. Perhaps he can be brought to support the bill, if he knew that all the essential facts regarding radio will be brought to the attention of the next Congress.[154]

The Federal Trade Commission did make an investigation of the Radio Corporation of America as proposed by Rogers.[155]

By mid–February 1923, Secretary Hoover knew that there was no chance of the White-Kellogg Bill passing that session of Congress.[156]

IV. Regulation Without Legislation

Throughout the failed attempt at legislation from 1921 to 1924 the Department of Commerce staff was attempting to regulate and control broadcasting to the best of their abilities. How well they accomplished control influenced the development of further regulatory efforts.

Interdepartmental Cooperation Between Government Agencies. At the First National Radio Conference it became evident to Hoover that "as a necessary part of the whole settlement of the allocation of wavelengths we must, if possible, secure agreement within the different departments of the Administration."[157]

This attempt began in early April of 1921 when Hoover reported to the cabinet that there was a need for a special committee to control government radio activities. He felt there was much conflict between government departments using radio, "and since the war, when all radio was under the supervision of the Navy Department, there has been no hard-and-fast rules in operation."[158]

Hoover informed the cabinet "that authority for coordinating the various Government systems did not now exist, although the necessity for it was apparent."[159] The cabinet, after much discussion, decided that the Secretaries of War, State, Navy and Commerce, and the Postmaster General should appoint a special coordinating committee.

"It will not be the intention to institute Government control such as was applied during the war, but regulations which systems would have to comply with in future to receive licenses."[160]

The Interdepartmental Radio Advisory Committee (IRAC) was formally established by the Secretary on March 10, 1922, following the First Radio Conference's recommendations that some means had to be found to regulate the frequencies used for government broadcasting.

After a number of meetings, representatives of the six government departments tentatively agreed on a report entitled *Recommendations on Governmental Radio Broadcasting*. The report noted that there were six classes of material being broadcast by government stations to the public:

a) market price movements
b) weather and hydrographic news
c) standard radio signals
d) executive announcements
e) statistics, crime control, etc.
f) educational material

The April report recommended that 1) radio be utilized whenever another means could not be found; 2) that an experimental system, using "primary" broadcast stations be started to furnish "local," stations with material for rebroadcast; 3) that these "primary" stations receive material by leased wire or relayed radio; 4) and specified the locations of these "primary" outlets.

The government departments agreed that any Government-owned station, either "primary" or "local" should be subject to the same regulations as privately-owned stations, and that the regulations should be established by the Secretary of Commerce. It was also recommended that the IRAC be made a permanent advisory committee to "advise the Secretary of Commerce on the general regulation of radio broadcasting by Government stations on schedules of operation, priority of types of Government material to be broadcast, etc."[161]

The Navy Department requested that each department be made responsible for the material broadcast, and the Post Office Department noted that government stations were temporary until Congress provided permanent facilities.

Dr. Stratton's suggested letter was sent to all departments under Hoover's signature. It said, in part:

> It is a matter of considerable satisfaction that such an agreement was reached.
>
> It is to be noted that the machinery contemplated for primary distribution of Government news is an experimental system. It is recognized that the stations involved which are near the borders of the country are subject to consideration of international rights, and that this must be considered in planning a permanent system later.[162]

The committee initially dealt only with government broadcasting, but successive meetings extended their scope. In January 1923, with the concurrence of all departments, the IRAC extended its activities to all matters pertaining to the government's radio business on an advisory basis.[163]

In addition to advisory functions the committee acted as a clearinghouse for the government. The entire question of which frequencies could be used by government radio stations was handled by the IRAC, which furnished a means to adjust any conflicts in frequency use. This voluntary adjustment in the use of government frequencies became the major feature of the IRAC's work and continues to this day.[164]

The IRAC passed a resolution supporting the White-Kellogg bills because congestion made it increasingly difficult to find frequencies for government stations.[165]

Commissioner of Navigation Carson, in November of 1922, recommended to the Secretary that the IRAC be expanded to include six members not connected with government agencies.

> The existing Interdepartmental Radio Committee, not having representation of the commercial and private interests, has considered exclusively radio matters in which the several Departments ... were interested.... About half of these departments and independent offices have no direct contact with radio problems such as must be considered in

connection with the preparation for the International Radio Conference [planned for 1923, but not held until 1927], the pending radio bill and the regulations which will follow its passage.

You are familiar with the attitude of the commercial and private interests that they should have representation on committees having to do with national or international legislation and regulations.

The appointment of such a committee as recommended ... will be of great assistance to this Bureau in connection with the problems which will affect largely commercial and private interests and whose opinions and interests this Bureau would like to carefully consider and safeguard as far as may be found practicable and reasonable.[166]

Carson's request was seconded by Dr. Stratton in December, just before he left the Commerce Department. Stratton said, "in view of the close relation between the different forms of radio communication and the fact that the same experts in the different Departments deal with the subject as a whole, that the scope of its [IRAC] activities be enlarged ... to cover matters pertaining to radio communications in general." This would include the power to regulate.[167]

Secretary Hoover disagreed and responded:

I believe, however, that it is important that the original character of this committee be preserved as a Committee advisory to the Secretary of Commerce rather than one having authority to assign duties to the various Government departments or enforce regulations.... Experience has shown that there must be complete authority in one department to control all stations, both Governmental and Nongovernmental. Without such unified control, radio regulation becomes hopeless; and the radio situation is a unique one in that the country is united in demanding regulation. The requirement that the establishment and enforcement of regulations bearing on radio interference be centered in one authority was emphasized by the recent Radio Telephony Conference. In a draft of a new law prepared by that Conference, it will provide that the Secretary of Commerce establish regulations covering Government as well as all other radio stations except for the handling of strictly departmental business by stations operated by the various Government departments.[168]

The provision for some sort of an advisory board was generally included in the bills introduced in Congress following the establishment of the IRAC.

Implementation of Cooperative Regulation. Shortly after the First National Radio Telephony Conference, the Department of Commerce attempted to implement some of its recommendations.

Amateur operators were given 200 meters (1500 kHz), but not allowed to broadcast programs to the general public. The concept of "broadcasting" was being codified as a separate classification. It was the opinion of some in the department that "when proposed new legislation is enacted, very few amateur licenses will be issued if the recommendations of the radio conference are followed."[169]

Amateur licensing during the 1920s decreased slightly even without legislative approval as the Department of Commerce implemented some Conference recommendations:[170]

$$
\begin{array}{ccc}
1923 & - & 16{,}570 \\
1924 & - & 15{,}540 \\
1925 & - & 15{,}000 \\
1926 & - & 14{,}902 \\
1927 & - & 16{,}926 \\
\end{array}
$$

Other services, such as police department radio, were assigned to the general broadcast band of 360 meters because no reallocation of frequencies had been attempted.

The Radio Conference Technical Committee recommended that the same wave or overlapping wave bands should not to be assigned to stations within specified distances of each other: for broadcasting by departments of the federal government, 1,500 miles; for broadcasting by public institutions including state governments, universities and others disseminating informational and educational service, 750 miles; and for broadcasting without charge by a communication company, a store, a newspaper, or such other private or public organization or person licensed for the purpose of disseminating news, entertainment and other service or broadcasting where a charge is made, 150 miles.

Terrell pointed out in a letter to Acting Secretary Huston that to carry out these recommendations would have meant "eight or ten long range stations in the United States similar in range to the Westinghouse station in Pittsburgh [KDKA]." If stations were kept to low power there could be some 100 equitably distributed to cover most of the United States. But, it was obvious that those stations with the more expensive programs were those which also had higher power.

> Possibly the newspapers would be unable or unwilling to provide such an elaborate program as that being sent out by the Westinghouse Company. Therefore, it seems advisable to continue this or a similar service by long range stations.

The 150-mile limit was ignored by the Department of Commerce and power increases provided long range service for the listener.

Terrell realized that the most important problem in the regulation of broadcasting was how to limit the number of stations in a given locality. There had to be some means of determining the "kinds of service of greatest value to the public." He wrote:

The matter of limiting the number of stations in any given locality is going to be a difficult problem requiring the cooperation on the part of the interests desiring to carry on broadcasting and the broad policy of giving the public the service it desires without annoying interference.

The management and staff of the Department of Commerce knew they had no power to limit the number of stations. The only options were to have stations in the same city on the same frequency divide time and, where possible, vary the frequencies assigned to each station. This would also require "the elimination of stations carrying on non-essential service."[171]

Necessity for Time-Sharing by Broadcast Stations. The principle of time-sharing was first used for wireless telegraphy special stations, amateur stations and ship stations. Time-sharing was often the only available choice. Assistant Commissioner of Navigation Arthur Tyrer recommended in 1921 that broadcast stations be required to share time. After the Second National Radio Conference, some stations were assigned 400 meters (749.6 kHz) and a few other frequencies than 360 or 485 meters. "The trouble appears to be due to all of the stations of the Westinghouse Company having the same wavelength, and you recommend that different wavelengths be assigned to the different stations so as to avoid this interference," Tyrer wrote to Detroit radio inspector Edwards.[172] He continued:

> At the time Westinghouse representatives proposed to this office that they be given authority to broadcast music and other entertainment from several of their stations it was agreed that one wavelength only, that of 360 meters, would be assigned and for the purpose of preventing interference between the stations using the same wavelength they would necessarily have to arrange their schedule for different hours.[173]

Even as broadcast stations increased, the Bureau of Navigation continued to assign them the same wavelength with the recommendation that they share time with stations already operating.

> With the limited number of wavelengths available and the rapidly increasing number of stations it has become impossible to assign different wavelengths for different stations and the only solution seems to be in assigning one wavelength for a particular kind of service and requiring all stations conducting service of that character to use the same wavelength at different hours.[174]

The marked increase in stations had the Department requiring four-letter station identifications as they ran out of three-letter call signs in September of 1922.[175]

Individuals who complained about conflicts between stations were requested to write to the stations causing interference to request that they broadcast at different hours.[176]

Other Proposals to Solve Interference. The earliest suggestion to separate stations on different frequencies came from radio inspector John F. Dillon when he gave Hoover a letter in March 1922 while the Secretary was in California on one of his trips home. Dillon suggested that the country be divided into zones, with different wavelengths allocated to adjacent areas, and "whenever necessary the same wavelength be assigned to alternate zones, or to zones remotely situated."[177] He also suggested that each station be classified, "indicated by a letter of the alphabet, according to the character of the matter which it is engaged in broadcasting."

This was to become the Class B station classification and marked a major difference between U.S. and European countries. Europe allocated frequencies by area while the United States assigned frequencies according to the service provided.

Instead of specifying specific hours of operation on the license, Dillon suggested that station owners should be required to cooperate and formulate non-interfering schedules satisfactory to the majority. "In the case of failure to agree, the Radio Inspector to act as mediator or referee in composing their differences."[178]

Navigation Commissioner Carson's response to these suggestions was favorable and he recommended that these excellent ideas should be seriously considered because both he and Chief Inspector Terrell were making similar plans for future consideration, "which we hope to put into effect as soon as the pending radio bill is enacted."[179]

Another suggestion was that those government agencies using 600 to 1600 meters (499.7 kHz–187 kHz) should give up their wavelength reservations. The Department was aware this might not be possible due to strong Navy opposition. The Bureau of Navigation was continuing to make plans that would soon have to be put into effect even without a new law being enacted.

Meanwhile, stations and the Department of Commerce were having intensified difficulties on sharing time on 360 meters. A few examples follow of cases the Department of Commerce dealt with and indicate the magnitude of the problem.

The *American Radio and Research Corporation* (AMRAD) station WGI, in Medford, Massachusetts, asked the Department to extend their time beyond the one hour they were allowed. "We see no reason why WGI should be limited to one hour when other stations broadcast over much greater span of time."[180] They noted the types of programs they presented and felt that public opinion required the Department to extend their time. Boston radio inspector Charles Kolster passed on the request with the recommendation:

> The only reasonable objection to this extension … beyond 9 o'clock would be that many of the listening-in stations in this vicinity would

no doubt swamp this office with complaints to the effect that these operations would interfere with the reception of broadcasts from Pittsburgh, Pa., Newark, N.J., Detroit, Mich. and others.[181]

Predating WEAF's first sponsored program on August 21, 1922, AMRAD informed Kolster in April that they were considering directly soliciting material and requiring a fee from commercial firms for the extra expense involved to broadcast programs strictly of an educational or entertaining nature. An arrangement was made by AMRAD with a Mr. F. A. Hutchins, an advertising agent, whereby he paid a fixed charge of $350.00 a week for the use of their broadcasting station and could solicit material to be broadcast on WGI for whatever he wished to charge. That same month Kolster notified the Commissioner of Navigation that WGI had solicited the larger businesses in Boston for advertising at $25.00 for a 15-minute program. Commissioner Carson informed Kolster that:

> Under existing law the broadcasting of advertisements cannot be prohibited. From time to time the Bureau has brought the attention of parties making inquiry concerning the broadcasting of advertisements that such use of the broadcasting service may prove objectionable to the public and if undertaken by a number of stations it would no doubt do much to discourage the public in listing in to the good programs of entertainment, educational talks, and other valuable information in which they are at the present time very much interested. It is the opinion of this office that broadcasting is a public service which should be confined to matter of real value to the public and not used solely for personal gain.[182]

Kolster was holding several pending applications for stations in the Boston area until a decision could be reached at the Radio Conference on whether or not there would be further frequency allocations.

The *Detroit Free Press* on March 28, 1922, requested that the Department provide them with a frequency. Upon learning that they would have to share time with the *Detroit News* station (WWJ—standing for [W. J.] Scripps of Scripps-Howard) they wanted to make sure "the *Detroit News* not be given any advantage over the *Detroit Free Press* in the allocation of operating time."[183] Commissioner Carson realized the difficulty in deciding a controversy on the division of time between rival stations of rival newspapers, and suggested "that the owners of these papers mutually agree if possible to a schedule which will be fair to both."[184] A meeting was held between Acting Secretary Huston, Chief Inspector Terrell, Detroit radio inspector Edwards and representatives of the *Free Press* and the *Detroit News*. The *Detroit News* contended that it should not be required to release any of its time and the *Free Press* contended they should get equal time. The *Detroit News* argued priority rights; they were there first. The stations were informed by Huston that "if they could not mutually agree among themselves and he was compelled to do so, they would be given an equal division of time which would be stipulated in their licenses and that the matter of priority could not be considered in the allocation of time as each station would have equal right under the existing law."[185] After more meetings, a division of time was agreed to by representatives of the stations, and WCX (Classics) was given 11 P.M. to one A.M. Tuesdays and Wednesdays, with the understanding that should any other station desire to use those hours, a further division of time would be necessary.[186]

One of the major difficulties in dividing time was the desire of most stations to operate between seven and ten P.M. which was prime time. While the staff of the Bureau of Navigation felt Secretary Hoover had the right under the Act of 1912 to fix the hours of broadcasting stations to prevent interference, it was considered inadvisable "to restrict the stations further than absolutely necessary because of the service being in the developing stage."[187] All broadcast licenses had to be renewed every three months to allow for any further necessary divisions of time to be placed on the license.

After the First National Radio Telephony Conference, the Department replaced specific hours of operation on the face of the license with the phrase, "Hours must be in accordance with the agreement of the broadcasting association, or other operating licensed stations."[188] If any group of station owners would not cooperate, the Bureau of Navigation informed them that on the license it was clearly stated, "a division of time may be required whenever in the opinion of the Secretary of Commerce such action is necessary."[189]

To deal with this problem in heavily populated areas with many stations, the radio inspector would set up and chair committees of station owners. The most active committee was in the Second District (New York). A committee meeting in May 1922 divided time between the 14 stations in the New York area. This meeting, held in Washington, was not attended by Westinghouse, but Westinghouse was given one-third of the total time in New York.[190] This did not please the Radio Corporation of America, and its station, WJZ, appealed on-the-air to the public to express their opinion as to whether WJZ should adhere to the time schedule or close up entirely. The company claimed the station had cost $50,000 to build and had operating expenses of $50,000 annually. Also, RCA complained that rival stations programmed phonograph records and other poor quality material.[191]

There was a backlash when WJZ did not adhere to the announced schedule and various public organizations interested in radio listening appealed to Secretary Hoover to close the station because it interfered with other stations. A threatened "radio war" was averted when WJZ, on July 25, 1922, gave way to the scheduled station, WOR ([W]orld [o]f [R]adio), which broadcast a speech by the governor of New York.[192]

The Kaufman and Baer Company station WCAE ([W]e [C]an [A]lways [E]ntertain) complained to the Department that KDKA continued to broadcast during the beginning period of their 10 to 11 P.M. slot on Tuesday, Thursday and Saturday. "This interference occurs every evening in our scheduled time—KDKA over-running their time by 5 or 10 minutes."[193] Carson asked KDKA to take steps to prevent their encroachment.

> You realize the importance of a regular schedule and also the possibility of renewed and continued complaints if the prearranged schedule is not observed.[194]

The manager of publicity for KDKA notified the Department that the overlapping of time was unfortunate and would be corrected.[195]

Requests for assistance continued to involve the Department of Commerce staff. Charles Kolster had two meetings between stations WGI, WAAJ and the new Shepard Store station in Boston. The owners could not agree on a schedule so Kolster, "took it upon myself to modify slightly the broadcasting schedule." He notified the various stations of the new schedule, but they continued to interfere with each other. He asked Commissioner Carson to allow his office or the Bureau to place the hours he had drawn up on the face of the stations' licenses. "Either this office or the bureau should be in a position to allot to them the actual hours of operation they are entitled to."[196]

Carson responded:

> While broadcasting is in the experimental or developmental stage this office believes it advisable to leave to the parties interested, who may have the assistance of the Radio Inspectors of the District, to arrange their local broadcasting schedules so as to provide for a satisfactory service to the public. Such schedules, will of course, have to be altered from time to time when new stations are opened and for this reason the Bureau does not consider it necessary to approve or disapprove a local schedule which may necessarily require a change within a short time.
>
> When the bill now pending in Congress becomes law and the broadcasting service more stabilized, new regulations will be necessary and possibly some plan can be devised to provide a uniform schedule.[197]

At a meeting on October 2, 1922, called by the radio inspector in Detroit, the *Free Press, Detroit News*, and the Ford Motor Company attempted to decide on which night all three stations would remain silent. "This quiet period of one evening each week was made necessary due to the large number of requests the office of the radio inspector had received for such a period."[198] Silent nights, when all stations in a community would stay off the air, were very popular because many people tried to listen to stations broadcasting from other communities. One of the goals was to see who could hear the station farthest away. This was termed "DXing." Silent nights in most communities were to be the only manifestation of effective self-regulation on the part of the broadcasters. In all other matters there was the potential threat of some governmental action applied by the radio inspectors.

By early 1923 Commissioner Carson felt that long-distance listening would not remain an important consideration.

> While it is realized that there is a fascination in listening to stations at a great distance it is not believed that this is the reason for the great interest now taken in wireless reception and unless the range is limited to some extent it will be difficult to prevent serious interference. The real value of receiving radio broadcasts is in having first class programs of entertainment and educational features, crop, market and weather reports, and the latest news and the value of this service does not depend on the distance from which it is received.[199]

Class B Stations Devised. The time-sharing difficulties reached a high level in 1922 as the number of stations grew. In an effort to alleviate congestion on 360 meters, John F. Dillon's suggestion on station classification earlier that year was carried through. The Department of Commerce's Commissioner of Navigation proposed to Secretary Hoover that another wavelength be made available for broadcast purposes.

The 400 meter (749.6 kHz) wavelength was set aside for a new class of radiotelephone broadcasting station to provide the better stations with a separate wavelength which they were demanding. To keep from becoming as congested as the other wavelengths, stations would need a special license to use this additional wavelength.

The plan proposed to Hoover was that these new licenses be designated Class A. Secretary Hoover returned the proposal to Commissioner Carson on August 5, 1922, with the handwritten suggestion: "Regarding your memo attached, I think this is a good plan, but would suggest you call these Class B licenses instead of Class A."[200] This suggestion, of course, was taken.

The requirements to get a Class B license called for a power supply which was dependable and non-fluctuating, with a minimum power of 500 watts to a maximum of 1000 watts. Modulation was to be accurate and spare parts had to be available to insure continuity of service. The antenna had to be rather rigid so it would not sway and the studios had been constructed to be non-reverberating.

To obtain a Class B station license, owners had to meet specific requirements concerning radio programming:

> Programs—The programs must be carefully supervised and maintained to insure satisfactory service to the public.
> Music—Mechanically operated musical instruments may be used only in an emergency and during intermission periods in regular programs.[201]

The regulations and orders to permit Class B licenses was signed by Commissioner Carson and Secretary Hoover on August 15, 1922, and published in the *Radio Service Bulletin*, September 1, 1922.[202]

Terrell was asked by Congressman Wheeler at a subsequent hearing, "What, if anything, did your department have to do with censoring the kind of speeches or music, or anything that went over the radio?" Terrell replied:

> We had not any legal authority to do that, and we, of course, would not do it. About the only thing I can say that would approach that was the creation of a special class of license known as Class B license under our administration. Under that class of license we would not permit the station owner—and he agreed to it—to use mechanical music, phonographs, and things of that kind. The reason we did that was because at the beginning all the stations were turning to entertainments, and at the beginning the people were appreciating it. But later they were tiring of it, and if we had not checked it, it would have had an effect on broadcasting. So we created this special license, and they had to have talent.[203]

Station KDKA requested a Class B license on August 25, 1922, for 500 meters and 320 meters instead of the 400 meters set aside for Class B stations. They were informed that the station must be operated on 400 meters only.[204] A description of how a high-quality Class B station appeared comes from the required inspection on September 28, 1922. The radio inspector found that the emitted wave was particularly free from harmonics, the transmitter delivered 600 watts to the antenna from a one-kilowatt Westinghouse transmitter and the power supply was alternating current and motor-generated. Condenser and arc-type microphones were used which had no internal diaphragms. The antenna was a six-wire inverted L-shape. A signaling system of a series of lamps was used to transmit signals between studio and transmitter and enough spare parts were available.[205]

The more powerful stations were licensed for 400 meters, and the typical listener liked the move because for a period of time reception improved. However, it did not relieve the crowding on the airwaves for long.

By October there was congestion on 400 meters in the larger population centers. California radio inspector Dillon recommended to the Bureau of Navigation that no further Class B licenses be awarded in his area. He was told by the Department that he had no right to restrict the licensing of any class of radio station. He asked to be allowed to put stations on different wavelengths, but it was still felt that "separate wavelengths for each radio station is not practical."[206]

The congestion on the Class B wavelength caused KDKA to notify the Department of Commerce on October 17, 1922, that:

> We have found that because of the large number of stations now using 400 meter wavelength and because these are all high powered we would only add to the general confusion and cause much trouble due to the production of beat notes.
>
> For this reason the Westinghouse Electric and Manufacturing Company has decided to remain at least for the present, on the wavelength

of 360 meters, at the same time, however, maintaining the high standard of programs and transmissions which 400 meter stations are required to have and which you know has been our policy right along.[207]

Powel Crosley, Jr., president of the Crosley Manufacturing Company and owner of WLW, Cincinnati, wrote "when any number of either the Class 'A' stations and the Class 'B' stations are in operation, the Class 'A' stations interfere with each other, and the Class 'B' stations interfere with each other, to such an extent that any night 360 meters or 400 meters are simply a 'bedlam' of interfering stations."[208]

Time-Sharing by Class B Stations Required. It was hoped that time-sharing problems would be reduced upon setting up the Class B classification on 400 meters. However, the number of stations who wished use of the less congested wavelength created congestion, which, in turn, required the sharing of time on 400 meters.

The *Detroit News, Free Press* and Ford Motor Company stations, all of which become Class B stations, received licenses which stated their hours were limited. They requested a meeting with the Detroit radio inspector to determine a mutually satisfactory schedule.[209] The Bureau of Navigation soon made it standard procedure that with the approved application for a Class B license a schedule of operating hours, mutually agreed upon by all the local stations, had to be submitted to the Department. A copy of this agreement was then attached to the license when the approval was returned to the station. The class B classification had not solved the problem of interference and the necessity for time-sharing.

Other solutions to interference were sought as the Class B stations proliferated. Inspector John Dillon attempted to implement his plan for different frequencies for stations on his own. The Los Angeles *Times-Mirror* station refused to recognize the rights of the *Examiner-Herald* station. After being informed that the government did not recognize any rights by virtue of priority and that regulations required the division of time between stations in each class be made with absolute equality, an agreement between the stations was reached. However, the agreement was not to share time. The 360 meter wavelength was relatively unoccupied in that area so the Los Angeles *Examiner-Herald* station was adjusted by the radio inspector to operate slightly above 360 meters, and the *Times-Mirror* station was adjusted an equal amount over 400 meters. This also prevented other Class B stations in that area of the country from heterodyning these signals.[210] Dillon wrote in describing his adjustments of frequency:

> The primary object of broadcasting is to serve the radio public with enjoyable music and entertainment; and while the equipment ... is quite capable..., unless we temporarily permit the various stations to vary

their wavelengths sufficiently to avoid the obnoxious interference which has been experienced in zones where two or more stations are using precisely the same wavelength, their efforts will be entirely nullified and the large sums invested in those stations will have been in vain.[211]

The Department reprimanded Inspector Dillon for adjusting the frequency of the stations and requested him to return them to the specific assigned frequency of 360 meters.

The Bureau of Navigation was unsure of its ability to regulate increases in power, but was quite certain of its ability to regulate a change in wavelength. When informed by the Boston radio inspector that the Shepard Store station had increased power and was operating between 335 and 340 meters, rather than the authorized 360 meters, the Bureau notified the inspector that he must have the station submit an application to change power. It refused, however, to allow the change in wavelength. The reasoning used was that lowering or raising the frequency would cause serious interference with some ship stations operating on the 300 wavelength.[212]

Time-sharing was to remain a problem and increasingly difficult task for the Department of Commerce staff.

Major Changes in Frequency Allocations. It had often been proposed by Westinghouse, Crosley and others that stations be placed a few meters or frequencies apart and a zoning system be used so stations located at a distance from each other could utilize practically the same wavelength. Thus, the Department of Commerce was aware that the most effective remedy for the continuing interference problem would be to remove the restrictions on the band of wavelengths from 600 to 1600 meters, which were reserved for the exclusive use of naval and military stations, so that non-broadcast stations could be placed in that wave band area, clearing a broadcast band elsewhere.

With a limited inspection staff "it was impossible ... to inspect all of the broadcasting stations and adjust them. The actual conditions existing at this time [November 1922] are a wide variation which is believed to extend from about 325 to above 400 meters."[213]

The implementation of the proposed plans was held off in the hope that Congress would act on pending legislation, but that was not to be.

Allocations at the End of 1922. At the end of 1922 the frequency allocations were:[214]

Meters	Kilocycles	Service
200	1500	Amateurs
300	999.4	Ships
360	832.8	Class A, C Broadcasting
375	800	Special amateur, etc.

Meters	Kilocycles	Service
400	749.6	Class B Broadcasting
410	731.3	Technical and Training
425	700	Point-to-point
450	666.3	Ships
485	620	Government reports
500	599.6	Point-to-point
525	570	Airplane
550	545.1	Point-to-point
600	499.7	Ships; up to Government
1600	187.4	Government: military, etc.

The greatest activity in licensing and inspection continued to be generated by broadcasting stations. The proposition of having "higher" class broadcast stations on the separate 400 meter wavelength relieved the situation temporarily, but the demand for the higher-powered Class B licenses soon negated any relief.

Tests were conducted at Henry B. Joy's experimental radio ranch by Joy and Detroit radio inspector Edwards to determine causes of interference. It was discovered that two Class B stations (WFAA, Dallas— [W]orking [F]or [A]ll [A]like, and WOI) and an amateur station (DM4) were intercommunicating on 400 meters. The Bureau warned these stations that such a test between broadcasting stations and amateur stations was not in accordance with the provisions of their licenses.[215] At the end of 1922 there was heavy interference from broad-band Navy spark stations. From a study of the correspondence received by Edwards, it was "very clear that this very great amount of NRQ [Navy station] interference is laid by the writers to Amateur radiologists."[216] This was primarily because most people did not know how to read code and could not identify what source was causing their interference problems. Spark sets were being replaced with tube transmitters by amateurs, but lowered appropriations forced the military to maintain almost all code sending stations with spark equipment.

The situation was worsening and reliance was placed on the passage of pending legislation.

Decision to Open Up a Broadcast Band of Frequencies. Commissioner Carson had notified Secretary Hoover on December 19, 1922, that it might be possible to reallocate the wavelengths of stations without further legislation.

Section 4 of the Act of 1912 stated that definite wavelengths shall not exceed 600 to 1600 meters. The Secretary of Commerce, it was felt, had the discretion to change the limit in accord with international conventions. "It is probable you would have authority to assign wavelengths within the band mentioned for broadcasting after consultation with the Navy Department."[217]

Article 2 of the International Radiotelegraph Convention of 1913 provided two wavelengths, 600 and 300 meters (499.7–999.4 kHz) for general public service. However, it was Carson's opinion that it was the intention of the Act of 1912 and the International Convention that these two frequencies could be used only by the military. Secretary Hoover soon came to a decision.

On February 12, 1923, Hoover learned that there was no chance of the White-Kellogg bills passing that session of Congress because the amended bill which had passed the House on January 31 was pigeonholed in a Senate committee.[218]

Hoover then telegraphed his decision to Chief Inspector Terrell from his home in California. "Inasmuch as our legislation is not likely to go through, would it not be desirable to call a conference to consider what should be done by way of invasion of the Naval Reserve?"[219]

Conferences immediately began through the Interdepartmental Radio Advisory Committee to determine if the Navy would release its hold on the frequencies between 600 and 1600 meters.

Within a month after learning that the White-Kellogg bills would not be considered by the Senate, Secretary Hoover called the Second National Radio Conference. His stated purpose was "for considering legislation for lessening interference."[220] Hoover also decided to utilize the conference in another way. He advised those he invited, "In spite of the failure of legislation, I believe it is possible to devise some administrative measures for lessening interference in broadcasting."[221]

Navy Agreement Necessary. Chief Radio Inspector William D. Terrell met with Capt. Sanford C. Hooper and Capt. D. C. Bingham of the Navy. There were three alternatives considered: First, to sandwich the broadcast stations between ship and shore stations; second, to allocate a wide band for the exclusive use of broadcasting stations and remove the existing non-broadcast stations from that band; third, keep the existing arrangement.

If the Navy agreed to broadcast stations getting a wide-band, it would have to give up half of the best spark wavelength space it had been using since the beginning of wireless. It would be necessary for ships to change all their equipment so that transmitters and receivers would not interfere with the new broadcast band. This was considered a very bold act on the part of Capt. Hooper (who later became Admiral) and he had some difficulties gaining Navy acceptance for this action. However, he felt that this was the best possible solution to modernize Navy communications and continued to press for it.[222] Hooper saw little future in radio broadcasting. He commented in a personal letter to the Director of Naval Communications that "the number of long-distance radio broadcasting stations was greatly in excess of what it would be in a few years and that these stations would be reduced in a short time from the hundreds then in existence to perhaps two, and that these would be owned by the Telephone Corp. and Radio Corp." [223]

Nevertheless, he was able to convince the Navy officials that by replacing the Navy spark sets with tube sets, more stations could be located in the half-band which the Navy would keep. This would cost the Navy millions of dollars in new equipment.[224] For giving up their reserved frequencies, the Navy gained support for large expenditures from the Department of Commerce and others interested in solving the interference problem.

There had been enough public pressure so that the broadcasting interests could demand that the Navy relinquish the 499.7 to 187.4 kHz band.

Arrangements were made for the radio inspectors from the more populated districts to report to the Bureau for discussions on a proposed agenda for the Second Radio Conference.[225]

The reallocation of wavelengths was deemed necessary by the inspectors because "many stations are using wavelengths not authorized in their licenses and many amateur stations are exceeding their wavelengths."[226]

V. The Second National Radio Conference

This conference of some 50 amateurs, government and industry representatives allowed the Department of Commerce, with the cooperation of the Navy Department, to abandon the policy of group allocation in broadcasting. Afterward, the Department could assign a discrete frequency from a predetermined wave band to each broadcast station. Thus, the "bloc" principle of spectrum allocation was finally adopted.

On March 21, 1923, Chairman Carson called the conference's first meeting to order:

> Gentlemen, I am going to ask you to be as brief as possible this afternoon and confine yourselves strictly to broadcasting and the allocation of wavelengths.[227]

The broadcasting band slowly evolved through testimony and declaration at the Second Conference. Its broad outlines had been in the report submitted by the radio inspectors, the Radio Chamber of Commerce and the Institute of Radio Engineers. The recommendations of the National Radio Committee of the Second Radio Conference were technically complicated, but of great importance in the history of domestic allocations. Favored for general pubic broadcasting were 222 to 545 meters (1365–550 kHz). Proposed classifications were:

Class A stations—Power to not exceed 500 watts; distinctive wavelengths to be assigned between 222–300 meters [1365–999.4 kHz]. No stations were required to change from 360 meters unless it so desired.

Class B stations—Power between 500 and 1000 watts; proposals were made to license these stations on special wavelengths from 300–345 meters [999.4–870 kHz] and from 375–545 meters [800–50 kHz]. Some ship work to be permitted on 450 meters [666.3 kHz]. Again, no station to be compelled to move from 360 unless it so desired.

Class C stations—This class comprised all stations officially licensed to use 360 meters. No new licenses were to be issued for this wavelength by the Department. Stations desiring to remain on the wavelength could do so at the risk of interference.

The unique aspect of this plan was the lack of formal compulsion on the part of the stations already assigned to 360 meters to change wavelengths. It was expected that most would do so willingly because interference continued and area coverage diminished.

Resolutions proposed by the Second Radio Conference were:

(1) Class A stations were to be distributed over five zones for the country, with no stations in adjacent zones closer in frequency than 10 kilocycles. [This was similar to the Dillon proposal of 1922.] Ten stations were to be assigned to the same zone, each separated by 50 kilocycles. Each broadcast station was to have a band 10 kilocycles in width.

(2) Only one exclusive frequency would be assigned to Class A stations in each community.

(3) Every station should have a tuned circuit coupled to the antenna to reduce harmonics. The operating frequency must be within two kilocycles of the government assignment.

(4) The Department of Commerce was requested to insist on suppression of harmonic radiation.

(5) Amateur radio organizations were requested to study the hours of broadcast Sunday religious services and provide silent periods so as to not interfere with them.[228]

The Department of Commerce attempted to implement all of its recommendations which had been approved of by the Second Radio Conference.

In February there were 578 stations and by March 1923 there were 588. The addition of ten stations to the total increased the workload of the Bureau of Navigation's radio service. "The great expansion of radio communication has not been accompanied by a proportional increase in the radio personnel and facilities at the disposal of the Bureau of Navigation and Standards of the Department of Commerce, and ... the resulting strain on the inspection and technical forces of the Department of Commerce has been excessive, and has even forced the omission of important activities and investigations...."[229]

A report in September of 1922 indicated that while a number of stations had ceased broadcasting, they were replaced by new ones which had to be inspected before licensing.

1922	September	—	23
	October	—	22
	November	—	20
	December	—	20
1923	January	—	34
	February	—	13
	March	—	29
Total			161

Tyrer optimistically felt, "it is reasonable to assume that we have about reached our maximum of broadcasting stations."[230]

Implementation of Second Radio Conference Approved Recommendations. Immediate steps were taken to carry out the recommendations passed by the Conference, and the change in wavelengths to fit into a broadcast band was set to take place on May 15, 1923. At the same time the Bureau of Navigation started specifying station frequencies, rather than wavelengths since they were now dealing with a band of frequencies running in 10 kHz steps from 550 to 1350 kilohertz. The general public had to be educated into making the transition to frequencies and it was some 15 years later that references to meters in various publications finally stopped.

The Department of Commerce felt their recommendations represented "a step in ideal development of measures for the prevention of interference in public broadcasting."[231] However, a number of problems developed in putting their plan into operation.

> First, the hardship that it may cause stations to move arbitrarily to new wavelengths; second, the difficulties introduced by the ship to shore communication that is now working on 300 meters [999.4 kHz] and also on 450 meters [666.3 kHz]....
>
> For internal broadcasting the Department proposes to cooperate with the various stations with a view to developing a systematic assignment of wavelengths to the various stations within the broad confines of the recommendations of the conference.[232]

As of April 1923, there were 23 Class A stations, 30 Class B stations, and 536 Class C stations, for a total of 589 broadcasting outlets.[233]

In April alone 21 new stations were licensed and 14 were deleted, making a net increase of seven for the month.[234]

Steps were taken for the radio inspectors in each district to inspect as many stations as possible before the end of the year to ensure their operations were on the proper wavelength and thus preventing interference. The Bureau of Navigation also decided to continue license renewals every three months as "it seems advisable that this be done until this service becomes more stabilized."[235] The move to a broadcast band vastly increased the spectrum space but made many receivers obsolete. In the public's mind AM broadcasting had become established.

Program Control. The Department of Commerce had received many complaints from listeners about the advertising practices of some radio stations, and they made a concerted effort to counteract some of them. One individual listening to the *Detroit News* heard advertising including complete information as to price and where to purchase. Radio inspector Edwards wrote the *Detroit News* that this practice might jeopardize the continuation of its broadcast license.[236]

In 1922 the AMRAD Radio Corporation station was soliciting advertising. Commissioner Carson told radio inspector Kolster to call their attention to the First Radio Conference recommendation that direct advertising be absolutely prohibited.[237] However, the lack of power to regulate advertising became apparent when Commissioner Carson reappraised the situation and wrote another letter to Kolster in April informing him that such practices could not be prohibited by the Department of Commerce. Although it might prove objectionable to the public, new regulations and laws would have to be enacted.[238]

The *Free Press* of Detroit formed a "Red Apple Club" which broadcast the names of people who wrote in that they listened to the station. It was pointed out to the station management that the Department of Commerce, in *Radio Service Bulletin,* number 69, page 8, prohibited point-to-point communication for broadcasting stations.[239] Assistant Secretary Huston gave the opinion that "the Red Apple Club program cannot be considered high-class entertainment which should be carried out on the 400 meter wavelength through Class B broadcasting stations."[240] However, he felt the program would be permissible if it was broadcast after midnight.

The Second National Radio Conference considered the question of whether the reading of telegrams and letters on-the-air from listeners far away was permissible. It had concluded "so long as the signer is not addressed in person and so long as the text matter is of general interest."[241] In October of 1923 KDKA was accused of reading mail over the air even when it was received from listeners just a small distance from the station. Chicago radio inspector E. A. Beane informed Westinghouse that these "violations" could not be permitted and he would recommend its license be suspended should such actions continue.[242] Westinghouse claimed that these readings had been unauthorized and would not occur again.[243]

Allocations. The Second Radio Conference recommended that New York be allocated four wavelengths for Class B stations because of the population served and the unlimited expert talent available in that city. The Bureau of Navigation was only able to allocate three wavelengths for Class B stations, one of which could not be used satisfactorily during the day because it caused interference with ship stations located on 450 meters (666.3 kHz). The Department noted during October 1923, "we are getting a large number of complaints of interference much of which is said to be due to ship communication on 450 meters [666.3 kHz]."[244]

The Radio Corporation of America asked for two complete broadcasting stations in New York, which was strongly protested by other concerns in other large cities. One of the RCA stations was assigned 405 meters (740 kHz), which it shared with the Bamberger station and with the Ship Owners' Radio Service station.[245]

The other RCA station (WJZ) was assigned 458 meters [655 kHz] which was to be shared with the People's Pulpit Association. A third, 492 meters (610 kHz), was to be used jointly by AT&T and Western Electric.[246]

So, this arrangement in New York placed seven Class B stations on three wavelengths, one of which was ineffective during the day. This created the same type of situation that existed before the Second Radio Conference.

The Ford Motor Company station at Dearborn, Michigan, was sent General Letter No. 249, which informed stations that any variation from adjusted frequency would be a violation of Section 2 of the Act of August 13, 1912, justifying the revocation or suspension of the license.[247] The Detroit radio inspector then adjusted the station to operate on 273 meters (1100 kHz). As most stations of this period, the Ford station had no equipment for checking their frequency and drifted around on 980 kHz, 800 kHz and at times in-between.[248] Stations were warned but there is no instance where General Letter No. 249 was ever used to revoke or suspend any broadcasting station.

Many listener complaints were not answered because of the department's inability to give demands personal attention. Consideration was given to drafting these listeners to assist in monitoring broadcasting. Experience showed Terrell that "our having in each district observers listening in on accurately calibrated receiving sets ... would be very helpful and would no doubt to some extent forestall the complaints."[249]

Interference was noted between WCX and WWJ (Detroit), sharing 580 kHz, and WOO and WIP ([W]ireless [I]n [P]hiladelphia), sharing 590 kHz. Radio inspector Edwards "did everything possible to remedy this situation."[250] This interference had continued for three months, until the stations received upgraded equipment in November that helped them stay on their frequencies.

Interference from Non-Broadcast Sources. Many interference complaints were caused by the rebroadcasting by receivers that would radiate signals much as a transmitter.

Thus, in the seven months following the reallocation of wavelengths following the Second National Radio Conference, interference was being reported from 1) ships operating on the wavelength of 450 meters which had been allowed to remain in the broadcasting band; 2) interference being caused by regenerative or radiating receiving sets; and 3) interference from stations that did not have the equipment to maintain their proper frequencies.

A minor change in the construction of regenerative receivers overcame the problem. As newer model radio sets replaced older model sets the difficulty would be alleviated. Interference also was caused by equipment other than radio sets, such as violet-ray and X-ray machines, precipitation plants, telephone magneto ringing systems and leaky power lines with bad insulation. Most of this interference was local.

The Bureau of Navigation asked the Bureau of Standards to investigate these matters, but Standards refused to undertake the work because of the expense involved and the press of other work.[251]

Station WEAF, AT&T's flagship New York station was given permission to increase its power but many complaints were received. Westinghouse's Pittsburgh KDKA was being received over a wide range of frequencies in Washington, D.C. because of their "excessive power," or the simultaneous broadcasting they were experimenting with on two close wavelengths.[252]

Despite the many reports about interference, Hoover stated in the *Eleventh Annual Report* of the Department of Commerce that the recommendations of the Second Conference adopted practically in their entirety, "have been put into operation with the result that interference has been greatly reduced."[253] However, that perception of reduction was short-lived.

Class D Stations Authorized. H. P. Davis, of Westinghouse, wanted to discuss with Secretary Hoover a "requirement on which a plan of higher quality broadcasting might be based...." Davis, apparently not satisfied with the Class B designation, argued:

> Our experience in broadcasting has been more extensive than any other organization.... The thing that has become most apparent to us from this is the wide public interest, and our conviction that the public's interest must be made paramount and not the interest of the broadcasters. This, I am sure, is a powerful weapon in the Department's hands in enforcing any plan which has the object fundamentally in view and worked out to best meet the public's requirements.[254]

Davis claimed there was a "defect in the recommendation of the recent [Second] Radio Conference which proposes a single wave band for a given locality, and requires qualified stations existing there to divide time." He then proposed "national stations," so located, restricted and supervised that they would provide a nationwide service. "To furnish a ... service which will be non-interfering among themselves or with the general broadcasting stations."[255] Davis wished to be freed of the problems causing interference among radio stations in the classifications then in existence.

On April 6, 1923, H. P. Davis; Mr. Southgate, a Westinghouse engineer; and Dr. Frank Conrad met with Secretary Hoover; Commissioner Carson and Chief Inspector Terrell. The discussion revolved around the request of Westinghouse for a special license or separate wavelength for KDKA. They were so unhappy with the Class B wavelengths that they had refused a Class B license when they learned that more than six stations would be on the 400 meter wavelength, which would necessitate time-sharing. It was suggested that it might be possible to establish a new class of station which would be those owned by companies with laboratories and experts engaged in developmental work.[256]

The argument against creation of a special class of broadcasting station was that it might appear to the public and other broadcast interests as "an evasion of the existing regulations beneficial to only two or three companies."[257]

Three plans were discussed fully: 1) assign these stations longer wavelengths and higher power along with more stringent regulations; 2) assign Pittsburgh two wavelengths along with Detroit, Chicago and other cities having two or more Class B stations within the reserved wavelengths available. By assigning a few of the same wavelengths in the East being used by a few stations in the West, it was assumed that some of these wavelengths could be duplicated without serious interference; or 3) issue Westinghouse an experimental license, which had been requested previously, but denied. This license would permit variations in power in recognition of Westinghouse's developmental work. The call letters of the station, however, would have to be changed to experimental class call letters.[258]

It was finally decided that the third plan was the most feasible because the first plan had been attempted with the Class B station classification and had failed, and the second plan would run counter to the recommendations of the Second National Radio Conference. It was also felt that the third plan was the most likely to survive criticism. However, Westinghouse studied the proposals again and attempted to arrive at a combination of the points. They did not wish to give up the popular KDKA call letters.

Samuel M. Kintner, manager of the Westinghouse research department, submitted a proposal to the Department of Commerce on April 20 for regulations to govern a Class D (Developmental) radio broadcasting station. Terrell noted in the margin of the document that the regulations must limit the number of stations in this class, their frequencies and power, because non-limitation is what caused the Class B station difficulties. It was also suggested by Westinghouse that: "Licenses will be granted for Class D stations only in such cases, as, in the judgment of the Secretary of Commerce, *the public interest* makes it desirable."[259] The stations must be for developmental purposes, must have superior facilities and be experienced in broadcasting, with talent available and the financial capability to undertake extensive programming.[260]

The Department of Commerce accepted the major part of Westinghouse's recommendations and incorporated them into regulations for a Class D license.

Secretary Hoover wrote, "As far as practicable stations in this class will be allowed the exclusive use of an individual wavelength and it is not contemplated to give any one company more than one license in the broadcasting development class and such stations will be required to adhere strictly to all of the regulations and specifications governing such stations."[261]

Carson proposed that KDKA operate on 326 meters (926 kHz) and that 462 meters would be removed from Charleston, West Virginia, and given to the Kaufman and Baer Class B station in Pittsburgh.[262]

The Department of Commerce records show three stations eventually received Class D (Developmental) licenses, but only two, KDKA (Pittsburgh) and WJAZ (Chicago), were specifically identified in the records. The other station would have had to have been on an individual wavelength and owned by a company involved in experimental development work on radio.

While supporting the small broadcasters and entrepreneurs in promotion of free speech, Hoover and the department recognized that for radio to expand, the economic support and developments would come primarily from the largest companies.[263] On April 25 and 26, 1923, a small group of broadcasters met in Chicago to establish a common front against the American Society of Composers, Authors and Publishers (ASCAP). The ASCAP controlled the performing rights to music. They demanded payment when their licensed music was broadcast. Broadcasters contended that they were in a non-profit business and the publicity they gave the music boosted record and sheet music sales. The broadcast group, calling itself the National Association of Broadcasters (NAB) picked the president of Zenith, Commander Eugene F. McDonald, Jr., as its first president. They established their own music licensing organization, Broadcast Music Incorporated (BMI). The representatives of the some 20 stations attending the NAB's first convention in New York that fall also discussed broadcasts by politicians, the need for technical cooperation and control, and possible revisions in the copyright law. The new group was small and largely ineffective at first, but this was the beginning of a powerful lobbying organization that would influence future regulation.[264]

VI. The Bureau of Standards Through 1923

The Bureau of Standards itself was an early broadcaster, when in 1920, at the request of the Bureau of Markets in the Department of Agriculture, it pioneered an experimental radio market and crop report service. As broadcasting stations proliferated, this service was turned over to the various stations that requested it, to be programmed on 485 meters.[265]

Even before that the Bureau of Standards had successfully transmitted music and speech for short distances over its station, but because voice transmission was so unreliable, the Bureau resorted to Morse telegraph for the market reports. After operating a general service for the government for four months, the Bureau turned it over to the Post Office, whose stations already served the air mail service.[266]

It was not transmission but reception that harbored the real problems of radio communications. The first of the technical difficulties as commercial broadcasting began was that of fading or variations in the intensity of received signals. A study conducted by the Bureau of Standards traced the other sources of interference to amateur equipment, radiating receiving sets, power lines, arc lights and other non-radio electrical equipment.[267]

Although inquiries about fading and noise began arriving at the Bureau in 1921, little was accomplished to resolve the causes because the biggest difficulty was the interference between stations on the same frequencies. As a restriction on numbers of station licenses seemed impossible, the obvious solution to station interference seemed to reside in the technical question of whether the stations could be made to operate exclusively on the frequency assigned, using as little power as possible to reach the required distance with sufficient sharpness. Because the remedies were beyond the ability of the Bureau to manage, it concentrated on the measurement and control of radio waves emanating from the stations. The main problem was the fluctuation in the width of the broadcast frequency, which seemed to have a strong correlation with the capacity of the signal to interfere with other nearby stations.[268]

Typical was the experience of a listener in Baltimore who reported interference between two broadcast stations, one in Cincinnati, the other in California. The interference arose, the Bureau learned, because the California station was off its assigned frequency by one-half of one percent.[269]

Bureau research concentrated on the development of new and improved types of measuring instruments, such as wave-meters, wave-meter scales and devices for rapid radio-frequency measurements. These instruments gave the radio inspection service of the Department better means for detecting and monitoring broadcasting frequencies.[270]

Then, in 1923, in order to provide the means for self-policing by radio stations, the Bureau of Standards set up a standard of frequency and began sending out precise signals over its laboratory transmitter, WWV, set up at

Beltsville, Maryland. The frequency signals were transmitted in groups each day so that the range from 125 to 6000 kilocycles was covered every two weeks for all stations within range of the Bureau signal. The obvious advantage of the service soon led to more frequency transmission of the signals and to their broadcast over a nationwide system of standard frequency stations.[271]

The Bureau also assisted in providing listeners for the new broadcasting stations. In the spring of 1922 it issued a series of mimeographed circulars on how to construct a simple crystal receiver set for $10. One of Hoover's secretaries wrote to Dr. Stratton that "Mr. Hoover was much impressed by the plans for the construction and operation of the very simple radio receiving equipment which you submitted to him. He suggests that it would be a very good thing if this were given out to the public."[272] Soon plans for a tri-circuit crystal receiver set capable of picking up stations beyond 50 miles, at a cost of $15, and an electron-tube set, reaching out 100 miles, for between $23 and $37 were made available to the public. The tube set cost included the tube ($5) and the battery ($15 to $20).[273]

Other Bureau circulars published in 1922 and 1923 furnished sources of elementary radio information for amateurs and described auxiliary condensers, loading coils and an audio-frequency unit for receiving sets. Two commercial publishers reprinted the crystal set plans and copyrighted their booklet, but they were enjoined by the courts.[274]

Even before these circulars appeared as formal publications, they were widely printed on the radio pages now found in many newspapers. In the first year of the radio boom (1922) the Bureau is estimated to have issued almost 100 reports, most of them typewritten or mimeographed, to meet the demand from radio technicians for radio data and instruction.[275]

Standards were being devised for the measurement of inductance, resistance and capacity.[276]

At the First National Radio Telephony Conference, the Bureau of Standards was asked to study:

> (1) The reduction of harmonics in continuous wave transmitters and of irregularities of oscillators;
> (2) The reduction of the rate of building up of oscillations in radiating systems;
> (3) Comparison between the variable amplitude and the variable-frequency methods of continuous-wave telegraphy;
> (4) The preferable methods of telephone modulation to avoid changes in the frequency of oscillation;
> (5) The proper circuit arrangements of regenerative receivers to avoid radiation of energy;
> (6) The use of highly selective receiving apparatus, including a list of approved types;

(7) The use of receiving-coil aerials with special reference to high selectivity;

(8) The reduction of interference, and

(9) The study of standardization of frequency meters.[277]

At the Second Radio Conference in 1923 the Department of Commerce and the stations agreed to abolish the term "wavelength" and to start using "frequency," which represented the number of oscillations of the radio wave per second, expressed in kilocycles per second. The band of frequencies between 550 and 1350 (later 1500) kilocycles—later to be renamed kilo-Hertz—was to be set aside for commercial broadcasting. They believed that by dividing the country into five zones and setting station frequencies five kilocycles apart, 570 broadcasters could be accommodated in the 89 available channels.

The Bureau soon realized that five kiloHertz between stations was not sufficient because interference continued as stations increased power.[278]

The Bureau's technical experts participated as advisors at all the radio conferences, chief among them Dr. J. Howard Dellinger and Dr. Charles B. Joliffe. The Bureau called a conference in New York in January of 1922 to try to standardize uniformity in the methods of describing, rating and testing the performance of radio apparatus. Trade associations and radio manufacturers were represented.[279]

Traditionally, the government retained the rights to the use of inventions by federal employees but left title with their inventors. The Bureau of Standards did not follow this policy. For 20 years under Dr. Stratton it was understood that any innovation or invention by a Bureau staff member was to be patented in the name of the government for use by the public. This understanding was not seriously challenged until 1921 when two members of the radio section, Percival D. Lowell and Frances W. Dunmore, while working on a radio relay project for the Air Corps, conceived a method of substituting home current for the storage batteries then used with radio equipment. The means they devised for operating radio on ordinary house current also eliminated the principle obstacle to its use, the hum of alternating current in the radio signal.

In March 1922 Lowell and Dunmore filed the first of three related patents in their own names and in October 1924 granted the manufacturing rights to the Dubilier Condenser Corporation of Delaware.[280]

Shortly after their patent was filed, in a memorandum to all employees, Dr. Stratton formally established the policy of assignment of all patent rights in inventions and discoveries of the staff to the government. He requested the Attorney General to sue for judgment in the U.S. District Court of Delaware.[281]

Eight years later, in 1933, the U.S. Supreme Court decreed that the commercial rights to a patent belonged to the inventor, whether or not the work was developed on government time. Lowell and Dunmore were to gain little from their invention because in 1924 RCA had developed a heater type of vacuum tube that performed as well as the Lowell-Dunmore unit on AC-DC current. Within a year most radios sold to the public were operating on house current utilizing the RCA tube.[282]

In 1923 research on radio continued and the Bureau of Standards reported:

> Experimental concerts are at present being sent out on Friday evenings from 8:30 to 11, by the Radio Laboratory ... using a wavelength of 500 meters.... The Bureau of Standards has made an interesting improvement [upon the method of transmitting music], which consists primarily of substituting the carbon microphone, which is the mouthpiece of an ordinary telephone, for the vibrating diaphragms ordinarily used on the phonograph. As a result, the phonograph sound record produces direct variations of electric current in the telephone apparatus instead of producing sound, thus while no sound is heard where the phonograph record is being played, the music is easily heard by those at the distant receiving stations.[283]

VII. Summary

The major problems facing the Department of Commerce were interference, increasing numbers of broadcasting stations and the difficulties of achieving legislation which would give the Department discretionary power to grant or refuse station licenses. This period was especially significant because the industry conferences began to achieve voluntary cooperation, and the broadcast band developed with stations classified by power and service rendered the public.

Chapter III

CONGESTION AND THE BEGINNING OF REGULATORY BREAKDOWN, 1924-25

The demand for radio regulation continued unabated but no legislation passed Congress to officially regulate radio during the 1924–25 session.

On April 1, 1923, there were 552 broadcasting stations using the wavelength of 360 meters which were designated by the Department of Commerce as Class C stations. In January 1924 there were 185 Class C stations, or a decrease of 367 primarily due to the transfer of Class C stations to Class A or B, or discontinued stations.[1]

Station licensing for 1924-1925, according to available figures:[2]

Month	Class A	Class B	Class C
1924			
January	200	48	185
February	315	40	181
March	351	49	166
June	378	54	101
August	386	56	89
September	382	57	78
November	N.A.	67	N.A.
December	N.A.	72	N.A.
1925			
January	N.A.	89	N.A.
February	463	92	16

Month	Class A	Class B	Class C
1925			
March	N.A.	91	N.A.
May	459	99	N.A.
June	468	103	101
December	N.A.	N.A.	N.A.

(N.A. indicates information not available)

From September 15, 1921, to June 30, 1924, the Bureau of Navigation had licensed 1,076 broadcasting stations. Of that, over half, 541, had closed down, leaving a total of 535 existing stations on June 30.[3] There was a slight decrease during September 1924 as another 30 stations discontinued operations. This then left 519 stations.[4]

By November 1924 there were six Class B stations that had passed inspection but were placed on Class A or C wavelengths pending openings in the Class B wave band. There were 37 Class B stations under construction or contemplated.[5] In December 1924 there were seven more Class B stations that passed inspection and qualified, but the Department of Commerce could not find Class B wavelengths for them and they were not assigned any wavelengths.[6]

In February 1925 there were 571 stations operating, and in March 1925, 34 new stations were licensed and 37 were deleted. At least 24 Class B stations were reported under construction.[7] During April 1925 more than 100 applications were received for new licenses and in May 1925 more than 136 prospective broadcasting stations were under construction or under consideration.[8]

By the end of 1925 the Department of Commerce had more than 350 new station applications on file, in addition to 32 existing stations requesting power increases.[9]

During 1924-1925, technical advances had made it possible for stations to broadcast with as much as 50,000 watts of power and stations interconnected to networks to serve wide areas. Proposals to construct these so-called "superpower" stations and the possibilities of linking them together generated further fears of monopoly.[10]

By the end of 1924 the Class B wavelengths were completely filled. It was discovered in 1925 that stations often fluctuated from their frequencies by at least 2 percent and had to be separated more than 7 kilocycles to actually keep them a minimum of 5 kilocycles apart. This further restricted the number of stations that could be placed within the available wave band space, and the Department of Commerce refused to place more than two stations in the same city sharing time on the same wavelength. The Fourth Radio Conference was asked by the Department of Commerce to recommend it cease all licensing.

The Department of Commerce was also finding it difficult to obtain further funding for its work because President Coolidge, who took office after the death of Warren G. Harding in 1923, mercilessly slashed appropriations.[11]

By the end of 1925 probably one-half of the population of the United States was able to receive radio transmissions. Competition for the ever-increasing audiences was great among broadcasters. Audience size grew quickly as power increases by stations expanded geographic coverage. About 30 stations increased their power from approximately one-half to 50 kilowatts during 1925.[12] The Second National Radio Conference recommendations had been based on lower power usages (generally 500 watts or less). Widespread power increases soon led to renewed and increasing interference problems.[13]

Secretary Hoover attempted a last minute effort in 1925 to obtain legislation, but no action was forthcoming from Congress.

As licenses became harder to obtain, sales of already licensed stations increased. Individuals and companies came to adopt the concept of broadcast advertising. Because of the scarcity of broadcast stations, some standard began to be applied as a basis for the privilege of broadcasting. Service to the listener became a consideration.

The Fourth National Radio Conference was the last effort by the Department of Commerce to sustain some control of broadcasting. The Department requested and received permission from the industry leadership at the conference to stop licensing new stations. Those still seeking to enter the industry refused to cooperate and the Department of Commerce was powerless to control growth.

The failure of legislation efforts in 1924-25 led the department staff to continue actions to sustain broadcasting for the public while Secretary Hoover influenced the debate through his major policy statements.

I. Attempts at Legislation

The Court of Appeals, which held in the 1923 Intercity Company case that the Secretary of Commerce had no authority to refuse to license any station, was settled in early 1924. In conversations with Solicitor General of the United States Beck on the strategy of an appeal to the Supreme Court, Secretary Hoover had "expressed a desire that the argument in the case should be deferred as long as possible, in the hope that Congress would solve the legal difficulties by supplementary legislation." The Solicitor expressed the belief in January 1924, that:

> Unless you have some strong reason for wishing the Court to interpret your power in the matter, I should advise against submitting the case to the [Supreme] Court. If the Supreme Court should affirm the decision of the Court of Appeals, it would probably attract public attention,

because of its novel nature, and you thus might be more embarrassed than at present.[14]

The case was postponed several times, each time after consultations with Hoover. Solicitor General Beck noted that there was "the hope that new legislation would make the [legal] question of little practical importance."[15]

Hoover was told by Beck in August that Intercity was no longer operating a radio station, in New York, but the Intercity lawyer wished to continue the appeal. He argued:

> So long as the present statute remains in force, the right of the Secretary to refuse licenses, or to place other than statutory limitations thereon, is continually brought up by applications....
>
> These are powers arbitrarily taken and not given by statute, but exercised rather in anticipation of the passage of the new radio law.[16]

However, since they were no longer operating a station the dispute was declared moot and dismissed before the Supreme Court on September 15, 1924. Hoover was acutely aware that the department's ability to regulate broadcasting had been tested. He had been told by everyone that if the case had gone forward he would have lost before the Supreme Court. Legislation to give the Department of Commerce adequate powers to control broadcasting was now even more necessary.

Early in the first session of the 68th Congress (1924-25) several bills to regulate communications were offered. Eight were introduced in the Senate and five in the House of Representatives. Of these, Senate Joint Resolution 177, which extended for two years the authorization for the Secretary of the Navy to allow press associations and newspapers to use government-owned code stations for overseas transmissions, passed.

The only bills detailed are those the Department of Commerce either sponsored or was interested in.

H. R. 7357. Congressman White's revised radio bill, H. R. 7357, was introduced in the House, February 28, 1924. It was similar to the bill which passed the House in 1923 which proposed placing in the Secretary of Commerce authority to better control radio operations. This bill had the support of the Department of Commerce because it had been drafted with the assistance of the Second Radio Conference and the Bureau of Navigation.

S. 2930. Senator Howell introduced a bill into the Senate in the same session. Bill S. 2930 was not, as was the House bill, an attempt at comprehensive regulation of radio. It merely affirmed the use of the ether for radio communication or other endeavors to be the inalienable possession of the people of the United States and their government. It limited grants of privilege of this use in time, and provided for temporary suspension by the President of the privileges granted licensees in case of war or other national emergency.[17]

The idea that the "ether" was a public possession and that its use should be considered a mere privilege granted to individuals for some public purpose was not a new concept. It had been voiced often by Secretary Hoover at the First National Radio Conference. The bill passed by the House in 1923 provided that every license contain the condition that "There shall be no vested property right in the license issued for such stations in the bands of wavelength authorized to be used therein."[18]

The Senate passed S. 2930 quickly and sent it to the House where it was referred to the Committee on the Merchant Marine and Fisheries. Before the Senate bill was voted on, the House held hearings on H. R. 7357 in March 1924.

Hearings on H. R. 7357. This bill provided that stations should be licensed by the Secretary of Commerce, and that because of *public convenience, interest or necessity* he should have the power to: a) classify radio stations and operators; b) prescribe the nature of the service to be rendered and the priorities as to subject matter to be observed by each class of licensed station and of each station within a class and assign frequencies thereto; and c) make regulations concerning the service to be rendered and the priorities as to subject matter to be observed by each class of station.

Another item in the bill provided for revocation of a license if the licensee failed to operate substantially as proposed in the original application. The bill did not include definite provisions on censorship, but the inclusion of "prescribe the nature of the service" and "priorities as to subject matter" indicated a growing concern over programming.[19]

On March 11, Hoover testified on the proposed bill. He expressed general support for its provisions but did not care for the wording of the monopoly section and vigorously objected. Section Two (c) authorized the Commerce Department to refuse a license to any concern that would monopolize radio through patent control of the apparatus. Hoover stated that the determination of whether a company was an illegal monopoly should not be entrusted to the Department of Commerce because it was an administrative body and did not have the capability to carry on a proper investigation, and the matter should be settled judicially.

He revoked his support for the bill when the provision was left in.

Secretary Hoover's statement at the hearing clearly set forth his attitude towards regulation and the legislation before the House Committee.

> It is urgent that we have an early and vigorous reorganization of the law in Federal regulation of radio. Not only are there questions of orderly conduct between the multitude of radio activities, in which more authority must be exerted in the interest of every use whether sender or receiver, but the question of monopoly in radio communication must be squarely met.

It is not inconceivable that the American people will allow this new born system of communication to fall exclusively into the power of any individual group or combination. Great as the development of radio distribution has been, we are probably only at the threshold of the development of one of the most important of human discoveries bearing on education, amusement, culture and business communication. It can not be thought that any single person or group shall ever have the right to determine what communication may be made to the American people. I am not making this statement in criticism of the great agencies who have contributed and are contributing so much to the development of the art and who themselves have been well seized with the necessities of its development and proper use, but I am stating it as a general principle which must be dealt with as an assurance of public interest for all time....

Telephonic communication, however, is impossible between individuals from the point of view of public interest as there are a very limited number of wavelengths which can be applied for this purpose and the greater usefulness of the available wave bands for broadcasting communication inhibits their use for personal communication. We can not allow any single person or group to place themselves in the position where they can censor the material which shall be broadcasted to the public, nor do I believe that the Government should ever be placed in the position of censoring this material.

The problem involved in Government regulations of radio are the most complex and technical that have yet confronted Congress. We must preserve this gradually expanding art in full and free development; but for this very purpose of protecting and enabling this development and its successful use, further legislation is absolutely necessary....

Where there were no broadcasting stations, there are to-day 561 of them, located in every town of importance in the country. There are certainly three to five million telephonic receiving sets, therefore there is a radio audience of anywhere from ten to twenty million people....

For practical purposes, however, the wavelengths available for telephonic purposes in the present development of the art are much more limited than those for telegraphic purposes and are today practically limited to the range between 200 and 600 meters [500 to 1500 kHz]. Within this area we have about seven possible bands for sending in any one locality. The number of telephone broadcasting stations that can be operated from any one place is, however, more limited than this because of interferences of one locality with another. With the system of staggered zones set up by the department it has been found possible to work broadcasting stations on three different wavelengths within each zone. No doubt the number of available wavelengths will steadily increase with improvement in the art and better adjustment because different purposes.... Were it not for the regulation and the very tenuous voluntary cooperation of to-day, we should have pandemonium despite the development of the science.

The tremendous development in electrical communications is to a large extent due to the fact that individual initiative has not only been unhampered by the Government, but has been encouraged to the extent of the Government's ability and regulated so as to give the maximum service. The further legislation needed should, in my view, regulate only to the extent that is necessary in public interest for the development of the science itself; for the service of those who make use of it. It seems to me, therefore, that the fundamental thought of any radio legislation should be to retain possession of the ether in the public and to provide rules for orderly conduct of this great system of public communication by temporary permits to use the other. It should be kept open to free and full individual development, and we should assure that there can be no monopoly over the distribution of material.

Radio communication is not to be considered as merely a business carried on for private gain, for private advertisement, or for entertainment of the curious. It is a public concern impressed with the public trust and to be considered primarily from the standpoint of public interest to the same extent and upon the same basis of the same general principles as our other public utilities.

The act of 1912 would naturally aim at the regulation of the art as it was then known. It has become entirely obsolete and unworkable applied to radio communication as we know it to-day. We are managing to preserve some order in the ether under the old legislation, but to do this we are depending to a large degree upon the voluntary cooperation of those interested in the development of the art. We do not always receive this cooperation.

It is of course impossible to provide on the face of any general law rules which will meet the innumerable specific cases which will arise, or will anticipate the development of the art. In my view the situation can only be met by regulation which may be altered from time to time to meet changing conditions and may be varied in accordance with the necessities of different localities and modified as the art progresses—all in accordance with some broad general principle to be laid down in the public interest. I do not advocate any large personal authority, but I do advocate the resting of such authority in administrative hands checked by advising bodies....

Under the 1912 law, it has been held that the Secretary of Commerce has no discretion in the granting of licenses to stations. It is now obligatory to grant a license to every applicant irrespective of the interference which may be anticipated from the operation of the station. The present bill grants a discretionary power to be exercised in accordance with the public interest. I believe that this is necessary in order that there shall be no question of vested right in the use of the ether.

Section 2 (c) of the bill provides that the Secretary of Commerce shall refuse a license to any concern which is monopolizing or attempting to monopolize radio communication through control of the manufacture of apparatus or otherwise. I am in sympathy with the purpose shown in the paragraph to which I am referring; but I do not believe that the method there adopted is the proper one.... We have a conflict between the general American principle of opposition to monopoly and an equally American principle, recognized by our patent laws, that an invention belongs exclusively to him who makes it.... That problem does not properly belong to any administrative body.

The Department of Commerce has no machinery with which to carry on the investigations necessary, nor is this the organization suited for the decision of such questions ... and I would suggest that the bill be so amended that the refusal of a license to a monopoly be placed upon the [judicial] basis, and determined in the same manner as is the revocation of a license under this section.

One of the great difficulties in the regulative efforts of the department heretofore has been and will continue to be the lack of funds....

The need for radio legislation is imperative, although no law will be a panacea for all radio ills. The bill which you are now considering is a valuable step in the proper direction and, excepting as I have above indicated, I heartily commend it to your favorable consideration.[20]

Hearings on S. 2930. The substance of this proposal was contained in its first paragraph:

Be it enacted ... That the ether and the use thereof for the transmission of signals, words, energy and other purposes within the territorial jurisdiction of the United States, is hereby affirmed to be the inalienable possession of the people of the United States and their Government, but privilege to enjoy such use may be granted as provided by law for terms of not to exceed two years.[21]

The question of control over interstate and intrastate transmission arose. The definition of "ether" was a constant stumbling block. Learned scientists were unable to define it properly, and most of the lawmakers found it even more difficult to do so. Many radio interests, aside from certain companies in maritime communications, were eager to have some form of regulation to prevent wavelength interference, but some insisted on permanent preemption of channels as private property.[22]

Sen. Bruce held that:

Under the Federal Constitution if the Government has any right in the ether, or if the people of the United States have any right in the ether, if it is true that the ether is the inalienable possession of the people of the United States or of the Government, then it must be by virtue of the commerce clause of the Federal Constitution.[23]

Here was the unique approach to the right of federal control of the air-waves, by affirming the right of authority via the commerce clause of the Constitution, which to this day underpins government control.

When S. 2930 was referred to the Committee on the Merchant Marine and Fisheries, they replaced it with the White Bill and reported it out on May 13, 1924.[24] According to Rep. Davis there was so much opposition by "certain representatives of the radio monopoly," that a majority of the Committee on Rules refused to allow consideration of the bill by the full Senate.[25] No law was possible at this juncture.

II. The Third National Radio Conference

In the beginning of May 1924 the Bureau of Navigation realized that "there will be no action on the [White] bill at this session of Congress."[26] They believed that the bill, as amended by the Committee on Merchant Marine and Fisheries "if enacted would increase our difficulties and add new problems greater than those now encountered."[27] A Third National Radio Conference was planned for September. The Deputy Minister of Marine and Fisheries of Canada wished to have a representative attend the conference. Carson thought it appropriate "that a Canadian representative be asked to attend because of a conflict between American and Canadian broadcasting stations. Our previous conference gave no consideration to the needs of the Canadians."[28]

Subjects for Consideration at the Third Conference. The Supervisors of Radio, as the radio inspectors were called from 1924 on, were furnished with a list of subjects to be considered. They were asked to study the proposed questions and submit opinions to the Bureau of Standards prior to the conference. Today's regulators still seek answers to many of those questions.

As drawn up by Chief Inspector Terrell, their exact wording follows:[29]

> 1. What action is necessary to encourage "National High Grade Program," having national interest, transmitted either by individual stations or by a chain of stations, and insure a general effort to maintain a higher standard broadcasting service than we have had in the past?
> 2. What changes in wavelengths are recommended to provide necessary operating channels for Marine, Broadcasting, Point-to-point, Amateur and other classes of service?
> 3. What are your views concerning discontinuance of Class "C" broadcasting stations and requiring them to transfer to either Class "A" or Class "B"?
> 4. Should the problem of interference caused by electrical devices other than radio transmitters be considered at the conference? If so, why?

5. Is it desirable to permit broadcasting stations to use power of 5 to 10 K.W.? If so, what in your opinion would be the effect?

6. What are your views concerning rebroadcasting using wire lines or radio on short wavelengths?

7. Should consideration be given to public safety or emergency broadcasting and utilization of existing systems for emergency communication?

8. What effort should be made to regulate broadcasting advertising matter?

9. Should any effort be made to encourage a limitation of the number of broadcasting stations in localities believed to be adequately served at present? If so, how could this best be accomplished?

10. Should any effort be made to secure an agreement as to priorities of subject matter or service? If so, how could this best be accomplished?

11. What can be done to insure the identity of amateur calls in different countries? The same system and calls are now used in the United States and Canada.

12. Should it be recommended that Government stations use bands of wavelengths assigned for their exclusive use only, or is it desirable that Government stations share commercial and private wavelengths?

In further preparation for the conference the supervisors were instructed by the Bureau to investigate the extent to which broadcasting stations were using the wavelength and time allotted them. It was being reported "that some of them operate only a part of the time and in such cases other stations may be given a part of the time on the same wavelength infrequently used."[30]

On July 31, 1924, a meeting was held in the office of W. E. Harkness, Assistant Vice President of the American Telephone and Telegraph Company. Attending were Arthur Batcheller; P. W. Spence and Elam Miller of AT&T; and John V. L. Hogan, consulting engineer. Dr. Alfred Goldsmith, former Secretary of the Institute of Radio Engineers and now employed by RCA, was unable to attend. The agenda used was Terrell's list of questions.

These powerful entities felt that question five, about higher power in cities, would cause disturbance and interference. But higher power in rural areas would have advantages. To reduce interference it was agreed that any rebroadcasting should be done by wire interconnection and not by radio relay.

It was the consensus at this pre-conference meeting that the Secretary of Commerce be given full authority through discretionary powers to grant or refuse to grant licenses to new broadcasting stations. However, limitations on power were also recommended. For instance, cause had to be shown that creation of new stations in a locality would result in interference with stations already in operation. New radio legislation was recommended.[31] Detroit supervisor (inspector) Edwards said it was evident that much of the interference in the Detroit area was caused by obsolete spark transmitting equipment used for ship-to-shore communication in that area.

Edwards commented on question eight, "I have never yet met anyone who has had a good word to say for broadcasting of advertising matter."[32]

Membership of the Conference. Invitations were issued to approved individuals and companies.[33] A delay of the conference until October 6 generated much publicity and "it is believed [the Third Conference] will be better attended than the two previous ones."[34] When the conference was delayed, it was decided that all the radio supervisors should also be asked to attend.

Secretary Hoover's letter of invitation was extended through the Secretary of State to the Canadian and Mexican officials with jurisdiction over radio matters in their countries.[35]

Some radio districts had difficulty choosing individuals to represent them at the conference. The various groups in the radio field were asked to name representatives who would constitute the formal advisory committee at the conference. Listeners, marine service, broadcasting (one representative from each district), engineering transoceanic communication wire intercommunications, manufacturers, amateurs, point-to-point communication, and government departments were all invited.[36]

The Chicago radio supervisor wrote to each station in his area asking that they combine to nominate one person as their representative:

> To date [September 20], the number of votes cast total 103. 31% of these are in favor of Charles E. Erbestein, owner and operator of Station WTAS; 31% in favor of Prof. C. M. Jansky of the University of Minnesota; 17% in favor of Mr. J. E. Jenkins of Chicago; 8% in favor of single individuals and 13% for the present supervisor of radio.[37]

It was recommended that the individual to represent the district should be chosen from among those who attend the conference, and Dr. Jansky was selected.[38]

A similar problem developed in the Second District of New York. In a letter from an official of WNYC:

> The broadcasting interests in the second district are diversified. They might be divided into four groups, namely: Those independent broadcasting stations, second those of Western Electric Company manufacturers and sold under restrictions imposed by the American Telephone and Telegraph Company. Thirdly, those stations of the large electrical companies engaged in the manufacture and sale of radio apparatus, which companies have formed a combination for their own protection and, finally, the interests of the Municipal broadcasting of the City of New York.[39]

It was the belief of this official of the City of New York station that there was no one man who could represent all these interests and he desired to have a representative of his own at the conference.[40]

The number of people to attend the conference grew. Other letters were sent by the Bureau to non-broadcast companies which had some impact on the industry. One example:

> Your plant at Barberton, Ohio, known as the Ohio Insulator Company, where insulations are being tested, is said to produce interference with radio reception in that locality.
>
> It is possible that there will be discussion of the interference caused by your plant in view of which you may care to have someone representing your company present.[41]

Secretary Hoover's Opening Address. The opening meeting of the Third Radio Conference took place October 6, 1924, at 8:30 P.M. More than 90 representatives were in attendance.[42] This was more than four times the number of delegates that had attended any of the previous conferences. The opening meeting took place in the auditorium of the Department of the Interior in Washington, D.C., and Hoover's opening address was broadcast by a number of stations. Hoover noted: "Through the cooperation of the broadcasting stations throughout the country, at this opening session we are inviting the listeners of the country to sit in because they are obviously interested in all questions of radio development, and we all wish them to participate in the consideration of our problems."[43] A number of letters were later received such as, "I listened in on your interesting lecture before the Third Conference as relayed by our station KLZ [Denver] which came in very clearly."[44] It was even reported that Hoover's breathing came through distinctly, apparently the measure of good reception in the 1920s.

The following are selected portions of Hoover's opening address:

> I have called the conference of each of the last three years in the confidence that it was only by your cooperation that the requirements of this great service could best be met. There are certain minimum regulatory powers in the Department of Commerce. They are inadequate to meet the shifting situation that this developing art constantly presents. Nor could any legislation keep pace with the changes imposed by scientific discovery and invention now going on in radio. I have been convinced, however, that we could meet these problems by organized cooperation of the industry itself. I need tell no radio listener that this industry is unique in that unless it has stringent rules of conduct to which all elements adhere it will die of its own confusion. We must have traffic rules, or the whole ether will be blocked with chaos, and we must have safeguards that will keep the ether free for full development....
>
> It is in a large sense the purpose of this conference to enable listeners, broadcasters, manufacturers, marine, and other services to agree

among themselves as to the manner in which radio traffic rules may be determined. Like the two previous occasions, this may be called an experiment in industrial self-government. Through the policies we have established the Government, and therefore the people, have today the control of the channels through the ether just as we have control of our channels of navigation; but outside of this fundamental reservation radio activities are largely free. We will maintain them free—free of monopoly, free in program, and free in speech—but we must also maintain them free of malice and unwholesomeness.

Radio had passed from the field of an adventure to that of a public utility. Nor among the utilities is there one whose activities may yet come more closely to the life of each and every one of our citizens....

Radio must now be considered as a great agency of public service, and it is from that viewpoint that I hope the difficult problems coming up before this conference will be discussed and solved.

At the first radio conference I hazarded some modest anticipations as to its development and use. Some thought them visionary, yet we passed every point of these anticipations within 18 months. We have, in fact, established an entirely new communication system, national in scope. In the whole history of scientific discovery there has never been a translation into popular use so rapid as in radiotelephony.... The sales of radio apparatus have increased from a million dollars a year to a million dollars a day. It is estimated that over 200,000 men are now employed in the industry, and the radio audience probably exceeds 20,000,000 people.... Its worth depends on the use that is made of it. It is not the ability to transmit but the character of what is transmitted that really counts.... An obligation rests upon us to see that it is devoted to real service and to develop the material that is transmitted into that which is really worthwhile. For it is only by this that the mission of this latest blessing of science to humanity may be rightfully fulfilled....

BROADCASTING PROGRAMS. When broadcasting first started, the phonograph was a sufficient attraction to the radiotelephone listeners, who were swayed chiefly by curiosity and marveled at the new discovery. Public interest has long since passed this stage. Broadcasting would die in 24 hours if it were limited to transmission of phonograph records. We have made great improvements in material transmitted. Original music, speeches, instruction, religion, political exhortation, all travel regularly by radio today. Program directing has become one of the skilled professions....

But we require a still further advance in the character of material beyond the capacity of local station directors if the art is to emerge entirely from the curio and entertainment stage to that of fundamental service.... The local material available for the local program is of the highest importance but is not, in my view, enough to maintain the assured interest necessary for the support of the industry nor to fulfill adequately the broadcasting mission.... I want to see the little fellow get something more than he has now. My proposition is that the local stations must be able to deliver every important national event with regularity.... This can only be accomplished by regularly organized interconnection on a national basis with nationally organized and directed programs for some part of the day in supplement to local programs.

It may be stated with assurance that the greatest advance in radio since our last conference is the complete demonstration of the feasibility of interconnection....

It is our duty to consider the possibilities and potentialities of interconnection as a regular daily routine of the nation. Unless it is systematically organized we can not expect its continuation. I realize that this matter, except in so far as it may be fostered and encouraged, does not lie in the Government. It would be unfortunate, indeed, if such an important function as the distribution of information should ever fall into the hands of the Government. It would still be more unfortunate if its control should come under the arbitrary power of any person or group of persons. It is inconceivable that such a situation could be allowed to exist; but I am not now dealing with monopoly.... Interconnection is going on to local extent....

I believe that the quickest way to kill broadcasting would be to use it for direct advertising. The reader of the newspaper has an option whether he will read an ad or not, but if a speech by the President is to be used as the meat in a sandwich of two patent medicine advertisements there will be no radio left. To what extent it may be employed for what we now call indirect advertising I do not know, and only experience with the reactions of the listeners can tell.... I suggest for your consideration the possibility of mutual organization by broadcasters of a service for themselves similar to that which the newspapers have for their use in the press associations, which would furnish programs of national events. It would arrange for their transmission and distribution on some sort of financial basis just as the press associations gather and distribute news among their members....

THE PROBLEM OF INTERFERENCE. One of the most important subjects for your consideration is the rearrangement of our system so as to provide more operating channels for broadcasting stations—more wavelengths. This is the first step to eliminating most of the interference. As you know, our previous conferences have classified our broadcasting stations, have zoned the country in effort to secure these results. The wavelengths of the stations in the same zone were placed at least 50 kilocycles apart, adjoining zones at least 20 kilocycles apart, and distant zones at least 10 kilocycles apart. This was a great step and has been in a large degree successful, but many new difficulties have arisen. Of the present 530 stations 57 are class B, with a power of from 500 to 1,000 watts and having a wide range, and 387 are class A, many using small power and covering small areas. There are still 86 class C stations, most of which have low power, all of a wavelength of 360 meters. Our chief trouble is with the class B situation. They are all assigned within the band of 288 to 545 meters, within which there are, under the present system of allocation and excluding the class C band, only 44 available wave bands and only 33 that seem desirable at present. To assign these among the 57 stations necessarily means duplication, although it was the theory of the last conference that individual wavelengths could be assigned to each. As it now develops, only 23 stations either have exclusive wavelengths or are sharing with stations so distant that both may operate simultaneously, while the remaining 34 are compelled to divide time, and the congestion is growing in the large cities, New York and Chicago particularly.... It has been suggested ... that the band now reserved for class B might be somewhat broadened. Removals of class C stations from the class likewise give some relief, depending on what proportion of the present Class C stations quality for class B licenses....

POWER OF BROADCASTING STATIONS. Most class B stations are now operating on 500 watts. A limitation of 1,000 watts is imposed in the license. I understand that there are several stations erected or in course of construction which contemplate the use of power up to 5,000 watts, and I am aware of the suggestion of those who would go beyond even this to so-called "superpower" of 50,000 watts. There is opposition, especially to the latter.... From the viewpoint of nationwide broadcasting, the question becomes one as to whether we should aim to cover a large territory through a number of interconnected small ones....

I can assure you that this is a question of considerable popular interest. During the past ten days I have received thousands of letters from men, women, and children all over the country protesting against what they honestly believe would result in depriving them of the chance to listen to the local stations or to use their will in selecting the ones they want to hear. They fear a monopoly of the air.... There is no man nor body of men strong enough to monopolize it even if there was any desire to do so. And always bear in mind that permission to use the air is reserved to the Government. There is, however, much misunderstanding in the loose use of "higher power" or "superpower." There are two very different things involved.... Static can be overcome by somewhat higher power than the 1,000 watt limit at present. It is desirable that all stations should increase in power for this reason. The "superpower" is an entirely different thing ... and it has many implications of interference with local stations and of monopoly which must cause us all a serious thought....

GENERAL TENDENCIES IN DEVELOPMENT OF BROADCASTING. There seems at present some tendency toward a decrease in the total number of broadcasting stations.... So far as is known to the Department, of the present stations 196, or over one-third, are owned and operated by manufacturers of or dealers in radio apparatus.... Department stores and similar mercantile concerns add 39 to this number of publishers 41, making a grand total of 276 known stations, of which 44 are class B.... On the other side we have 85 educational institutions, 35 churches, 12 city and State agencies, 12 clubs, of which seven are class B (four schools, two State or city agencies, and one church), all of which may be said to operate from more altruistic motives....

OUTSIDE SOURCES OF INTERFERENCE. ...There is no means of control at present [of] the interference from non-radio sources ... Harmonics, too, are troublesome ... Accurate and sharp transmission must be insisted upon.

AMATEURS. ...I have during the past year somewhat extended [the amateur] wave band. I hope that this conference may dismiss the objections that have been raised to this section.

COOPERATION OF THE DEPARTMENT. The officials of the Bureau of Navigation, which has direct charge of administrative features and full familiarity with the entire situation, are ready to give you the benefit of their information and advice. In short, the Department of Commerce is at your command.[45]

Open Hearings. Work was assigned to various committees. The large attendance forced the meeting to move to the new National Museum auditorium, and the Third Conference reconvened on October 7. The first speaker was C. P. Edwards, Director of Radio Services, Department of Marine and Fisheries, Canada. His remarks were introductory in nature and pledged cooperation between Canada and the United States in the allocation of wavelengths that would affect the communication of both countries.[46]

Terrell recognized that the conference would have to take into consideration problems other than broadcasting; indeed, the Marine Service was pressuring for additional channels, while the broadcasters desired a completely clear broadcast band.

The question of higher power as discussed by David Sarnoff, commercial manager of the Radio Corporation of America, continued to provoke controversy. Chain broadcasting had begun to evolve at this time and remarks at the Third Conference by Secretary Hoover were indicative of the necessity to think in terms of national interconnection of broadcasting stations.[47]

During his remarks, Hiram P. Maxim, president of the American Radio Relay League, made it known that the amateurs had opened up short wave transmission over the ocean in the fall of 1923. In late July 1924, the Department of Commerce, following a thorough study, allocated for amateur use certain wavelengths in addition to the 150 to 200 meter assignment. During his address, Maxim indicated that progress was being made in amateur radio communication by obtaining voluntary cooperation of the league members in maintaining frequency stability. He chided that if other interests could cooperate like this, there would be little need for the conference.

Secretary Hoover pointed out remarks he had made August 16, 1924:

> In a discussion with one of their officers [the ARRL]—a youngster of about 16—the method of preventing interference between them, he stated with some assurance that there would be no difficulty about enforcement if left to them. I pressed him as to the method they would employ in order to secure results. He showed a good deal of diffidence but finally came through with the statement "if you leave it to us and if somebody amongst the amateurs does not stick to the rules, we will see that somebody beats him up."[48]

On the third day the Third Radio Conference met in the hearing room of the Department of Commerce. One of the topics was the maritime communications problem. George S. Davis of the American Steamship Owners' Association stated that marine communication was ready to surrender 300 meters (999.4 kHz) to broadcasting, provided certain other bands were made available to them. Thus, the broadcasting band would be finally completely free of any other use.[49]

Experiments in radio relay interconnection were reported upon by C. W. Horn of Westinghouse. Francis C. Jenkins reported on radio-photography and claimed he would only need a single broadcast channel for experimental purposes. Hoover declared:

> I felt for some time that Jenkins was on a new track, and that he is opening for us a real, new vision of radio; and I think the conference will be grateful for his statement that he does not want a waveband. (Laughter and applause.)[50]

Jenkins proceeded to demonstrate his early television efforts by transmitting an image of Secretary Hoover over his device.

President Coolidge Addresses the Conference. In recognition of the growing importance of broadcasting in politics, members of the Third Conference gathered at the Executive Offices of the White House that afternoon for an address by President Coolidge on the subject of radio communication. In his opening remarks the Chief Executive stated:

> Your conference has been summoned by Secretary Hoover to advise with him on the problems involving the relationship of the Government to one of the most astounding developments in the history of science. It seems almost incredible that within so short a period as 4 years it has been made possible to communicate simultaneously with practically the whole population of the United States.[51]

The President assured the delegation that the government would carry out radio policies to prevent any monopoly of the air.

Secretary Hoover told the conference that previous remarks concerning government and control of radio had brought a deluge of telegrams with pleas to ban all monopoly in the industry. He answered in a report to the conference:

There is just one cardinal principle in the attitude of the Department of Commerce, in the relation of Government of radio. We intend to encourage whenever it lies within our power the development to its maximum of service to the American people. It cannot so develop if there is any monopoly in it. With 530 broadcasting stations operating, and with four or five alternative methods of interconnection there is no monopoly in radio today.[52]

Committee Reports to the General Conference. Sessions during the next two days were devoted to reports of the various committees and general voting on their recommendations.

Subcommittee Number 1 (General Allocation of Frequency or Wavelength Bands), under the direction of Terrell, assigned that portion of the spectrum below 150 meters. Since international agreement was uncertain on that portion of the spectrum, assignments were considered temporary or experimental.[53]

Subcommittee Number 2 (Allocation of Frequency or Wavelength Bands to Broadcasting Stations), under the direction of Dr. George Burgess of the Bureau of Standards, did not make any substantial changes from the allocations adopted by the Second Radio Conference. Some proposals, however, increased slightly the number of available broadcast channels. The old Class C designation was to be eliminated. It was proposed that the letter designations of Classes A, B, and C be changed to numerical designations for the different classes of stations:[54]

Class	Kilocycles	Meters	Number of Channels
1	550–1070	545–280	53 (10 k.c. apart)
2	1090–1400	275–214	32
3	1420–1460	211–205	5

It was suggested that November 15, 1924, be designated as the date after which no further Class C (360 meters) licenses would be issued. It was suggested that all stations using less than 100 watts of power be assigned frequencies in Class 3. Not more than two Class 1 stations (which had been Class B) were to be licensed on a given frequency, which meant that no station would be required to divide more than half the available time . The five-zone plan was augmented by an additional sixth zone on the West Coast. A 50 kilocycle separation was suggested between stations in adjacent zones.[55]

The proposed classifications would be adopted and used by the Federal Radio Commission and the Federal Communications Commission. Class 1 (Class B) would be the equivalent of Class I stations, a dominant station operating on a clear channel with relatively wide coverage, while Class 2 would be the equivalent of Class IV stations.

Dr. Burgess' Remarks to the Conference. Dr. Burgess of the Bureau of Standards discussed technical aspects of the fast-moving radio field. He stated that the two previous conferences were wise in not limiting their allocation structure and general discussion to broadcasting because all radio problems were interrelated. He spoke of developments in frequency control and recommended high power as being essentially economical. Burgess reported a study of the causes of radio interference by the Bureau of Standards indicated that the major obstacles to broadcast reception were 1) other broadcast stations; 2) atmospherics; 3) radiating receiving sets; 4) amateurs; 5) commercial stations; and 6) non-radio electrical interference.[56]

Various other aspects of the technical development of radio communication: short waves, variable condenser research and propagation characteristics were also discussed by Dr. Burgess.

Subcommittee Number 3 (General Problems of Radio Broadcasting), chaired by Gen. George O. Squier, had some impact on the Department of Commerce's public policy. On the agenda were four topics:

(1) Power requirements and limitations
(2) Revision of Class requirements
(3) Operators' licenses
(4) Improvement of programs.[57]

The first topic proved to be of some importance in spectrum allocation because an increase in power was often accompanied by a corresponding increase in interference on non-selective receivers. The term "power" is somewhat relative because 5,000 watts was considered by some authorities in 1924 to be "super-power."

Dr. J. H. Dellinger addressed the question of power and stated, "that a high power station located at a distance from a city would not cause material interference to stations located within the city itself."[58]

Gen. Squier suggested that when higher power was authorized, wavelengths should be far removed from those of lower power stations and, if possible, geographically separated.[59]

Edwin Howard Armstrong thought that a general increase in power by all stations would result in interference remaining the same.[60]

David Sarnoff testified in support of "super-power" on an experimental basis.[61]

Powel Crosley expressed the viewpoint that it had never been the policy of the Department of Commerce to limit in any way the number of stations, and this should be their policy on power.[62]

Higher power, in principle, was approved during the second session of the committee's deliberations.[63]

A new class of operator's license was approved in 1925 by the Department following the deliberations of this committee. General Letter Number 266 specified that a theoretical exam would consist of questions on transmitting apparatus used by broadcasting stations, instead of the previous questions which had to do with marine wireless.[64]

Conference members were opposed to monopoly in broadcasting and suggested the development of interconnected stations to provide a system of national broadcasting which would make it possible for the public to obtain programs of national interest. A new system of zoning which allowed 30 additional wavelengths was proposed, bringing the theoretical total to 100. The amateur and ship transmitting stations were to finally be removed entirely from the broadcasting band, thus removing another form of serious interference.

Stations were to be reclassified according to their power. This recommendation rated the stations in descending order, with Class 1 being the most powerful. "Super-power" stations had been discussed but no definite recommendations were made other than noting the benefits to be gained by the public seemed to warrant development of higher powers.[65]

The conference did not adopt a formal policy mandating programming quality or priorities because the conferees did not wish to bring about any government censorship or control of programs. Instead, they recommended a policy of government non-interference.[66]

Implementation of the Third Radio Conference Recommendations. A meeting was held on October 21–22, 1924, at the offices of the Department of Commerce to try to work out a satisfactory plan for "allocating non-interfering channels to the various broadcasting stations."[67]

One of the Third Radio Conference proposals was to extend the broadcasting band from 550 to 1500 kilocycles. The upper portion of the frequency band for broadcasting was extended by 150 kilocycles over the recommendations of the Second Radio Conference. It was agreed that broadcasting receivers available to the public would not adequately cover the frequency spectrum over 1350 kilocycles. Therefore, it was decided that allocations of stations in that area of the band would not really be practical until manufacturers were able to produce suitable receiving equipment. A few felt there might be some opposition by Class A licensees assigned to Class 1 licenses in the fringe area of the broadcast band.

It was anticipated that a two- or even three-way time-sharing plan would be necessary as the only solution to the allocation problem.[68]

A new zoning plan was devised, which was another modification of the Third Conference proposals. Six zones were established with channel separation within each zone of at least 50 kilocycles and in adjacent zones of 20 or 30 kilocycles. The following recommendations for Class 1 licenses were established:

    (1) Frequency range 550–1070 k.c. inclusive
    (2) Channels ten kilocycles wide, making a total of 53

(3) Assignment of six channels to Canada

(4) 47 available channels to be used East of the Rocky Mountains; East Coast channels to be assigned to West Coast stations with discretion.

By making use of all available channels, it was felt that 58 stations could be assigned on a time-sharing basis and 18 stations could actually be given exclusive channels.

The interference limits were arrived at rather arbitrarily. Stations less than 50 miles apart were to use channels not less than 50 kilocycles apart; stations from 200 to 500 miles distant of each other were to use channels not less than ten kilocycles apart.[69]

The meeting's final recommendations became the public policy of the Department of Commerce's Bureau of Navigation radio service:

> It is believed important that this reassignment should not be publicly proclaimed as making available a host of new channels for broadcasting [for it did not] but rather that the public be convinced that a fairly satisfactory solution of a very unsatisfactory problem has been arrived at. It was even felt advisable for the Department of Commerce to publicly request that all persons considering going into broadcasting should first consult with representatives of the Department before carrying out their plans.[70]

The most difficult problem during November 1924 was the reallocation of wavelengths to Class B broadcasting stations. There were 67 licensed Class B stations operating on Class A and Class C wavelengths pending the adjustment of allocations. In addition, there were 37 Class B stations under construction or contemplated, making a total of 104 for which the Department of Commerce had to make space.

In the Class B wavelength band from 350 to 1060 kHz there were about 53 wavelengths of ten kilocycle separation. With Canada receiving six of these, that left the Department with 37 which could be utilized. This permitted a total of 94 stations if two stations were placed on each wavelength.

In order to temporarily provide the needed channels four plans were considered:

> (1) Further division of time. This would require two stations on each wavelength until 94 were licensed, then three, etc.
>
> (2) Authorize use of the same wavelength by stations some distance apart. Heterodyning was considered likely as increased power would cause more of a problem.
>
> (3) Reduce the kilocycle separation between stations. Tests were being conducted to determine the practicality of a seven k.c. separation.
>
> (4) Require future stations of Class B nature to use Class A wavelengths. However, Class A was also a congested area and additional stations utilizing 500 or more watts would cause more interference.

The classification system recommended by the Third Conference was finally rejected by the Bureau of Navigation. Carson noted:

> There are about 275 Class A stations [October 1924] using power less than 100 watts which would be required to go into Class 3 on the band from 205 to 211 meters [1420–1460 kHz] providing only five operating channels. To require this change would deprive 275 stations of an audience and they might as well be closed. As no advantage is gained by changing the present classification system, permitting Class B to use wavelengths from 280 to 545 meters and Class A to use wavelengths from 205 to 278 meters, it is believed more desirable to continue A and B classifications and reject the 1, 2, and 3 classes recommended by the conference.[71]

Stations WEAF, AT&T of New York; WTAM, Willard Storage Battery of Cleveland; KYW and WBZ, Westinghouse Company in Chicago and Springfield; KFI ([F]armer's [I]nformation Station), owned by Earle C. Anthony in Los Angeles; and KGO, General Electric at Oakland, California, were the only six Class B stations authorized to increase their power experimentally in November 1924, to 1500 watts.[72]

By December an experiment had been placed into operation. It provided for a ten kilocycle separation on wavelengths from 352.7 meters to 424.7 meters, an eight kilocycle separation on wavelengths from 424.7 to 498 meters and a seven kilocycle separation on wavelengths from 498 to 549.1 meters. This was to determine if local reception would be satisfactory with this variation in frequency separation.[73]

Narrowing the distance between stations' frequencies produced interference and heterodyning and increased power (as Edwin Armstrong had predicted) just added to the interference.

It was suggested by the Bureau of Navigation that "the Department should decline to issue any more Class B licenses until some definite position can be taken on wavelength allocations; stations qualifying for Class B licenses should be permitted to use Class A wavelengths until a Class B channel is open for them."[74]

The deliberations of the Third Conference had not resulted in workable solutions to the problems faced by the Department of Commerce because few of the proposed vital allocation solutions were accepted or implemented.

Secretary Hoover Withdraws His Support for Major Bills. The situation was becoming intolerable. Secretary Hoover wrote to Congressman White in another effort to get a stop-gap measure passed through Congress. He gave his exact reasons for desiring such action:[75]

December 4, 1924

Dear White:

I am enclosing herewith a suggestion of a very short bill clarifying the powers of this Department as to radio regulation as to interference. It does not pretend to confer complete regulatory authority, nor does it cover many matters which must sooner or later receive legislative attention. It is intended only to enable the Department to retain firm control of a situation which is very rapidly changing, in which there are some elements of danger. If such a bill is passed it will give time for more consideration of the whole subject.

We have long agreed that this industry will ultimately require exhaustive legislation, and you have given a vast amount of valuable time, care and study to the subject not only as manifested by the bills which you have introduced but by your cooperation in the annual radio conference we have held. I have, of course, been in full sympathy with your efforts.

I feel, however, that the new developments in the art during the last 12 months have taken such a departure as to require somewhat further time for ascertaining its ultimate result to the public before we can adequately determine the proper course of legislation. There is a probability that by the end of that time, we may require wholly new legislative provisions.

The short bill proposed will reinforce the fundamental situation so that no public damage can result from delay, whereas much public advantage might result from a further clarity of our knowledge as to the application of this new system of communication. As you are aware, there is no monopoly in the radio world at the present time, there being over 500 broadcasting stations of which not more than four are the property of any one institution.

With only 57 wavelengths and 500 stations—rapidly increasing—we are today forced to certain duplication of waves and to the division of time between stations. If there were enough wavelengths for all the matter would be much similar. Any attempt to give preference among stations in the allotment of wavelengths on the basis of quality of programs raises the question of censorship, the implications of which I cannot at present accept.

Three major things have developed during the last twelve months. The first is interconnection of stations by which a single voice may be broadcast from all parts of the United States. This interconnection has been most successfully carried out by the use of the wire systems between broadcasting stations but other methods of interconnection are in use and process of development. It is difficult to see as yet what the public implications of interconnection will be.

During the past year there have been discoveries in the use of higher power and therefore larger areas of broadcasting, which may result in a single station being able to cover a large portion if not all of the country. This raises questions of the rights of local stations and the rights of local listeners.

Still another development has been the fact that it has been found possible by indirect advertising to turn broadcasting to highly profitable use. If this were misused we would be confronted with the fact that service more advantageous to the listeners would be crowded out for advertising purposes.

Because of this situation, there is growing up a demand for the elimination of the number of stations in a given area and that such a limitation would be based on the service needs of the community, just as public utilities are generally limited by the rule of public convenience and necessity. Again this enters a dangerous field of recognizing monopoly and implied censorship.

On the other hand, we are in a rush to broadcasting which may in time die down and the number of stations may decrease. Alternately improvement in the art may increase the number of individual wavelengths and no priorities need then be contemplated.

These are not all of the shifts in progress and we may have to come to the conclusion that many station owners must be considered as having abandoned the field of private enterprise and entered that of public service. In view of these changes we may have to reconsider the regulation of the whole art from the point of view of the listener.

The public interest of radio broadcasting is rapidly widening. Entertainment and amusement have ceased to be its principal purposes. The public, especially our people on farms and in isolated communities, are coming to rely on it for the information necessary to the conduct of their daily affairs. It is rapidly becoming a necessity and they rightly feel that since the public medium of the ether is used to reach them, that they have a direct and justifiable interest in the manner in which it is conducted.

From all of this it seems to me that there is a tendency which may require an entirely different basis in character, theory and extent of legislation than any we have contemplated in the past. The basis of regulation and the fundamental policies to be followed must be finally declared by Congress, not left to an administrative officer. Hitherto, we have conceived the problem to be one of interference but there is now opening before us a whole vista of difficult problems. The development of the art is such that the whole situation is changing rapidly and the opinion of today on the solution for given difficulty is worthless tomorrow. I hope that another year's experience will show what direction of legislative course must be pursued. Meanwhile I feel that we would be actual gainers by allowing the industry to progress naturally and unhampered except by the maintenance of a firm principle of government control of the ether and the elimination of interference so far as it is possible.

The suggestion which I enclosed is necessary under whatever regulatory theory may develop. It merely affirms the authority now exercised by the Department over wavelengths, power, apparatus and time of operation. It is in the nature of emergency legislation urgently needed to preserve the situation in the public interest until a final and complete legislative policy can be adopted. It contains the provision reserving Federal control over the ether. Its other provisions are merely condensed statements of powers conferred in the bill which you introduced as reported by the House Committee.

Yours faithfully,

[signed] Herbert Hoover

The bill he submitted to Rep. White was simple and straightforward:

AN ACT RELATING TO THE REGULATION OF RADIO COMMUNICATION. Be it enacted by the Senate and House of Representatives in Congress assembled, That it is hereby declared and re-affirmed that the ether within the limits of the United States, its territories and possessions, is the inalienable possession of the people thereof, and that the authority to regulate its use in interstate and/or foreign commerce is conferred upon the Congress of the United States by the Federal Constitution.

Section 2. That Section 1 of the act of Congress approved August 13, 1912, entitled "An Act to Regulate Radio Communication" is hereby amended by adding at the end of said section, the following:

"The wavelength of every radio transmitting station for which a license is now required by law, its power, emitted wave, the character of its apparatus, and the time of transmission, shall be fixed by the Secretary of Commerce as in his judgment and direction he shall deem expedient, and may be changed or modified from time to time in his discretion."[76]

Secretary Hoover knew that "our part of the radio industry is becoming more difficult each month and we certainly do need moral support."[77] At the same time legislation was losing support from the industry, possibly because Hoover did not want Congress to take the regulation of broadcasting away from the Department of Commerce. The stop-gap legislation he wanted would have given him most of the powers he needed while keeping regulation under his control. Whatever Hoover's intentions, the effects were disastrous.[78]

E. F. McDonald, Jr., president of the Zenith Radio Corporation and licensee of WJAZ, Chicago, and also the first president of the National Association of Broadcasters, attacked the proposal in *Radio Broadcast* magazine:

I have unbounded confidence in him [Hoover] and would be in favor of putting this tremendous power into the hands of the Secretary of Commerce on one condition, and that is, that Hoover give to the radio broadcasting industry a guarantee that he will live 100 years and that he will serve as Secretary of Commerce for that hundred years. In other words, Hoover, we don't know who your successor is going to be![79]

In the same article J. H. Morecraft, past president of the Institute of Radio Engineers, commented:

McDonald's point is well taken. The actions and policies of Hoover during the last few years have given the radio broadcasters every confidence in his judgment, and all of them would cheerfully abide by his decision in any matter he deemed it wise to regulate, but to confer on any Secretary of Commerce such Napoleonic power as this brief paragraph would do, seems certainly unwise. His word would be final. There would be no recourse of appeal from any decision he might make, as the bill is now worded. Such papers are too sweeping and should not be granted.[80]

The *New York Times* reported that "as a result of the position taken by Secretary Hoover, it is considered doubtful that there will be any important legislation dealing with the radio industry at the short session of Congress."[81] Even though the White Bill had little chance of passage, it appeared to many of Hoover's supporters as though he had abruptly withdrawn his department's support of legislation seriously under consideration by Congress.

Hoover's effort to obtain a stop-gap bill generated considerable adverse comments to which he and his staff reacted strongly. Hoover's assistant, Harold Stokes, wrote to the editor of the *Chicago Herald Examiner* replying to an editorial attacking Hoover's emergency request.

The short substitute bill which he proposed to Congress, pending further experience with the industry and therefore more certain determination as to what measures are needed, was far less drastic in character than the present pending White bill and confers much less authority on the Secretary of Commerce, it being his view that further experience will determine the character of regulation necessary.

Hoover's proposal merely clarifies the existence of powers not exercised by the Department which bear at the present time a legal interpretation even more drastic than the short measure which he has suggested. Incidentally the proposal does not contemplate the slightest supervision or control over radio programs. Its power is limited entirely to measures necessary to prevent interference between the multitude of stations so that each may operate as freely as possible.[82]

Hoover attempted to clarify his reasoning through a number of public statements. He noted that "I would like to avoid legislation until we have a clearer view of the future."[83] Since the present law was enacted to regulate marine radio communication and was inadequate for the current situation, Hoover conceded that there were some problems, "but would rather continue to stretch them [laws] over the bare spots than to risk hampering radio broadcasting at a time when the greatest possible freedom for development is essential."[84]

He believed that crystallizing certain attitudes into a law "will impede the development of the art."[85] His general outlook was optimistic as of September of 1925:

Any day we may see discoveries which will simplify the whole of our problems of congestion. And in any event the undoubted improvements in our sending and receiving sets every year contributes to widen the paths through the air. We have a great unsolved problem in the amount of power necessary to give real service to listeners even against the opposition of static and summer conditions and without adding still further congestion and interference.[86]

Two months later, Secretary Hoover wrote a letter to the radio editor of the *Youngstown Telegram* disavowing any intention to dictate to the broadcast industry:

I do not ... like the growing tendency to refer to me as the radio "czar." Most czars seems to meet unpleasant fates. As a matter of fact, in all my dealings with radio I have tried to take the opposite of the czarlike attitude.

It has been my thought that those directly engaged in radio, particularly in broadcasting, should be able, to a very large extent, to regulate and govern themselves and this has been accomplished by a succession of annual conferences. It is true that there must be a firm Federal control over certain features, particularly the use of the air channels, but this control has always been exercised with the complete cooperation of those who were affected by it and it is largely through their aid and assistance that it has been possible to maintain order without much legislative authority.

I am inclined to the belief that absolute authority over radio broadcasting is too great a power to place in the hands of one man. Personally, I do not want it and would not like to have to exercise it.[87]

III. Secretary Hoover's Stand on Major Issues

During 1924 and 1925 Hoover made many major addresses about radio broadcasting and its regulation. He outlined a consistent philosophy of the control government should have over radio.

Monopoly. Secretary Hoover had made a clear statement of his opposition to a monopoly of the airwaves during the hearings on H. R. 7357. The purchase, ownership and control of key equipment patents by a few companies had begun to impact on others attempting to enter broadcasting. There was a great deal of negative publicity caused by AT&T's efforts to use the transmitter patents under its control to prevent competition. There was agitation by stations that did not have the favored channels large corporations had obtained.[88]

On March 6, 1924, Grover A. Whalen, founder of WNYC, the municipal station of New York City, accused AT&T of obtaining its allocation in

New York by "questionable and unscrupulous tactics, special exclusive concessions and the use of higher power than that permitted to other broadcasting stations." He charged that AT&T had assumed the prerogatives of the federal government in the control and regulation of radio. The company, Whalen stated, was "refusing the lease of its land wire to all stations but its own" and was "attempting to secure subscriptions to pay their artists."[89]

The AT&T company had offered to sell its patented transmitters to radio stations, and to license transmitters already in use for prices ranging from $500 to $3,000. Most station owners did not believe they were infringing on the patent rights of what was being called the radio "trust" and refused to pay. To protect its patents, AT&T sued station WHN, New York, in 1924. This case generated so much unfavorable publicity for AT&T they settled out of court.[90]

Secretary Hoover received many requests for his views on the patent cases that were before the courts. He held it was not proper for him to make statements on specific pending cases but he did feel it was necessary to go on record with the following:

> Emphatically that it would be most unfortunate for the people of this country, to whom broadcasting has become an important incident in life, if its control should come into the hands of any single corporation, individual or combination.
>
> It would be in principle the same as though the entire press of the country were so controlled. The effect would be identical whether this control arose under a patent monopoly or under any form of combination, and from the standpoint of the people's interest the question of whether or not the broadcasting is for profit is immaterial....
>
> I believe it safe to say, irrespective of claims under patent rights on apparatus, that broadcasting will not cease, and neither will our public policy allow it to become monopolized.[91]

In an interview for the *New York World*, March 16, 1924, Secretary Hoover pointed out two conflicting arguments.

> One is the right of inventors to earn a profit on their patents, and the other is the broad principle that nobody must be permitted to monopolize or control the means of public communication. I think that is a question for the courts to solve, and I am not a lawyer.[92]

He went on to discuss censorship and legislation.

> You will recognize that if anybody should be able to have the exclusive use of a certain wavelength he would have a monopoly on that part of the ether. That cannot be permitted. We have protected the ether. Of course certain people have patents on the instruments by which you get in and out of the ether. Like all patentees, they have certain rights which should be protected. That is a matter for the courts. It is also a matter for the exercise of broad vision by people in control of great industrial enterprises.[93]

But it was pointed out to Hoover that if individuals or corporations could monopolize the instruments by which access to the ether was obtained, they might have for all practical purposes a monopoly on the ether itself. Hoover countered, "Don't forget that the Government can prevent them from using the ether, and thus destroy the value of the apparatus if it chooses."[94]

Hoover made another strong public statement about monopoly a few days later. He repeated that the licensing system of the Department of Commerce made it impossible for anyone to have a vested interest and restated, "that broadcasting will not cease and neither will our policy allow it to be monopolized."[95]

To effect monopoly control Hoover felt the policy of the Department of Commerce "must limit the use of the ether to a definite period of years or months so that we can under any reasonable conditions return the use of this particular wavelength to the Government." However, certain care was necessary "to give a reasonable continuity of service to a broadcasting station so as to warrant its erection and support."[96] Hoover had no doubt that the companies who controlled the manufacture of equipment had so fundamental an interest in the expansion of the art and in the development of broadcasting, "that they will show great vision in handling of their patent rights."[97]

In an address before the California Radio Exposition in San Francisco, Hoover repeated that there must be a limit to the length of time any broadcasting station could retain its license. He repeated these opinions in an interview he gave to *Radio News* in October 1924.[98]

During the presidential campaign of 1924, Senator Robert LaFollette of Wisconsin, a third party candidate, charged that the radio "monopoly" had kept him off the air on station WHO, Des Moines, Iowa, on October 15. Secretary Hoover replied to this public charge with some anger. He said that LaFollette obviously did not understand the broadcasting situation or the law which regulated it. "Anyone who likes is free under the law and the practices of the Department of Commerce to erect a broadcasting station and say anything over it that he pleases."[99] He listed the many times that special permission for LaFollette's speeches to be broadcast on various interconnected stations had been given. "There are 530 radio stations [October 1924] in the United States; less than a dozen of them belong to the people that LaFollette calls the monopoly."[100] Hoover went on:

> There is no monopoly and there can be none under the law. The stations are all independent and have the right to decide for themselves as to what they will or will not broadcast.[101]

By May of 1925 Hoover recognized that "if we limit the number [of broadcasting stations], the possession of a license becomes commercially valuable, and in a sense, a monopoly."[102] He also knew that it would be impossible to continue to license everyone who wished to be a broadcaster.

"A year ago I was told that it immediately would be necessary to limit the number of broadcasting stations. But the number of large stations has continued to increase and we have found means of getting them all on the air without in any way interfering with their service to the public."[103]

However, this situation had begun to change in 1925 and "it may become necessary to limit the number of stations; But I hope not, for as soon as that is done we set ourselves up as censors and dispensers of privilege."[104]

Above all, Secretary Hoover believed, it was the American system to leave broadcasting in the hands of free enterprise. With the convening of the Fourth Radio Conference it had became apparent that the federal government had no choice but to dispense privilege to those who had already made their entry into the broadcasting industry.

Censorship and Programming. A conflict was developing between regulation of broadcasting and free speech. A number of law review articles were justifying deregulation on the basis of broadcaster's rights to free speech. Others were arguing that broadcasters must be heavily regulated to promote the free speech of those who were not broadcasters.[105] This contentious issue is still debated.

The basic issue of what should be programmed motivated Senator LaFollette's attacks on radio station WHO who had refused to carry his political speech. Other writers were asking the Department how they could keep political speeches off the air. "I was of the understanding that radio broadcasting was to be kept to a point where it would be of interest to any home. And with the Presidential election almost eleven months off it is sure disgusting to think about if they are going to accommodate [sic] all of the political speakers."[106] The Bureau of Navigation's reply became a form letter to be used over and over, which stated:

> Under the existing law the Government has no control over the matter broadcast.
>
> So far the programs have been controlled largely by public sentiment and if the majority of listeners object [to whatever the complaint was about] it is believed that such owners will endeavor to rearrange their programs so as to please their audience as good will is their chief asset.[107]

Programming control had occurred when "broadcasting" was restricted on amateur licenses and special programming conditions were attached to Class B and Class D stations. The Department also attempted to enforce any promises about programming which had been made to the Department by licensees. Radio Inspector Edwards wrote to KDKA that a contest they were running for the *National Stockman and Farmer* newspaper should be discontinued. Station KDKA notified the *Stockman* which wrote the Department that the contest, guessing the future market prices, was instructional in nature.[108] The department replied:

the Westinghouse station is one of three licensed in the development class and the regulations applying to stations in this class do not permit competitions where prizes or other valuable considerations are offered. This regulation was recommended by the Westinghouse company.[109]

The newspaper was not satisfied with that answer and complained that they had heard other contests such as "the number of seeds in Cantaloupe [*sic*] in Cincinnati."[110]

Hoover had some rather pointed ideas on what the responsibility of the broadcasting industry was in programming. "The very moment that the Government begins to determine what can be sent out, it establishes a censorship, and almost immediately it will be called upon to discriminate between opera and jazz, fundamentalist and modernist sermons, and so on throughout the whole field of clashing ideas."[111]

He had said for some time:

> Another problem that is beginning to arise is the question of determining priority of material to be broadcasted. This implies indirect censorship, or the organization of some method of expression of the wishes on the part of radio listeners as to the material which is broadcast. At the present time most of our receiving instruments when not blanketed by the local broadcasting station can receive programs from 3 or 4 alternative stations. The art and perfection in instruments are so developing as to render it possible even now, with certain kinds of instruments, to receive from several times this number of stations. This will, I believe, solve the problem by competitive programs.... I certainly am opposed to the Government undertaking any censorship even with the present limited number of stations. It is better that these questions should be determined by the 570 different broadcasting stations than by any Government official. These stations naturally are endeavoring to please their listeners and thus there is an indirect censorship by the public. This is the place it belongs. What we must safeguard is that there shall be no interference with free speech, that no monopoly of broadcasting stations should grow up under which any person or group could determine what material will be delivered to the public.[112]

It was apparent from correspondence from stations to the Department that they were seeking to learn, through such techniques as surveys, what listeners did want to hear. One such survey in Chicago, with three stations participating, KYW, WDAP and WJAZ, brought in 263,410 pieces of mail. Of the responses received, 32.6 percent were from women and 67.4 percent from men. Their preferences: popular music 29 percent, classical music 24.7 percent and jazz 18 percent.[113]

Carson wrote in January of 1925 that:

> It is hoped that the owners of broadcasting stations will benefit by the suggestions of Mr. Hoover concerning improved programs. There are

so many broadcasting stations in operation at this time that it appears very necessary to give serious thought to provide the best programs possible to insure holding the attention of the audience as it is an easy matter to change a dial.

There is undoubtedly too much trashy material filling the air at present.[114]

Hoover defined the job of the Department of Commerce as "keeping the traffic lanes clear so that the voice over the radio may reach the listener."[115] It was the listener in whom he was primarily interested and he believed the listener should be the primary concern of the broadcaster "not only as an industry but as a public service."[116]

Although Hoover held that the Department of Commerce should not censor, there was regulation of certain aspects of programming. In order for the public to report unsatisfactory performance the public had to be able to identify stations. On February 2, 1925, the *Radio Service Bulletin* announced:

> According to the reports received by the bureau the announcers of some of the broadcasting stations continue programs for long periods without announcing the call letters of the station and as some of the call letters are not readily understood, suggestion has been made that some other method be used which will make identification more positive.
>
> It will probably be more helpful if when making an announcement the call letters of a station are followed by the name of the city in which the broadcasting station is situated and it would no doubt be appreciated by the audience if the announcers would announce distinctly the call letters and name of the city at somewhat regular intervals.[117]

Later, this would be codified into the station identification rule which still exists.

A number of complaints were received citing specific stations and programs. One writer complained that the Dr. John Romulus Brinkley station, KFKB ([K]ansas' [F]irst, [K]ansas' [B]est) in Milford, Kansas, broadcast a talk on "glands [in which] the language used was distinctly unsuited to radiocasting or to decent conversation even among men. The terms used were nauseating...."[118]

Another writer assumed "by this time you have received numerous protests against the broadcasting under government license the false, malicious, and un–American propaganda by the Klu Klux Klan of Kansas."[119] This was also in reference to Brinkley's KFKB. The Department of Commerce sent its form letter which read, "Under the existing laws, the Secretary of Commerce has not the authority to censure programs."[120] The writers were asked to complain directly to the radio station.

The radio supervisors censured programs in various ways. Inspector Deiler, for instance, wrote, "if a change in wave can be arranged [for this station], it is recommended, but to change to Class B at present in our opinion would severely lower that standard and dignity of Class B stations as a whole."[121] Thus, only stations with appropriate programming obtained this particular supervisor's recommendation.

Public pressures continued and Hoover's personal secretary, Harold Stokes, responded to newspapers whenever they attacked regulation by the Department of Commerce. Hoover dictated to Stokes the following letter on programming control, published in the *New York Mirror*, on March 30, 1925:

> I believe you are under a misapprehension because there is no federal authority of any kind by which the Secretary of Commerce may suppress advertising, or in any way interfere with the character of radio programs. His very limited authority extends only to questions of interference between stations.[122]

Perhaps the final word on programming was written by Hoover to Aaron Fox, of the Fox Film Company, on December 9, 1925:

> Every radio station is in exclusive control of its own broadcasting and may decide for itself what it will and will not send out. The Department has absolutely no power in the matter. I am inclined to think it would be very unfortunate if any such authority were placed in any Government Officer, as it might finally lead to a rather complete censorship.[123]

Network Interconnection. It was often suggested that the government set up a broadcasting network of its own to "disseminate educational and scientific matter." Secretary Hoover wrote to President Coolidge's secretary in reply to such a suggestion: "I do not believe that the United States as a Government should directly enter the broadcasting field."[124]

However, Hoover began to speak out more often about national programming. Only a few listeners had radios capable of receiving distant stations consistently through the static and interference. Hoover felt that the local station was the key to consistent reception and "in order that we should have a national service we must have interconnection of these different broadcasting stations."[125] He commented:

> On last Thursday President Coolidge's acceptance speech was delivered [July 1924] to twenty million people East of the Rocky Mountains as plainly as you can hear me from this local station.... The great events in the United States occur only in one place at a time, and therefore if radio is to become a great source of serious distribution of public events, interconnection must be our first concern.[126]

Hoover urged the broadcasters to develop more frequent interlinking so "that we may also enjoy each night the product of our great artists and the thoughts of our leading men and women, and may participate in great national occasions."[127]

He saw the development of national programming being much along the lines of the "organization which our newspapers maintain through the press associations."[128] Some reports had Hoover, in effect, suggesting a national tax to support national programming at the Fourth National Radio Conference. The volume of mail opposing this concept was such that Hoover felt it necessary to publicly announce that networking would be left to the broadcasters.

> A misapprehension which I would like at this time to correct is that any suggestion had been made by me or the Department of Commerce that there should be a tax on the sale of radio material for the provision of a national program. Such proposals were discussed at the recent [Fourth] Radio Conference but were abandoned.[129]

Hoover wrote to Congressman Aswell late in 1925 to try to ease the concern which had arisen about networks becoming a monopolistic instrument.

> There is no plan for the linking up of all high powered broadcasting stations in the U.S....
>
> Personally, I see no danger whatever in the practice. The radio bills which have been introduced in Congress at this session contain no provision regarding it.[130]

The Radio Act of 1927 when it passed had no provision for the direct regulation of networks.

Financial Support for Broadcasting. How to provide funds to pay for broadcasting had to be resolved if the industry was to survive. On March 16, 1924, Hoover wrote:

> The largest unsolved question in this entire problem is the problem of remuneration for broadcasting stations. The man who evolves a practical and fair way of compensating them will have cracked the hardest nut in the bowl.[131]

Hoover felt that the British system of taxation was not the American system.

> We cannot do that. It would make the Government responsible for the program, which would lead to an impossible situation. I know that if the Government were responsible for some of the programs that come in over my set I would register plenty of kicks. But, knowing that they are the efforts of private individuals, I give them credit for doing the best they can.[132]

Hoover observed that in order to secure artists, regular payment would have to be made for their services. It was also necessary for some "proper return on the capital invested in the stations, the cost involved in the use of wires or other means of interconnection."[133] The operation of all broadcasting stations was costing at that time a total of five million dollars a year, according to the Secretary.

> Up to date they are supported through their advertising value to owners or through the desire of manufacturers to maintain a service for purposes of developing the art.... It can be said at once if radio broadcasting shall be overwhelmed with advertising the radio audience will disappear in disgust. It is as yet too early to foresee the solution of this problem of support but I am confident that a system will be worked out.... In the meantime I am opposed to any scheme of imposing a charge on the radio listeners by law.[134]

Hoover summed up his opinion of the matter a couple of months later:

> With more than 3,000,000 receiving sets already in existence and the number fast increasing, I see no way of collecting a charge from listeners for the support of broadcasting programs. I don't know how you would find the sets or police such a collection. It seems physically impossible. I don't believe it is necessary.[135]

He listed five possible means of financing broadcasting: 1) the manufacturers; 2) advertising; 3) public service corporations; 4) public institutions; and 5) municipal agencies.

> I have no doubt that somewhere, out of all these combinations, broadcasting will be maintained, and that there is no real question of putting a charge on the owner of receiving sets.
>
> It is asked whether, with broadcasting in the hands of these groups, high-class programs employing fine artists and orchestras are likely to be developed. That is a hard question to answer. All one can say is that there has been astonishing improvement in the last three years.[136]

Hoover did not have an answer to financial support, but he ruled out government license fees, and personally frowned upon advertising. Overall, financing was a matter he felt had to be left to the industry for solution.

Government and Business. Secretary Hoover gave a major address before the Chamber of Commerce of the United States on May 7, 1924. Although his topic was about the relationships between business and government, it explains what his views were toward the amount of regulatory freedom he felt business needed.

> Ten people in a whole country, with a plow a-piece, did not elbow each other very much. But when we put seven million people in a country with the tools of electricity, steam, 30-floor buildings, telephones, miscellaneous noises, street cars, railways, motors, stock exchanges, and what not, then we do jostle each other in a multitude of directions.

Thereupon our law makers supply the demand by the ceaseless piling up of statutes in attempts to keep the traffic open; to assure fair dealing in the economic world; to eliminate wastes; to prevent some kind of domination. Moreover, with increasing education our senses become more offended and our moral discriminations increase; for all of which we discover new things to remedy....

The question we need to consider is whether these rules and regulations are to be developed solely by Government or whether they can not in some large part be developed out of voluntary forces in the nation....

National character can not be built by law. It is the sum of the moral fiber of its individuals. When abuses which rise from our growing system are cured by live individual conscience, by initiative in the creation of voluntary standards, then is the growth of moral perceptions fertilized in every individual character.

No one disputes the necessity for constantly new standards of conduct in relation to all these tools and inventions. Even our latest invention—radio—has brought a host of new questions.... Our public utilities are wasteful and costly unless we give them a privilege more or less monopolistic. At once when we have business affected with monopoly we must have regulation by law. Much of even this phase might have been unnecessary had there been a higher degree of responsibility to the public, higher standards of business practice among those who dominated these agencies in years gone by.

There has been, however, a great extension of Government regulation and control beyond the field of public utilities into the fields of production and distribution....

Legislative action is always clumsy—it is incapable of adjustment to shifting needs. It often enough produces new economic currents more abusive than those intended to be cured. Government too often becomes the persecutor instead of the regulator....

I am one of those who believe in the substratum of inherent honesty, the fine vein of service and kindliness in our citizenship....

In these times of muddled thought it is sometimes worth repeating a truism. Industry and commerce are not based upon taking advantage of other persons....

The thing we all need to searchingly consider is the practical question of the method by which the business world can develop and enforce its own standards and thus stem the tide of Government regulations.[137]

Secretary Hoover felt there must first be an organization to establish standards of conduct, and, second, there must be some sort of enforcement on the minority who will not "play the game."[138] He concluded:

All of this is the strong beginning of a new force in the business world. The individual interest is wrapped up with the public interest. They can find expression only through association. Three years of study and intimate contact with associations ... convince me that there lies within them a great moving impulse toward betterment.

If these organizations accept as their primary purpose the lifting of standards ... we shall have proceeded far along the road of the elimination of government from business.

The Government can best contribute through stimulation of and cooperation with voluntary forces in our national life; for we thus preserve the foundations upon which we have progressed so far—the initiative of our people. With vision and devotion these voluntary forces can accomplish more for America than any spread of the hand of Government.[139]

His good friend, Charles K. Field, who broadcast as "Cheerio," wrote this about Hoover:

As secretary of Commerce, Hoover was in the thick of his ongoing fight to establish control of radio by the Government. He told me once: "If I could have on my tombstone that record: 'This may help save the ownership of the channels of the air for the people,' that would be enough!"[140]

Hoover did not believe that the Interstate Commerce provision in the Constitution should be stretched to regulate all things that crossed state lines, for "we shall by that very means automatically absorb to Federal authority most of the government that lies within State lines."[141] However, he understood that radio broadcasting was inherently different.

There are a number of intricate problems to be solved if the art is to become the great service to the public of which it is capable. The first of these problems is regulation to prevent interference between stations. There can be no adequate development of the art unless there is very positive Federal regulation. It is the one industrial service I know of which is anxious to be regulated, for without regulation we will have absolute chaos in the ether and no adequate service can be developed. The Federal law on the subject was passed a dozen years ago at the time when the telegraph was the only radio manifestation in the field. The Department of Commerce has been unceasing for three years in endeavors to secure adequate legislation to govern the radio telephone field. Congress has been too crowded to deal adequately with so intricate a subject but it is probable that such legislation will pass in the next session.[142]

IV. Increasing Regulatory Difficulties

What follows are examples of the problems of interference, allocations, time-sharing, and licensing to be found in the record:

Interference. HIGH POWER. Mr. C. W. Horn, operations director of KDKA (which was a Class D station authorized to use power up to 1000 watts) wrote the Department on January 15, 1924, that "our comparatively lengthy experience has shown us that the power of 1,000 watts is not sufficient to give this station a constant and efficient transmitting radius of several hundred miles under all conditions."[143] They requested higher power. He mentioned that "in fact, we have been using more than 1,000 watts for some time and there has been no objection."[144] The bureau desired to be liberal with the Westinghouse Company "in view of the developmental work this Company has done in the past and may do in the future. However, it would not be wise to give to this Company the unrestricted use of power up to ten kilowatts."[145]

Radio supervisor Edwards had a meeting with Dr. Conrad, Davis and Horn of Westinghouse and recommended that the requested increase be granted.[146]

The Department informed Edwards that a conference had been held with Judge Stephen B. Davis, Solicitor for the Department of Commerce and representatives of Class B stations just previous to this request. "These representatives informed Judge Davis that it was their opinion that it would not be advisable at the present time to permit the use of high power by Class B broadcasting stations as it has not yet been definitely determined that high power could be successfully used."[147] It was reasoned that if KDKA, a Class D station, were given higher power it would then be necessary to afford the same opportunity to all Class B stations that requested increases.

On April 3, 1924, Horn replied to a letter from the Department of Commerce that asked what attitude Westinghouse would have if Class B stations were given higher power. Horn noted that higher power should be permitted those stations that demonstrated their ability to provide proper programs and who were willing to bear the expense of the facilities. He noted the greatest harm of power increases would be the "competitive race among the different stations for larger powered sets. This would create a situation which would not be desirable."[148] It was suggested that regulations specifying requirements to prevent "shoe-string" operations from using higher power would be necessary.

Many letters were received from listeners who stated that higher power would cause interference on their radio sets. The Department had authorized WEAF, the American Telephone and Telegraph station located in New York, to increase power. This resulted in many complaints about interference with other broadcasting stations. It was claimed that increased power prevented local reception of out-of-town stations. One such letter commented: "I know that one of the arguments presented by those in favor of higher power is that it is for the benefit of the ruralist ... [and] I wonder if those presenting that argument know that the ruralist with his little two-tube Armstrong regenerative circuit now has a consistent range of 40 to 60 broadcasting stations."[149] The question of higher power had come before the Third Radio Conference which approved the concept in principle.

KDKA was authorized 1500 watts of power on January 17, 1925.[150]

By March 1925 the following stations were authorized by the Department of Commerce for five kilowatts of power:[151]

KFI—(F)armer's (I)nformation Station—Earle C. Anthony, Los Angeles
WLS—(W)orld's (L)argest (S)tore—Sears-Roebuck Co.,Chicago
WCBD—Zion Institution—Zion, Illinois
WOC—(W)orld (O)f (C)hiropractic—Palmer School, Davenport, Iowa
WCCO—(W)ashburn (C)rosby Milling (CO)mpany, Minneapolis
WEAF—AT&T—New York
WORD—People's Pulpit—Batavia, Illinois
WLW—(W)e (L)ove (W)attage—Crosley Radio, Cincinnati
WSAI—U.S. Playing Card Co.—Cincinnati

Soon other stations were to join in the high power category. Westinghouse was constructing higher power equipment to be sold to the Radio Corporation of America and invited Edwards to look at it. He was quite impressed and reported favorably to Carson.[152]

Horn of KDKA felt that higher power "is the only way we can overcome the poor conditions which exist during the summer months."[153] He applied to the Bureau of Navigation for authorization to use 75 kilowatts.[154] Tyrer replied that the Department did not consider it advisable to authorize such a high power. However, "it is believed proper that experiments should be conducted to determine what the effect of the use of that amount of power would be."[155] Periodically, the Westinghouse Company notified the radio supervisor that they were increasing their power at KDKA to 40 kilowatts, eight kilowatts, or some other higher power for one hour for experimental purposes. As a Class D station they were given this option for short periods of time for experimental purposes only.

The Department soon decided to allow the experimental use of high power for longer periods. The Bureau of Navigation issued a public statement:

> Secretary Hoover today [August 16, 1925] announced that the Department of Commerce had made arrangements with WGY at Schenectady to broadcast experimentally with fifty kilowatts, the greatest amount of power ever used in the history of regular broadcasting.
>
> The purpose of the experiment is to attain more satisfactory and definite information than is presently available concerning the effect of increased power upon the intensity and quality of signals, distance, and area covered, interference caused with other stations, overcoming summer static, modulation, fading and possible blanketing....
>
> Secretary Hoover is anxious that all radio listeners as well as other broadcasting stations, report their observations which will be checked with the official findings of the Department's radio inspectors....[156]

By November 1925, 197 stations were using at least 500 watts of power.[157]

The RCA station, WJZ, in Bound Brook, New Jersey, was authorized in December to use up to 50 kilowatts. Secretary Hoover noted:

> There has been, during the past year, a very decided movement towards a raise in the power level used by broadcasting stations and while the Department has maintained a firm control over the increase, it has not deemed it wise to make any arbitrary prohibitions or limitations until the situation is fully developed. This particular station [WJZ] has been broadcasting for some ten days, using about forty kilowatts power. This is a very large amount and the Department has received a considerable amount of complaints from broadcast listeners in its immediate vicinity.[158]

David Sarnoff called at the Department of Commerce in December to discuss this situation, and Hoover reported:

> The station has now reduced its power to five kilowatts, which is the amount used by some twelve or fifteen other stations in the United States which are similarly situated and which have caused very little complaint. I think this reduction will obviate a very large proportion of the just complaints in that vicinity. Future policy with regard to the use of power will be determined from time to time as necessity and convenience may indicate.[159]

Further experimentation continued and the Radio Corporation of America sent out crews of technicians to answer every complaint in the area of WJZ. This series of experiments proved to the Bureau of Standards that the use of higher power produced louder signals and greatly reduced atmospheric disturbances and other interference in a larger radius around the broadcasting station. However, the gain in distance was not proportional to the increase in power.[160]

THE REGENERATIVE RECEIVER. It was the circuit design of Edwin Howard Armstrongs' regenerative receiver that caused broadcasting stations and the Department of Commerce some difficulties. Armstrong testified:

> I want to bring to you the attention of this committee [House, Hearings on H. R. 7357] a technical matter, a matter relative to interference which, in my estimation, is just as serious for the future of radio as any question of monopoly which has been considered....
>
> I might as well identify myself as the inventor of the circuit which causes this interference. This circuit on the other hand has created radio broadcasting.
>
> It is used in every transmitting broadcasting station in the country, and it is used in about 80 percent of the receiving stations.
>
> Technically speaking it is this—that just as you approach the most sensitive adjustment of this receiver, it begins to oscillate and it becomes a miniature transmitter, and it sends out signals which interfere with every other receiver within a radius of a few hundred yards.[161]

When improperly turned, the regenerative receiver would emit a "squeal" and interfere with any other receiver within a small distance. Harold J. Power of the American Radio and Research Corporation suggested:

> If you will first adjust your tickler dial to low setting, use headphones for tuning in, because with your tickler loosely coupled the signals will be weak. After adjusting your tuning dials bring up the tickler adjustment until the music is sufficiently loud.[162]

A conference was called by the Bureau of Standards at the Engineers Club in New York, January 16, 1924, to discuss ways and means of curbing this source of interference. The conference was attended by radio engineers and editors and writers from radio publications. The participants reached the unanimous opinion that radiating receivers were causing a great deal of the interference and that some immediate steps had to be taken.[163]

Two committees were selected, a technical committee to furnish diagrams showing how radiating receiving sets could be converted into nonradiating receivers, and an educational committee to provide publicity for the material provided by the technical committee. It was their opinion that the educational campaign "would be more effective at this time than any legislation covering receiving apparatus."[164]

Tyrer and Terrell went before a subcommittee of the House Committee on Appropriations in February of 1925 to ask for an increase of $125,000 for the Radio Service. In the testimony at the hearing it was pointed out that as of February 10, 1925, there were 454 Class A stations, 85 Class B, 16 Class C and two Class D stations for a total of 557 licensed stations. The chairman of the subcommittee assumed that the requested increase was going to be used by the Bureau of Navigation to investigate complaints of interference caused by the regenerative receivers.[165] Tyrer told him, "We have no jurisdiction over the inspection of receiving sets."[166] An argument on this jurisdiction then ensued:

> CHAIRMAN: Let me ask this question right there: You issue licenses to sending stations, and you issue the licenses under certain regulations; presumably, those regulations are complied with, and I want to know what business it is of your organization to ascertain the difficulties that may be found in receiving stations? What is it that leads you to conclude that you have the right to supply remedies to those people whom you do not license on account of the troubles that they encounter?
>
> TYRER: There is no other way.
>
> CHAIRMAN: It is not a question of whether there is any other way, but it is a question of what are your rights, or what does the law authorize you to do. Where does the Government come into it? Why do you presume to say that you have the right to interfere with my business or somebody else's business without regard to what the law is? You may think that it is patriotic, and you may think that it is important to do

this thing, but there are limits beyond which a Government agency can not enter into the privacy of another man's business....[167]

CHAIRMAN: Going further than that, let us follow up the matter: I may be wrong in my conception of it, but why does the Department of Commerce presume to do what I conceive to be the duty of the sending station? For example, if a receiving station is not able to get radio messages, is it not the business of the sending station to find out what the interference is that prevents the receiving station from getting it? Is not that the duty of the sending station instead of being the duty of the Government?

TYRER: The sending station, however, is transmitting those messages in accordance with the law, and I do not know wherein the burden would be on that sending station, inasmuch as it is complying with the law, to determine any other sources of interference.

CHAIRMAN: You must remember that this is a land of law and not of men. It is a Government of laws. We can not run the country upon the basis of what you or I think it ought to be, but upon the basis of what the law says. That question was fought out in the last campaign.... Is your present organization sufficient to regulate the sending stations and the radio equipment on ships?

TERRELL: I think if we had to regulate only the ship stations operating along the coast, I would say yes....

CHAIRMAN: If the number [of receiving sets] has grown to 5,000,000 and the Government should undertake to investigate every complaint, there will be 10,000,000 next year, perhaps. You can see what the Government would be getting itself into. This appropriation would run up to a billion dollars before very long. It would cost more money to investigate these complaints than it would be to run the rest of the Government.[168]

The committee did not approve the increased budget. The chairman stated, "I believe everybody on the committee agreed, without division, that there should be no money available to the department to take supervision over the individual receiving sets owned by the people in their homes."[169] The chairman held to the view:

There was no law then and I presume there is no law now to give the department that jurisdiction. I think it would be unwise to have such law, though I may not have any people agree with me, because if we enter upon the field of controlling, licensing, or regulating receiving sets, there would be no limit to the amount of money required for that purpose.

Tyrer replied:

Chairman, I would like to say that the department concurs entirely in your view that we have practically nothing to do with the receiving sets.[170]

The problem still existed in November as reported in *Radio Broadcast*, "the radiating receiver should get its share of adverse comment at the Washington [Fourth] Conference. Listeners continually complain of these miniature broadcasting stations."[171]

SPARK TRANSMISSION. The Third Radio Conference had finally gotten marine communication moved from the broadcasting band. However, international regulations allowed ships to utilize 450 meters (666.3 kHz) which was at the lower end of the broadcast spectrum. The British Embassy communicated with Secretary of State Charles E. Hughes in October of 1924 to inform him that reciprocal arrangements had been recently concluded between Canada and Britain that would prohibit ships from continuing use of this wavelength. "The object of this agreement is to lessen interference with the reception of radio broadcasting programs."[172] The British ambassador wanted to reach a similar agreement with the United States.

Hoover replied that the Department of Commerce already had issued a regulation on the subject that agreed with the Canadian and British governments.[173]

On November 14, 1924, the Interdepartmental Radio Advisory Committee passed a resolution "providing that the 450-meter wavelength should not be used by ships of British or American registry when within 250 miles of the coast of either country."[174]

By March of 1925 no further complaints were being received on interference from 450 meters.[175]

NON-BROADCAST INTERFERENCE. The Bureau of Navigation felt that there was "the urgent need of a force of radio observers listening in to get firsthand and accurate information covering operating conditions, sources of interference and infractions of the laws or regulations."[176]

A difficult problem which "promises everlasting investigations ... is the interference caused by leaky power lines, defective insulation, telephone lines using magnetos, X-ray and violet-ray machines and similar devices."[177] These sources often caused widespread interruption to the broadcasting service.[178]

Hoover noted that interference came "from different reactions set up by certain kinds of receiving sets, partly from some kinds of electrical machines and circuits, and partly from disturbing conditions in the ether, commonly called 'static'."[179]

Carson said that there was no control over these various electrical devices, but usually operators and owners willingly cooperated when they were informed they were causing interference.[180] The Bureau of Navigation announced on October 1, 1925, that "the only general remedy for electrical interference sources of disturbance, is for distributors of electrical power to reduce or eliminate the cause of the trouble."[181] It was suggested that the use of filters, shields, and chokes would help eliminate the problem.

PIEZO-ELECTRIC CRYSTAL CONTROL. The Westinghouse Company was experimenting with crystal control of radio frequencies to prevent fluctuation of the broadcasting station signal.

The Bureau of Standards assisted with this research and suggested the application of piezo-electric crystals to achieve standardization. Studies indicated that the crystals could be used to try to hold the station frequency constant.[182] The Radio Division of the Bureau of Navigation ordered 12 piezoelectric crystal oscillators in April of 1925 for use in measuring frequencies.[183]

Horn of Westinghouse reported to Terrell, "it would be ideal if all stations throughout the country were equipped to operate with control frequency by crystal. This would do away with unpleasant beat notes."[184] Westinghouse had the patents on crystal control.

However, interference continued.

FREQUENCY ALLOCATIONS. By March of 1924 the Bureau of Navigation discovered that "there is unusual activity in erection of broadcasting stations at this season of the year.... The most difficult solution will be providing wavelengths which will give the new stations satisfactory working channels with sufficient operating time to justify the cost and not handicap existing stations."[185]

There appeared to be only one way to provide for the expected expansion. Transmitters and receivers would have to become "more selective or provide for closer tuning so as to be operative on narrower bands."[186] It was assumed that eventually transmitters and receivers that did not meet these requirements would have to be outlawed and "immediate steps should be taken by manufacturers in anticipation of this demand."[187]

It was believed possible to rearrange the wavelengths in the broadcast band to provide for a dozen extra channels by providing for closer separation "without producing interference."[188] This, in turn, would stimulate the efforts of the manufacturers to "construct sets of greater selectivity."[189]

A general reassignment of wavelengths was authorized by the Department of Commerce on January 31, 1925, and all stations were separated by 10 kilocycles. The seven kilocycle separation experiment had not worked. David B. Carson assumed that if the stations would maintain the frequencies assigned by the various supervisors of radio there would be no reception difficulties.[190] Reassignment did not markedly change the frequencies of the stations, but realigned the general space between each one. Examples of the minute changes that were made: in New York, WEAF moved from 492 to 491.5 meters; WGBS moved from 316 to 315.6 meters; WJZ moved from 405 to 405.2 meters[191]

However, it was reported by Edwards in a letter to KDKA's Horn, "We find that even after we spend considerable time and money in re-adjusting stations to their proper wavelengths they will re-adjust the apparatus so that it will agree with their wavemeters which they have on their stations."[192]

Edwards commented, "We are doing everything possible to overcome the difficulties and the present situation in the Class B band. But we are short of personnel, apparatus and travel funds and we cannot do things which we would like to do because of this handicap."[193] The Bureau of Standards also did not have the facilities to assist in reporting stations which were operating off their frequency.

Edwards went on to comment about the general situation:

> When we ship our wavemeters to the Bureau of Standards for calibration we sometimes wait as long as twelve months before we get them back....
>
> You ask why the Bureau does not take it upon itself to check all the stations it can hear and inform them by wire if they are off their frequency. I do not know if you mean the Bureau of Navigation.... In connection with this I might say that every one of the inspectors on this station and the Supervisor monitor the broadcast stations every night and have been doing it for the past eighteen months. In order to gather all the necessary information necessary for us to properly function, insofar as Class "B" broadcasting is concerned, it is necessary for us, after we have finished the day's work at the office to go to our monitoring stations and remain there from 7 P.M. until midnight or later. We do this, not because it is required by law, but because we are all intensely interested in our work and desire to make broadcasting successful insofar as we are concerned....
>
> You have no idea of the number of obstacles we meet with every day in connection with broadcasting. We find people who absolutely refuse to cooperate with us and we do not seem to have authority under the existing law to compel them to do the things which they should do so that the public would benefit.[194]

The supervisors had to deal with such situations; for example, KDKA wandering two kilocycles off its frequency and interfering with WJAR. Horn notified the Commissioner of Navigation that "we hope this matter will be definitely settled when we get our crystal working."[195]

It was in 1925 that the evangelist Aimee Semple McPherson's radio station, owned by her huge Angelus Temple in Los Angeles, "roamed all over the waveband, causing interference and arousing bitter complaints from the other stations."[196] Most of these complaints came from her competitor, the Rev. "Battling Bob" Robert P. Shuler. The supervisor of radio closed down and sealed her station. She telegraphed Secretary Hoover:

> Please order your minions of Satan to leave my station alone. You cannot expect the Almighty to abide by your wavelength nonsense. When I offer my prayers to Him I must fit into His wave reception. Open this station at once.[197]

Secretary Hoover wrote that "the tactful inspector persuaded her to employ a radio manager of his [the inspector's] own selection, who kept her on her wavelength."[198] The temple's radio operator, Kenneth G. Ormiston, a married man, was soon meeting Mrs. McPherson at various hotels. Aimee Semple McPherson disappeared on May 18, 1926. At first it was thought she had drowned. However, soon the newspapers were linking the names of Ormiston and McPherson, and on June 23 she reappeared with a story of having been kidnapped. This was one of the more sensational news stories of that period. In an effort to vindicate herself Mrs. McPherson forced the local law enforcement officials to investigate her so-called kidnapping. The whole story of her affair was dragged through the newspapers until interest finally waned.[199]

Hoover said, "The Department of Commerce felt morally responsible for the incident because they had insisted a new radio technician be hired in the first place."[200] Ironically, the Federal Radio Commission in 1930 denied Rev. Shuler's license renewal for attacks on the Catholic church, the Jewish religion, the Salvation Army, Christian Science, the courts and the local Chamber of Commerce.[201]

Back in May 1925, Secretary Hoover had written that "there is at present no intention whatever of making any radical change in wavelength assignments."[202]

During the year there was "continuous complaint of interference by the stations in both the Class A and Class B wavelengths."[203] A circular was sent to all supervisors in April which informed them that there were no wavelengths available because of congestion and that all prospective builders of radio stations should have "been informed as to the difficulty of providing wavelengths and that reservations will not be made."[204]

All supervisors were told by the Bureau of Navigation in September that they should not assign wavelengths to broadcasting stations in either Class A or Class B.[205] A letter to all supervisors from David B. Carson in December notified them that:

> when requests are made to you concerning the licenses of broadcasting stations, copies of all such letters SHOULD be forwarded to the Bureau in order that a departmental letter may be forwarded in reply to each.[206]

The departmental letter sent by the Bureau stated that Class B wavelengths were "practically all assigned and operating channels are about exhausted."[207] By the end of 1925 the letters the Bureau was sending to applicants for broadcasting licenses announced that there was no room available for anyone on any frequency.

One of the radio supervisors remarked:

> I don't think we did too good a job in clearing the frequencies selected for assignment with a sufficient number of other districts. But, if we had done that, there would have been a terrific amount of correspondence

necessary, along with technical data which was not available to us in regard to all those stations.[208]

Division of Time. The Department of Commerce policy was not to interfere with the arrangements of time-sharing between stations. There were numerous meetings in Washington where the Department staff acted as mediators between dissenting stations sharing the same wavelength. Here are three examples from 1924-25 to illustrate the continuing problem.

CINCINNATI. The Department was giving careful consideration to the matter of wavelength allocations for Cincinnati in November of 1924.[209] There were three stations and Davis stated:

> If we had only their two stations to deal with the situation would present no great difficulty but there is a third station, that of the Ainsworth Gates Company, and there are only two available wavelengths. While the suggestion has come from several sources that because of the greater size and proposed power the stations of the Crosley and U.S. Playing Card Company should have preferential treatment over the Ainsworth Gates Station, their smaller competitor, it is obviously impossible for the Department to take that attitude and it regards all three as entitled to equal consideration. Such cases have arisen in other cities and it has been the invariable rule of the Department to leave it to the stations themselves to determine the manner in which the wavelengths shall be divided among them.[210]

Crosley suggested that various wavelengths be transferred from Boston to Chicago, and Judge Davis had the supervisor of radio confer with the owners of the Cincinnati stations. Davis also suggested that the power of the Crosley station, WLW, (W)e (L)ove (W)attage, be checked because "the broadcast listeners are experiencing more interference lately than they did before a change was made in this station and it appears evident that a considerable increase in power has been made at the Crosley station."[211] Five months later, WLW was authorized a power increase to five kilowatts. (It would be authorized in the 1930s to temporarily operate with 500 kilowatts.) A meeting was held in November between Inspector Edwards and officials of the three radio stations. An agreement was reached that WSAI and WLW be assigned two separate wavelengths, and station WMH utilize one-half of the transmission time of one of the stations for each month and then alternate to the other wavelength for half-time.[212] Soon afterward both WLW and WMH operated on Monday and Wednesday night at the same time on the same wavelength, which caused chaos. Secretary Hoover ordered Carson and Terrell to clear up the situation and the next day an agreement was reached on the hours that would be used by each station during the month they were on the same wavelength.[213] In March of 1925 the Ainsworth station was sold to the Kodel Radio Company and they were asked to abide by the November 1924 agreement.[214]

CLARINDA, IOWA. Another instance of Secretary Hoover's continued intervention occurred when the A. A. Berry Seed Company of Clarinda, Iowa, arranged through their congressman and the Republican National Committeeman of Iowa to meet with Hoover while he was giving a speech in the area in June 1925. They sought a broadcast license and time on the only frequency available in that area. Hoover attempted to convince the Berry Company to buy time on the Field Seed Company's station but Berry refused. Hoover then suggested "that such a division of time might be arranged [with the Field Seed Company] and that you should take up the matter with the Supervisor of Radio at Chicago and if necessary with the Department or with him personally."[215] After a letter on this was sent to the Field Seed Company, a satisfactory division of time was arranged.

ILLINOIS. A religious group in Illinois had sold all their possessions and wanted to buy a radio station with their funds to announce the end of the world. When the group approached Hoover for a license, he suggested they use the money to purchase time on another station. In this way they could use their funds to the best advantage because, he pointed out, a broadcast station would be of little use to the sect when the world's end came. [216]

In the early days of broadcasting, arranging a division of time between stations was comparatively easy. But dividing the limited broadcast time into smaller slices as more stations went on the air made it difficult for stations to arrange their schedules and furnish satisfactory service. Assistant Secretary, J. Walter Drake, wrote:

> It became necessary for the Department to take the position that no further division of time would be required and that where a division of time was desired it would be arranged between the parties interested.... It is contemplated that another radio conference will be held [and] some arrangements may alter the existing situation.[217]

V. The Fourth Radio Conference

The Fourth Annual Radio Conference was held November 9–11, 1925, in the United States Chamber of Commerce Building in Washington, D.C. Some 500 delegates, 400 more than had come to the previous conference, were in attendance. They represented all facets of the radio industry.

Secretary Hoover addressed the opening session:

> We have great reason to be proud of the results of these conferences. From them have been established principles upon which our country has led the world in the development of this service. We have accomplished this by a large measure of self-government in an art and industry of unheard of complexity, not only in its technical phases but in its relations both to the Government and the public....

Some of our major decisions of policy have been of far-reaching importance and have justified themselves a thousand-fold. The decision that the public, through the Government, must retain the ownership of the channels through the air with just as zealous a care for open competition as we retain public ownership of our navigation channels has given freedom and development in service that would have otherwise been lost in private monopolies. The decision that we should not imitate some of our foreign colleagues with governmentally controlled broadcasting supported by a tax upon the listener has secured for us a far greater variety of programs and excellence in service free of cost to the listener.

Secretary Hoover listed the expansion of international communication by radiotelegraph, the clearing of the broadcast band of code signals, better frequency control, higher powers and other items as areas of progress. He emphasized:

The most profound change during the year, however, has been the tremendous increase in power and the rapid multiplication of powerful stations. When the conference assembled a year ago, there were 115 stations equipped to use 500 watts or more. Now we have 197 such stations, an increase during the year of over 70 percent. This mere numerical expansion of stations falls far short of telling the whole story. A year ago only two stations were equipped to use an excess of 500 watts. Of the new stations, 32 are equipped to use 1000 watts, 25 to use 5000 watts, and two a still higher power, making 59 in all against two last year. Taking the situation as a whole, we find that a year ago all stations of 500 watts and over are using a total of 67,500 watts. Today they use 236,500 watts, or a 250 percent increase....

Our experience during the year has somewhat more clearly defined the geographical area within which a single broadcasting station can give complete service, and by "complete service area" I mean the territory within which the average set can depend upon getting the clear, understandable, and enjoyable service from the station, day or night, summer or winter.

PROBLEMS FOR THE INDUSTRY. ...are of two categories—those, on the one hand, which the industry can and should solve for itself in order to safeguard the public service and its own interest and, on the other hand, those which can only be solved in cooperation with the Government; and again, as before, we should find the solution of as many of our problems as we can in the first category.

INTERCONNECTION. ...is becoming more systematized and has gone far toward the creation of long-linked systems....

ADVERTISING. There lies within it the possibility of grave harm and even vital danger to the entire broadcasting structure. The desire for publicity is the basic motive and the financial support for almost all the broadcasting in the country today....

But the radio listener does not have the same option that the reader of publications has—to ignore advertising in which he is not interested—and he may resent its invasions of his set....

REMOVAL OF STATIONS FROM CONGESTED AREAS. I look forward to the not too distant time when all stations of sufficient size to cause disturbance will be banished from the cities and when their blanketing annoyances will cease. The conference could render a definite service by formulating proposals to that end.

PROBLEMS FOR SOLUTION BY COOPERATION WITH THE GOVERN-MENT. It is a simple physical fact that we have no more channels.... One alternative, which would only partly solve the problem, would be to increase the number of stations by further dividing the time of the present stations down to one or two days a week or one or two hours a day. From the listener's viewpoint, and that is the only one to be considered, he would get a much degenerated service if we were to do that. It is quality of program, location, and efficiency of transmission that count....

The choice is between public interest and private desire and we need not hesitate in making a decision.... It has been suggested that the remedy lies in widening the broadcasting band, thus permitting more channels and making it possible to provide for more stations. The vast majority of receiving sets in the country will not cover a wider band, nor could we extend it without invading the field assigned to the amateurs, of whom there are thousands.... The ether is a public medium, and its use must be for public benefit. The use of a radio channel is justified only if there is public benefit. The dominant element for consideration in the radio field is, and always will be, the great body of the listening public, millions in number, countrywide in distribution....

The greatest public interest must be the deciding factor....

WHAT ARE WE TO DO? It seems to me we have in this development of governmental relations two distinct problems. First, is a question of traffic control. This must be a Federal responsibility. From an interference point of view every word broadcasted is an interstate word.... This is an administrative job, and good administration must lie in a single responsibility.

The second question is the determination of who shall use the traffic channels and under what conditions. This is a very large discretionary or a semi-judicial function which should not devolve entirely upon any single official and is, I believe, a matter in which each local community should have a large voice—should in some fashion participate in a determination of who would use the channels available for broadcasting in that locality.

In other words, the ideal situation, as I view it, would be traffic regulation by the Federal Government to the extent of allotment of wavelengths and control of power and policing of interference, leaving to each community a large voice in determining who are to occupy the wavelengths assigned to that community. It is true, of course, that radio is not circumscribed by State lines and still less by city boundaries; but it is possible, nevertheless, to establish zones which will at least roughly approximate the service areas of stations and to a very considerable extent to entrust to them the settlement of their local problems.

I am seeking your view as to how far this can be made practicable or what other basis may be found for handling the problem. I have no frozen views on radio, except that the public interest must dominate. As many of you know, I am not one of those who seek to extend any sort of Government regulation onto any quarter that is not vital, and in this suggestion I am even endeavoring to create enlarged local responsibility.

Much work has been done in past sessions of Congress looking to radio legislation. I can not speak too highly of the constructive effort expended by Representative Wallace White and his committee associates in the study of radio needs and the preparation of measures to meet them; but until the present time I think we have all had some feeling of doubt as to the precise course which legislation should take, for changes have been so rapid and conditions so shifting that no one was ready to try to chart an exact course. I am glad that Congressman White and other members of the House and Senate committees are with us in this conference....

To sum up, the major problems for consideration are, to my mind: (a) Is public interest paramount? (b) Shall we limit the total number of stations in each zone pending further development of the art? (c) What basis shall be established for determining who shall use the radio channels? (d) What administrative machinery shall we create to make the determination?[218]

The various committees appointed by the Department of Commerce made their reports to the entire conference.

The radio conferences had provided the Department of Commerce with a great deal of industry information and working together to achieve a desired result or agreement became the recognized practice.[219]

The Committee on General Allocation of Frequency or Wavelength Bands proposed that the broadcast band be widened. This met immediate opposition from the amateur operators because the section of the spectrum to be taken was theirs. Hiram Percy Maxim, president of the American Radio Relay League, declared that the proposal would be an "unwarranted encroachment on the amateur."[220] Hoover agreed and the conference's recommendation was not implemented.

The Committee on Advertising and Publicity urged the use of advertising for the creation of goodwill but advised against obtrusive advertising. This stand was praised by Secretary Hoover who felt that a great service had been done for the industry. By a unanimous vote the conference declared itself opposed to "direct advertising or any form of special pleading for the broadcaster or his products."[221]

The Licenses and Classification Committee recommended that a permit must be obtained before construction, which would give the owner assurance that when his station was completed he would have a frequency. A license fee was recommended, which ranged from a minimum of $25 to a maximum of $5,000 a year. But conference members were opposed to a license fee, declaring it restricted the use of the ether and the recommendation failed general approval. Stephen B. Davis, Solicitor for the Department of Commerce, noted: "I think we can agree that the question as to whether there should be a substantial charge for a broadcasting license is a debatable one. I do not know what the reaction of Congress will be on the subject but am rather inclined to think that the bill which Congressman White will introduce will not contain any such provision."[222] (It was not until the latter 1990s that license fees were legislated.) The Committee also recommended that licenses should be issued for a term of five years with an understanding that they could be renewed at the expiration date.

The Committee on Cooperation Regulations came out strongly against speculation in stations' ownership. The conference delegates asked the Secretary of Commerce to establish a rule allowing for the sale of stations only under close supervision. The Department of Commerce had always recognized the right to transfer ownership of the broadcasting station as property, but the licenses covering these stations were not considered transferable. When a station was sold, an application had to be submitted for reassignment of the license in the name of the new owner. There was usually little difficulty in such a transfer.[223] Carson noted:

> The Department recognizes the right of the owner of a station to sell his station and where such stations continue to serve the same locality or if a station happens to be in a section where a station is serving the locality and its removal would not deprive the people of that locality of radio service, no objection has been raised as to the re-licensing of the station in the name of the new owner and extending to him the same privileges the original owner enjoyed, that is, he would be allowed to use the same amount of power and the same wavelength if this could be permitted without injury to other stations.[224]

This committee recommended that there be no change in the power of broadcasting stations, and also that any further time divisions were not in the public interest.[225]

The Legislative Committee suggested that no new station should be licensed until it was shown that it would be in the public interest for the station to operate. Hoover requested that, in view of the congestion on the airwaves, the Secretary of Commerce and his staff should withhold further licensing of stations, except in the case of government stations. This recommendation was approved by the conference with an almost unanimous vote. On November 11, 1925, Secretary Hoover announced "that no new stations be licensed by the Department of Commerce pending further legislation by Congress."[226]

The Committee on Interference recommended that, in view of improved reception and the fact that Hoover had sanctioned the continued operation of high-power broadcasting stations, the Department of Commerce should continue to license them.

The Committee on Copyright Relations to the Industry, which was chaired by Congressman White, wrestled with the problems of the American Society of Composers, Authors and Publishers and the broadcasting industry. It was agreed by the broadcasters that owners of copyrighted material were entitled to reasonable compensation for the use of their work. However, the definition of reasonable was not settled.[227]

Legislation Suggestions. The Fourth National Radio Conference proposed a comprehensive program of legislation for presentation to the closing session of Congress. This program included the suggestions and principles that had been recommended during the previous three conferences and was to be the basis for future proposed legislation. These recommendations also exhibited the confidence the industry had in Secretary Hoover and the Department of Commerce during this period of turmoil.

The recommendations were summarized by the *New York Times*:

> The existing laws are inadequate to permit the proper administration of radio communication. Congress, by statutes, is empowered to enact legislation necessary to provide the needed legislation and the conference felt that such enactment was needed in respect to the public interest.
>
> In the proposed legislation the following principles were recommended:
>
> 1. That the administration of radio legislation shall be vested in the Secretary of Commerce, who shall make and enforce rules and regulations necessary to the proper administration of the provision of such legislation.
>
> 2. That such administration shall be exercised by the Secretary of Commerce through the offices and employees of the Department of Commerce.
>
> 3. That the doctrine of free speech shall be held inviolate.
>
> 4. That those engaging in radio communication should not be required to devote their property to the public and their properties are therefore not public utilities in fact or in law, provided however, that a license or permit to engage in radio communication shall be issued only to those who in the opinion of the Secretary will render a benefit to the public or are necessary to the public interest or are contributing to the development of the art.
>
> 5. That in time of war and other national emergencies the President shall have the power to discontinue existing radio stations with just compensation.
>
> 6. That no monopoly in radio broadcasting shall be permitted.

7. That the legislation shall contain provisions for the due appeal from final decisions of the Secretary of Commerce to the appropriate court.

8. Except in the case of government stations the Secretary shall be empowered to classify all stations, and to affix and assign call letters, wavelengths, power, location, time of operation, character of emission, and duration of licenses. It is recommended that call letters shall be recognized as representing a property right and be treated accordingly during the life of the license. The Secretary shall not change call letters, wavelengths, power, and time.

9. No license shall be issued to operate a transmitting station not already operating in radio communication except mobile or amateur stations, unless prior to the application of such, there shall have been issued by the Secretary of Commerce, an erection permit to those, who, in the opinion of the Secretary will render a benefit to the public or are necessary to the public interest or are contributing to the development of the art.

10. Each license to operate a transmitting station in radio communication shall prescribe the responsibility of each station with respect to distress signals, but in any event all licenses shall provide that upon due and proper order from government authority each station shall cease operation until released by the same authority.

11. That the act should define the following terms, to-wit; commercial stations, broadcast stations, amateur stations and experimental stations.

12. That the Secretary shall have the power to revoke or suspend any license whenever he shall determine that the licensee has violated any of the terms of his license, regulations of the Secretary, Federal radio law, or international treaty.

13. That in order to insure financial stability to radio enterprises capital now invested must receive reasonable protection thereof. All stations which contribute to the public interest and benefit shall be given a reasonable length of time to conform to the provisions of the proposed act and the rules and regulations prescribed thereunder.

14. That rebroadcast of programs shall be prohibited, except with the permission of the originating station.

15. That the Secretary of Commerce shall be empowered to make and enforce such rules and regulations as may be necessary to prevent interference to radio reception from radio sources.

16. That authority should be provided to prescribe and enforce uniform regulations regarding the use of radio transmitters on ships in territorial waters.[228]

Secretary Hoover's Review of the Conference. Hoover discussed the Fourth National Radio Conference's recommendations in a radio address. He stressed that the primary subject of the conference was interference. This required consideration of complicated issues: 1) legislation by Congress; 2) treaties with foreign governments; 3) operation of broadcasting stations; 4) cooperation from electric power companies; and 5) cooperation from listeners.

> The air today is overcrowded. And even worse, we are faced with the desires and demands of nearly 200 broadcasters who wish to erect stations and to force their way into the already congested lanes....
> This was the primary problem with which the conference had to deal. It is the cause of major interference. It faced it boldly.[229]

Because the conference had declared that the public interest, represented by service to the listener, should be the basis for every broadcasting privilege, Hoover stated; "it there determined that it would ask the Congress of the United States to enact legislation in your interest to the effect that there must be a legal limit upon the total number of broadcasting stations until the art further develops new channels."[230]

He continued:

> I take pride in the fact that in this conference, made up as it was not only by representatives of the listeners, the amateurs, the great newspapers and magazines of the United States, but of the manufacturers and broadcasters, with millions of dollars invested in their enterprises at stake in this situation, not a dissenting voice was raised against the resolution by which they formally recognized that your [the listeners'] interests are dominant in the whole situation.[231]

He felt that the two outstanding results of the conference were 1) recognition of the listener's dominant interest in radio, and 2), as a corollary, the recommendation that interference must be reduced.

> It may be that we shall hear a great deal about freedom of the air from some of the people who want to broadcast and who will not be able to show that their desires accord with your interests. But there are two parties to freedom of the air, and to freedom of speech for that matter. There is the speech maker and the listener. Certainly in radio I believe in freedom for the listener. He has much less option upon what he can reject, for the other fellow is occupying his receiving set. The listener's only option is to abandon his right to use his receiver. Freedom cannot mean a license to every person or corporation who wishes to broadcast his name or his wares and thus monopolize the listener's set.[232]

Secretary Hoover restated the idea he had presented at the Second Radio Conference that "the ether is a public medium, and its use must be for public benefit."[233]

It was pointed out that the small broadcaster and the larger Class B station operator had no need to fear each other.

> The distinction between Class A and Class B is wholly arbitrary. It goes back to ancient times in radio history of four years ago when the favorite

occupation of the broadcaster was the transmission of phonograph music. Some of the more progressive stations declared that there was a higher form of entertainment and they were put into a separate class, designated as Class B, on the condition that they would provide better programs.[234]

The conference had recommended that the classification of stations be eliminated. Secretary Hoover continued:

> From now on, all stations will be on the same basis. There is to be only one test, if Congress passes the necessary legislation, that is service to the listener, and this test will be applied to every station, big or little.[235]

It was Hoover's hope that Congress would impose regulation "only to the extent absolutely essential."[236] He felt that radio broadcasters should be proud of their self-regulation and that "radio had grown up in the spirit of service."[237] Secretary Hoover summed up the conference:

> In general, the conference, representing every phase of this question, was unanimous that there must be new legislation to give more control in the protection of public interest and in the perfection of the service. The conference recognized that radio has introduced a new element in the American life, that it possesses great values in home entertainment, in education and the spirit of religious thought; that it contains a great moral purpose not only to bring new things into the lives of our people but to cement them together in a greater common understanding, and that the obligation of the industry is to provide these services.[238]

Some newspapers implied that Secretary Hoover sought to have radio control placed in his hands. Hoover issued a press release angrily responding to this charge:

> Far to the contrary, I have both before Congressional committees and in at least a half dozen public addresses stated that no one official should dictate who is to use the radio wavelengths, and I have for years advocated that this being a semi-judicial function it should be placed in the hands of an independent commission.
>
> Moreover, for five years I have reiterated that these wavelengths are public property to be used by assignment of public authority. This view has been enforced by the Department of Commerce for the past five years. It was again affirmed by the last Radio Conference. This principle, together with a provision for a commission to control assignments, was incorporated into a bill introduced to Congress some weeks ago by Congressman Wallace White and approved by me. Somebody needs to find out what has already taken place before he starts something.[239]

Legislative Action. Solicitor for the Department of Commerce, Stephen B. Davis, had been working on a bill in conjunction with Rep. White prior to the Fourth National Radio Conference. The main points were:

1. Radio, especially broadcasting, should be considered as a quasi-public utility, and permission to use a channel should be based upon and justified by a service to be performed. Before a station was to be licensed it must show that its operation will be in "the public interest, and obtain a certificate to that effect."

2. It should be the duty of the federal government to provide and police air channels so that there will be freedom of communication between all points without crowding or interference, "and this (policing activity) is about the extent of its responsibility."

3. The number of stations which can operate at any one time is necessarily limited by the number of channels available. It was therefore considered impossible to license stations for an indefinite period of time. "But it is a matter of indifference to the public whether a given channel is used exclusively by one concern or at different times by two or more, so long as the channel is used efficiently and economically."

4. The question of how many stations should be allowed to operate in a given locality on a limited number of channels, whether one to each or more than one, dividing time, is a local question which should be left to local determination.

5. The state commissions, which determine similar questions for public utilities generally, are the proper bodies to handle radio broadcasting questions. "There is such a commission, as defined in this draft, in every state excepting Delaware."

6. While it is true that state commissions would be regulating interstate commerce, there was, according to Solicitor Davis, no legal objection to the Congress selecting as its agencies any bodies which it would choose. "A large proportion of the listeners to a given station are within the state in which the station is located, and regulation in their interest would necessarily be in the interest of those outside. Whether or not the commissions would assume this duty is a wholly different question, which can be definitely answered only by inquiry."

Overall, the Davis suggestions followed closely the White Bill which had been introduced in the previous session of Congress. Davis knew there had been objections to this proposal earlier and was aware that Congress was wary of endorsing any plan coming from Secretary Hoover.

> Neither myself nor anyone else is committed to its [the draft bill] ideas. They may be wholly wrong, and we may abandon them entirely, but their expression in concrete form at least gives something to consider. Assuming the necessity of limiting stations, I can think of no better plan for doing so. I do not believe it can be efficiently done from Washington.
>
> Please consider this as confidential ... for any general dissemination would cause it to be considered as a departmental proposal, which it is not.[240]

Davis' comments are included here to show that the legal areas of the Department of Commerce must have been either quite divorced from the work that was being done in Congress on radio legislation at this time, or that some sense of desperation had entered into their deliberations. Davis later wrote an authoritative book, *The Law of Radio Communication*.

Sen. Robert B. Howell was the first to offer a Senate bill in December of 1925. Senate Bill S. 1 was a short attempt to insure that the use of a wavelength did not constitute ownership.[241] Congressman White's lengthy bill (H. R. 5589) was introduced next in the House on December 2. The bill was similar to the one introduced in the previous session of Congress. It was modified by incorporating many suggestions of the radio conference and some of the provisions contained in previous bills were eliminated.

Rep. White stated:

> All of the principal recommendations were adopted in their substance. They will be found in the express language of the bill, or power to carry them out will be found in the general authority conferred upon the Secretary.[242]

The provision for license fees contained in the previous White bill was not included. Instead of providing for the establishment of an advisory committee, the proposed bill provided for the formation of a National Radio Commission to assist the Department of Commerce. It was believed that some agency to whom the Secretary could transmit the more troublesome problems which might arise would insulate Hoover from the charge of dictator.

The next day Sen. C. C. Dill, a Democrat from Washington, introduced a second bill (S. 4057) into the Senate, also based on the actions taken at the Fourth National Radio Conference. Touching on most of the points of the White Bill, Sen. Dill added a section which prohibited censorship and reduced the number of members of the proposed radio commission from nine to five. In the White Bill, appointment of the members of the commission was left entirely in the Secretary's hands. Sen. Dill's bill proposed that the commission should be named by the President and confirmed by the Senate.[243]

Hearings on these bills were held in 1926.

VI. Summary

The period of 1924 to 1925 witnessed the increasingly difficult task of regulating radio. There were some 600 stations licensed at the end of this period, with more than 350 applicants awaiting for new stations.

The Department of Commerce held two radio conferences during that span. The Third Conference approved the expansion of the broadcast band to cover 550 to 1500 kilocycles. Power increases continued and experimentation was conducted to reduce the kilocycle separation between adjacent stations. The further licensing of new stations and the increase in power of existing stations continued to create difficulties.

In a last effort to achieve legislation from a lagging Congress, Hoover proposed a short amendment for the Act of 1912 that would have given him the power to classify stations, decide on power, frequency and the character of the apparatus used. His hope was that technological development would soon provide an answer to the overcrowded spectrum. Industry reaction to this suggested legislation was cool and Congress did not act on it.

Hoover made clear during these two years his feelings on the controversial subjects of monopoly, censorship, programming, network interconnection and financial support. He did not stray from his basic philosophy of self-regulation and remained optimistic throughout this period.

Higher power, regenerative receiver oscillations, non-broadcast interference and overcrowding made the reception situation worse. The Bureau of Navigation separated all stations by ten kiloHertz, but the stations could not hold to their assigned frequencies with accuracy. Research was conducted on piezo-electrical crystal control in an effort to overcome this problem, but the new allocation plan was ineffective.

The very success and popularity of broadcasting gave rise to its principal difficulty, which came to a head in 1925. Broadcasting stations, although ten kiloHertz apart, used 89 channels or frequencies. Since there were about 578 stations operating in 1925, not every station could have an exclusive frequency and most of them had to share time with one or more stations. This duplicate assignment of frequencies required that stations alternate in the use of the frequencies, for instance, transmitting on alternate evenings. This was generally recognized as undesirable. Despite this, the building of stations and the applications for broadcasting licenses increased. Because all of the channels for broadcasting were already completely filled, the Department of Commerce could not license most who applied.

The discussions at the Fourth National Radio Conference brought out clearly that broadcasting would be harmed unless a severe check were put on the numbers of stations being authorized. This brought about an increase in the practice by stations of renting time to those who wished to reach the public through this medium.

The demand for regulation reached a peak. The legislation introduced at the end of 1925 eventually passed as the Radio Act of 1927. It had evolved from the Department of Commerce's past experience which defined the necessary application of government's power.

Chapter IV

REGULATORY BREAKDOWN AND THE PASSAGE OF THE ACT OF 1927

The public's interest in broadcasting exploded in 1926 and 1927. A radio exposition held in New York in September 1926 drew 228,000 people.[1] The potential audience for broadcasting was estimated by the Department of Commerce in the range of 20 million.[2]

There was also a marked increase in the power of broadcasting stations. Many used five kilowatts, and several stations used 50 kilowatts each. This increase in station power averaged "716 watts as compared with 312 in 1925."[3] Local stations provided an improved signal to their local area and increased their coverage. According to Commerce Department figures, probably 70 percent of the stations were doing some "toll" (sponsored) broadcasting.[4] Most were selling small amounts of time.

The RCA corporation purchased AT&T's New York WEAF, the first station to rent facilities to advertisers, for $1 million in September 1926. Only $200,000 was to pay for the physical facilities and the rest of the price was for the clear channel frequency the station occupied.[5]

The Fourth National Radio Conference in 1925 endorsed the Department of Commerce's continued request for legislation to control the number of stations. The broadcasting band of frequencies had been apportioned by the Department of Commerce in 1924. Stations from 550 to 1070 kHz were Class B stations and 1090 to 1500 kHz was for Class A stations. The Class B stations were permitted 500 watts or more and the Class A stations were generally using less than 500 watts.

There were 53 frequencies available, ten kHz apart, in the frequencies used for Class B stations. Since there were approximately 100 Class B stations operating by July of 1925, and still increasing, each station could not have an exclusive frequency but had to share its wavelength with at least one other.

The ten kHz separation required that the stations accurately maintain their position. Heterodyne action between two station frequencies producing whistling interference diminished during 1926-1927. There was also an improvement in the sensitivity of receiving apparatus to discriminate between stations operating close to each other. But, delays in the implementation of legislation and the inability of the Department of Commerce to control the number of new stations created the conditions for further deterioration of reception even with technical advances. From July 1926 to February 1927, 181 broadcast stations were licensed by the Bureau of Navigation. This made a total of 716 stations operating on February 7, 1927. Only seven months earlier there were 528 active broadcasting stations.[6] It was reported in *Radio Broadcast* that between July 1, 1926, and January 15, 1927:[7]

> 181 new stations were operating
> 148 stations were being built
> 280 stations were being planned
> 150 stations had increased power
> 70 stations had requested higher power
> 104 stations had changed wavelength

The Bureau of Navigation reported that from July 1926 to March 1927, "more than 200 stations have begun operating using any wavelength they might select which has resulted in a great deal of interference."[8] The sheer numerical increase was bringing about a chaotic situation. More stations were operating where previously there were only one or two stations. To make matters worse, some of these stations squeezed between assigned frequencies. This interposition of stations disrupted the entire system. When the newly appointed Federal Radio Commission met March 15, 1927, there was a total of 733 broadcasting stations.[9]

Reception improved in many cities because stations increased their power enough to drown out stations operating near or on the same frequency but from some distance away. Long distance reception retrogressed as a result of the frequency assignment problems, power increases and "in some places, the Chicago district being a notable example, stations are so numerous and the frequencies so close together that even the reception of local stations was impaired."[10] The beginning of network broadcasting brought a variety of better quality programs to local stations decreasing the listeners' dependence on distance listening for satisfaction.

The Department of Commerce published a report showing that the use of crystal receiving sets and headphones was decreasing rapidly because of the enormous increase in the number of tube receiving sets with loud speakers. The newest receiving sets employed radio-frequency amplification and the super-heterodyne circuit. The super-het set had enough sensitivity and did not require an outside antenna or ground connection. More sets were of the uni-control type, and tubes had improved giving stronger output without distortion.[11]

Percent Increase-Decrease (-) Between 1923 and 1925

Loudspeakers:	Number		2,606,866	318%
	Value	$	19,162,591	242
Headsets:	Number		1,397	-22
	Value	$	2,264,527	-38
Receiving sets (tube type):	Number		2,180,622	1045
	Value	$	88,800,538	566
Transmitting sets:	Number		112,656	-50
	Value	$	1,355,430	-49
Transformers:	Number		3,413,933	117
	Value	$	7,457,805	90
Rheostats:	Number		3,531,871	226
	Value	$	2,084,188	118
Lightning Arrestors:	Number		2,971,379	69
	Value	$	506,034	20
Radio Tubes:	Number		23,934,658	411
	Value	$	20,437,283	108
Miscellaneous parts:		$	27,978,097	115
TOTAL VALUE			$170,390,572*	215%

*Values given: manufacturers' wholesale prices

This two-year period witnessed the breakdown of regulation, the passage of the Radio Act of 1927, and the transfer of control to the Federal Radio Commission. However, the Department of Commerce's involvement with radio regulation continued beyond this turbulent period.

I. The Breakdown of Regulation

Assistant Commissioner of Navigation Tyrer announced that as of January 25, 1926, the Bureau of Navigation had "89 broadcasting wavelengths, with an average of six stations to the wavelength. In addition, we have pending before the Department over 300 applications for new stations."[12] There were about six million receiving sets in the country at that time.[13] It was this huge demand for broadcasting stations that began to make the Department's regulatory activities fail. A number of events contributed to the breakdown.

The Zenith Radio Corporation: WJAZ Case. Ralph H. G. Mathews built amateur radio equipment while in high school in Chicago from 1912, and during World War I he met Karl Hassel while at the Great Lakes Naval Training Station. They operated the licensed amateur station 9ZN and founded the Chicago Radio Laboratory to manufacture equipment. In advertising they used their call as the tradename "Z–Nith." After World War I, Chicago entrepreneur Commander Eugene F. McDonald, Jr., to get into the radio manufacturing business, discovered that the Chicago Radio Lab had a license agreement to build Armstrong patented regenerative receivers. Armstrong had temporarily stopped licensing any further companies who wanted to use his patents. McDonald offered to finance the Zenith Radio Corporation to acquire the use of their Armstrong license.

Mr. W. M. Dewey, owner of the Edgewater Beach Hotel, suggested 9ZN be equipped for broadcasting in 1921 and he would supply the premises at no cost, plus contribute to the operating expenses for the publicity value. The station became a Class C station licensed to the Chicago Radio Laboratory, manufacturers of Zenith "Long Distance Radio Apparatus," on August 17, 1922, with the call letters WJAZ. As with all radio stations at that time, it operated on 360 meters.

The evolution of station ownership and call letters during the 1920s can be confusing. An example is what happened to the WJAZ call letters. On May 14, 1923, the station was issued a Class B license to operate on 448 meters (670 kHz) and was used to keep in contact with the 1923 MacMillan Arctic Expedition, which was using Zenith equipment. Station WJAZ broadcast to the expedition every Saturday night at midnight. The usual programming was music and "radio letters" from family members of the expedition brought to Chicago by McDonald. The public relations effort was highly effective and Zenith's radio sales increased.

The *Chicago Tribune* then leased enough time on WJAZ to dominate its programming. McDonald then terminated the leasing arrangement with the Edgewater Beach Hotel and on April 4, 1924, WJAZ moved to 370 meters (810 kHz) and the call letters were changed to WGN ([W]orld's [G]reatest [N]ewspaper) with a power of 500 to 1000 watts.[14] On the same day, the agreement with the *Tribune* was discontinued and the license returned to Zenith. The *Chicago Tribune* bought WDAP, the Chicago Board of Trade Drake Hotel station, to broadcast trade reports, weather and music and moved it to the McCormick Building. On May 28, 1924, Zenith sold WGN (formerly WJAZ) to the Edgewater Beach Hotel which changed the call letters to WEBH (Voice of the Great Lakes). On June 1, 1924, the *Tribune* retrieved the discontinued WGN call letters and changed its WDAP to WGN.[15] Zenith now had no Chicago station of its own.

Planning and Building of "New" WJAZ. McDonald informed the Chicago radio supervisor he wished to reserve the now clear WJAZ call letters by transferring them to a portable station.[16] He then intended to build a new high-powered station with studios at Zenith's laboratory at 48th and Kedzie and wished to then transfer the WJAZ call letters to that station.[17] The portable station, licensed as WJAZ, was first used to try to find a good location for the building of Zenith's high-powered outlet.

> It has long been my desire to have our station located in an isolated district where its operation would interfere with only a few people in the immediate vicinity, rather than have it in the heart of a residential section. To accomplish this purpose we now have three canvassers, representing this company, who are obtaining signatures to petitions from three small townships well outside of Chicago.
> The new Zenith Radio Corporation Station, WJAZ, will be put in the township most desirous of having it, and I will locate it in no township that does not endorse it to the extent of at least 75% of the population.
> Of course, the advertising value for the lucky section getting our new station will be enormous. We will endeavor to make the new WJAZ superior in every way. Very elaborate plans are now being executed. Our studio will be located in the heart of Chicago on the top floor of the McCormick Building, and the music, concerts, talks, etc., will be transmitted from our studio by wire to the thinly [*sic*] populated district, where they will be transformed into powerful radio waves, and offer no interference to the residents of Chicago.
> We now have options on two farm houses and it is our intention to furnish one of them as the home of our broadcasting station engineering staff. Our engineers have, for the past three weeks, been traveling over the country surrounding Chicago with a portable Zenith Radio set [WJAZ], for the purpose of ascertaining the relative merits of the various localities.[18]

The WJAZ portable station was sent on a coast-to-coast trip, stopping at Zenith dealers along the way. At each community a Zenith radio was awarded to the first person to report hearing the station and sometimes another to the person who reported hearing the station from the greatest distance. The WJAZ portable was the first to bring listeners the roar of the MGM lion from Gay's Lion Farm in California. The last year portable stations were permitted was 1927.[19]

When the 370 meter (810 kHz) wavelength was assigned to WGN there was concern that there might be some danger of interference between WGN, and WDAP (Board of Trade, Chicago), located on 360 meters (832.8 kHz) "but in order to give to Chicago another Class B wavelength and try to provide for a larger number of stations there without a further division of time it was believed desirable to make the experiment."[20]

Because of many complaints about WGN being about 20 kilocycles from WDAP, which was within 35 kilocycles of WLS, the Chicago radio inspectors monitored WGN for two weeks in April 1924. The primary cause of the complaints was the non-selectivity of some receiving sets which could not discriminate between stations operating only 20 kilocycles apart. Chicago radio supervisor Beane commented:

> Complaints relative to the interference between the above mentioned stations are due entirely to either one of the two following reasons: (1) the receiving station is located so close to the transmitting station that they have a high signal voltage impressed on the grid of their first vacuum tube so that the signal cannot be controlled and therefore the selectivity of the set is low under this condition; (2) the design of the receiver in use is so poor that its natural damping is high under these wavelengths.[21]

Commerce Department Solicitor Stephen B. Davis wrote to Zenith in January of 1925, that "due to the rapidity with which new stations are coming in the Department can not give any assurance that a Class B wavelength will be available upon completion of your station."[22] McDonald replied:

> As you probably know, we sold our old station located at the Edgewater Beach Hotel, retained our call letters and are moving WJAZ out to Mt. Prospect, 35 miles outside the City of Chicago, so that we will not cause undue interference in Chicago.
>
> WJAZ is the third oldest station in the City of Chicago and our application for a five-kilowatt license was the first entered. I appreciate fully your position with the avalanche of applications which you have for "B" and "A" Stations and you have my hearty sympathy, but we would like to have your cooperation in our case.[23]

By March, Commissioner of Navigation, David B. Carson, asked Chicago supervisor of radio, E. A. Beane, to personally contact the Zenith Corporation and inform them:

> if they are contemplating the erection of a broadcasting station in Chicago in addition to the one they are now operating that all of the Class B and all of the Class A wavelengths are assigned and that they will have to make arrangements with the owners of some local stations for a division of time when they are ready to begin operation.[24]

McDonald telegraphed that WJAZ would be ready to begin operations by June 24 and requested the wavelength of 322.4 meters (930 kHz).[25] Acting Commissioner of Navigation Arthur J. Tyrer replied that a "Ten kilocycle separation between Chicago and Cincinnati not sufficient. Cincinnati now complaining of interference caused by Minneapolis having ten kilocycle separation."[26]

McDonald replied that there would be no interference because the Zenith station would *only operate* between the hours of 10 and 12, except Wednesday night, "when we shall be on the air under 9XN experimental in talk with Commander MacMillan (North Pole Expeditionary Force)...."[27]

Solicitor Davis agreed that experimental communication could be conducted after midnight when the Denver and Cincinnati stations were off the air, but that 322.4 meters could not be assigned to Chicago for broadcasting because it was the Denver allocation and too close to Cincinnati's WSAI. "Conflict was believed unavoidable."[28]

McDonald reiterated that it "is not our aim to broadcast nightly or daily."[29] He went on to plead:

> Our station is constructed with the sole purpose of giving to the public the highest form of entertainment in but a limited time. We have felt that to do this, sufficient high class talent could not be secured continuously throughout the year for more than *two hours per week.*
>
> We recognize that the public has been very good to the radio industry in purchasing its product in the course of development. It has supplied the funds necessary for it to reach its present state of perfection in a comparatively short time. It is, therefore, our intention to reimburse the public for their past helpfulness by giving them over the air the best obtainable talent.[30]

He then requested that WJAZ be given 10 P.M. to midnight on Thursday nights, when Denver's KOA ([K]ing [o]f [A]griculture), and Cincinnati's WSAI were not operating.

The Department of Commerce sent letters to both the General Electric Company, owners of KOA, and the U.S. Playing Card Company, licensee of WSAI, informing them of the Zenith Corporation's request.[31]

S. I. Marks, treasurer of Zenith, called personally at the Bureau of Navigation on July 12, 1925, and spoke with Davis and Tyrer. Mr. Sadenwater of General Electric was in Washington at the time and he was called in to join the discussion. Sadenwater was under the impression that Zenith desired the use of the Denver wavelength to a much greater extent than two hours a week, "but if their time was confined to two hours per week from 10 to 12 P.M. midnight, he felt sure that the General Electric Company's objections would be removed."[32]

Marks declared that it was not the intention of Zenith to go into the broadcast business, as conducted by existing stations. Zenith's idea was to broadcast the very highest class of entertainment for a limited period at specific intervals, so audiences could look forward and schedule their listening. "He thought that this innovation might encourage others to do likewise and to some extent relieve the existing congestion and be helpful to the Department as well as a relief to the audience."[33]

The Department of Commerce was informed by Martin P. Rice, manager of broadcasting for General Electric:

> We see no objection to the Department's temporarily assigning the Denver wavelength to Chicago for use from 10 to 12 P.M., Central Standard, or daylight saving time, on Thursday nights until such time as the Denver station requires and is ready to use its assigned frequency. Thursday night is the silent night for KOA and at present no conflict would occur.
>
> The Zenith Radio Corporation, in using the Denver wavelength assures us they were willing to suspend operations at Chicago should an important National program be scheduled for Thursday night, in order that Denver listeners may have the opportunity of receiving the major program.[34]

The U.S. Playing Card Company also agreed to the proposal, but Davis insisted that the Department place a restriction on the license to operate on 322.4 meters (930 kHz).

> The wavelength of 328.9 meters is used by two Cincinnati stations, there being only a 10 kilocycle separation from the channel you propose to use. It is the understanding of the Department that you will so conduct your operations as not to cause any interference with the Cincinnati stations.
>
> The assignment to you is conditional upon your avoidance of such interference.[35]

An inspection of WJAZ was conducted by Supervisor Turner. The "Spanish garden studio" located in the Strauss Building was connected by wire to the Mt. Prospect transmitter and antenna site. On July 22, 1925, a restricted license was issued for a Class D (developmental) station for 930 kilocycles to operate for only two hours per week because no other wavelength was available in Chicago.[36] The license was confirmed by telegram September 3, 1925.[37] The paperwork required to renew licenses every 90 days had become a burden to the Department so licenses were provisionally extended pending the enactment of radio legislation.

Marks wrote Solicitor Davis recalling "the very pleasant conference I had in Washington several months ago relative to our broadcasting station."[38] He then pointed out that after three weeks of operation WSAI Cincinnati had no complaints of the feared interference with WJAZ. He wished on his next trip "to personally thank you [Davis] for the license that has been issued to us."[39] Zenith management appeared satisfied with broadcasting the two hours a week they had negotiated.

Unauthorized Operation of WJAZ. Just as the earlier arrangement with the *Chicago Tribune* before that sale failed, WJAZ's programming had come under the direction of the *Chicago Herald Examiner*. Within five months McDonald was demanding more time on the air for WJAZ from the

Department of Commerce. He wrote Davis, who was serving as the Acting Secretary for a short time:

> Confirming our conversation of November 6th and today [November 12, 1925], W.J.A.Z., the radio station of the *Chicago Herald and Examiner* and the Zenith Radio Corporation, is operating on a wavelength of 322.4 meters. We divide this wavelength with the Denver station, K.O.A., and consider the division of time inequitable, as we have only two hours per week for our share. In other words, Denver has one hundred and sixty-six hours of the week and we are allowed only two hours.
>
> The *Chicago Daily News*, the *Chicago Evening Post*, and the *Chicago Tribune*, each receive on their respective wavelengths eighty-four hours per week, and in addition to this the *Chicago Tribune*, through its subsidiary, the *Liberty Magazine*, also enjoys two additional wavelengths.
>
> It is obvious that we cannot adequately serve the public in two hours per week. We desire more time for operation.
>
> W.J.A.Z. is one of the pioneers of broadcasting in the United States, being the third oldest radio station in Chicago.
>
> In 1924, W.J.A.Z. decided that the interests of the public would best be served by moving its transmitting station from the thickly settled section of Chicago to a remote control station located in a thinly populated district, where it would cause less interference, still maintaining, however, its principal studio in Chicago. To this end, we constructed a portable station [with call letters WJAZ], and at great expense by actual test compared locations surrounding Chicago, both from a standpoint of least interference and greatest efficiency. [40]

McDonald added that the United States wave bands "as we understand them, are from two hundred to six hundred meters."[41] He requested either 960, 910 or 840 kilocycles, all of which were unassigned in the United States.

Davis, after asking Carson, "What interest has *Herald* now?" and "Are these Canadian wavelengths?" personally answered McDonald that the wavelengths requested were reserved for Canada and therefore would not be assigned to him, or to the Chicago area.[42]

Within a month Davis received a letter from a personal friend, William P. MacCracken, Jr., member of the Montgomery, Hart and Smith law firm in Chicago, which represented Zenith. MacCracken asked that the letter not be placed in the official files because the communication "is written on my own initiative, merely to express my personal views on the subject."

> It has just come to my attention that my partner Irving Herriott is leaving for Washington today, to take up with you the subject of increasing the time allocated to WJAZ broadcasting station, or allotting them a different wavelength. Perhaps I mentioned to you in casual conversation, while in Washington, that our firm has represented Zenith ever since its organization. While I have not had charge of handling this

business, I have been more or less in touch with the company's affairs, due to my interest in "air problems."

After going over the facts which are relevant to the present situation, at some length with Herriott, I am firmly convinced that his position is both reasonable and sound and will be sustained by the courts.

Personally I feel that it would be very unfortunate to have a mandamus suit brought against the Department in a case of this character. It would militate against the chances of your securing the passage of the revised radio law and a broad civil aeronautics act; opponents of federal regulation would cite it as proving their fears were well founded that the Department of Commerce would attempt to exercise arbitrary authority not conferred upon it by law.

No doubt you are familiar with the opinion in the Intercity Radio case, and realize that it would control should Zenith be compelled to take the case to court. Naturally my primary interest is in protecting the rights of my clients. I have also a very deep interest in protecting the reputation of the Department of Commerce for fair dealing in matters of this kind.[43]

A meeting was held with McDonald, Herriott and Davis on December 12, 1925. Davis' response to the threat that McDonald would have to sue and the department would look power hungry was:

I am very sorry that we were not able to reach any understanding. There is nothing unfair or arbitrary in the position which the Department in [*sic*] taking. The situation is very simple. McDonald wants something which it is impossible to give at this time and we are therefor compelled to refuse. I am not at all alarmed about the effect of a mandamus proceeding on the legislative situation and am rather inclined to think that it would be helpful.[44]

Within a week McDonald requested a power increase to 1000 watts, which was denied that same day.[45]

McDonald then called personally on supervisor of radio Beane on December 19.

McDonald stated that every effort he has made to secure additional hours of operation for station WJAZ have been without success and as it is necessary to protect his investment he stated that his only recourse as advised by his attorneys would be to take steps towards the end of forcing the Department to issue a license to the Zenith Radio Corporation which would permit the operation of the station over an extended period of time. He stated that he would file applications for the frequencies of 690, 730, 840, 910, and 1030 kilocycles which have been reserved for the Dominion of Canada. In addition, he would file application for half time on the present frequency assigned to his station WJAZ which is 930 kilocycles. He would apply for the transfer of the wavelength of 268 meters [1120 kHz] from his portable station WSAX to station WJAZ, maintaining that wavelength was first used by his station for broadcasting purposes. He stated that he could not consistently inform this office as to the exact course that he really intended to follow nor would he state the exact time any steps would be taken on his part.[46]

Radio supervisor Beane was denied funds he requested to employ another assistant radio inspector to monitor WJAZ.[47] Carson told Beane, "to refer McDonald to the Dept. for any information he desires. Judge Davis is handling this personally."[48]

McDonald became aware that a station in St. Louis was going on the air with "super power" at the end of December. He complained to Davis, "this seems rather inconsistent following your statements to Mr. Herriott and myself. Will you be kind enough to advise me how this new station can be allocated a wavelength while we are refused?" Davis responded, "There is no relation whatsoever between the situation in St. Louis and that in Chicago. Nor do I remember having had any discussion with you as to proposed action regarding any St. Louis station."[49]

On the day after Christmas, McDonald filed applications for the Canadian reserved frequencies. McDonald also attempted to secure the services of H. J. Bligh "to sell advertising for station WJAZ."[50] Bligh wanted to check out if it was true that McDonald expected to have 24 hours per day available for WJAZ, and "Bligh also stated that station WJAZ was operated on Saturday December 26, 1925."[51] This information was given to Davis who took no action due to the holidays.[52]

Two days later, Martin P. Rice of General Electric asked Davis whether WJAZ was operating unauthorized times, to which Davis replied:

> Department has not given Zenith Corporation any additional time nor made any other changes in its license. Have heard rumors similar to those you mention but have no definite knowledge.[53]

Beane then observed that WJAZ had broadcast on the evenings of Saturday, January 2; Wednesday, January 6; and Thursday, January 7, in direct violation of the restrictions placed on the WJAZ license. Solicitor Davis reported:

> The violation on the first two nights was a double one in that operations were carried on both at an unauthorized time and on an unauthorized wavelength.[54]

The Zenith station had used 329.5 meters (910 kiloHertz). This wavelength was for Canada's exclusive use and had seven Canadian stations operating on it. In a letter to U.S. Attorney General Sargent, seeking legal action, Davis gave some background on the problem.

While there is no treaty, convention or other formal agreement between the United States and Canada relative to a division of wavelengths, it has been uniform practice for each country to respect the wavelengths used by the other. We are using some 89 wavelengths for broadcasting stations in the United States which the Canadians do not assign to their stations, except in a few cases where there is no possibility of interference. Canada uses some nine wavelengths under the same circumstances. A violation of this practice would result in an international conflict on wavelengths with consequent utter confusion and on our part would be a breach of good faith with our Canadian neighbors.

The use of this wavelength by the Zenith Radio Corporation requires us, as a matter of international comity, to take immediate drastic action. Aside from the international phase, freedom on the part of broadcasting stations to use wavelengths and hours of operation uncontrolled and in accordance only with their desire would amount to a destruction of our broadcasting system.

The Zenith Radio Corporation and Mr. McDonald are fully cognizant of these conditions and are openly acting in defiance of them.[55]

Davis also reminded Sargent that Zenith's use of apparatus for radio communication without a license was a misdemeanor under Section 1 of the Act of 1912.

In my opinion, both the Zenith Radio Corporation and Mr. McDonald personally are guilty under this statute. May I therefore ask you to take immediate steps towards the enforcement of this law, both as to the criminal liability and as to the forfeiture of the apparatus. The station is being used continuously in violation of the law and I believe it of the utmost importance that its illegal use be stopped at the earliest possible moment.[56]

On January 4, Beane asked for the authority to apply for a preliminary injunction to cease WJAZ's broadcasts.[57] Commissioner Carson denied this but ordered supervisor Beane to monitor WJAZ. Beane had his secretary, Helen C. Smith, do word-for-word transcripts of WJAZ broadcasts for the U.S. Attorney who would be handling the case. Smith noted the times of transmission and title of each piece broadcast.[58] Carson wrote Beane that it might be desirous that the station equipment be seized to stop further operations. If McDonald were to obtain a bond to retain possession there would have to be the condition that he not use the equipment further. It was estimated that the station was worth between 50 and 75 thousand dollars for purposes of obtaining a bond.[59]

The WJAZ Litigation. An assistant to Attorney General Sargent, William Donovan, ordered Chicago District Attorney Edwin A. Olson on January 14 to begin "a vigorous prosecution in this case with a view to vindicating the law on this respect." Donovan made it clear that:

> This case is the first serious instance which has arisen where a broadcasting station has persistently violated the laws and has caused widespread confusion and trouble in the air. The Secretary of Commerce regards this case as being of the greatest importance, both with regard to the maintenance of proper order in the air in this country and with regard to our friendly relations with the Canadian authorities.[60]

Donovan noted that the Department of Commerce, "wishes also to add that inasmuch as this case will probably attract widespread attention, they desire to be kept closely in touch with developments." He also suggested that some thought be given to taking possession of the broadcasting apparatus since the violations were continuing.[61] A *New York Herald-Tribune* story claimed that the District Attorney's office was preparing papers demanding forfeiture of the station's licenses and seizure of its equipment, along with a criminal bill of information which directed Zenith to show cause why it should not be punished for usurpation of an unauthorized wavelength.[62]

Zenith President Eugene McDonald broadcast a statement over WJAZ on January 18, 1926, the day that the government announced it would begin formal litigation. He also issued the following statement to newspapers:

> My attention has been called to articles appearing in the public press, from which it appears that the United States Government is about to institute some sort of legal proceedings against the Zenith Radio Corporation, of which I am President, with the idea of punishing the Corporation or certain of its employees for operating its radio broadcasting station WJAZ for more than two hours per week, the time allotted to it by the Secretary of Commerce. If the Government does take some action it will not be a surprise to us as we notified the Government authorities that we intended to go on the air for the purpose of making a test case in order to determine whether or not there is such thing as "freedom of the air." Before doing this we made every effort to obtain from the Secretary of Commerce some fair and reasonable division of time. I spent weeks in Washington with my attorney Irving Herriott, pointing out the various channels that were open. All our efforts met with failure.
>
> The Department even arbitrarily refused to permit us to use a wavelength that another station enjoyed and offered to us.
>
> We feel that not only we, one of the pioneers in radio broadcasting, but scores of other stations have been discriminated against. The Secretary of Commerce claims to have wide discretionary powers in the division of time between broadcasting stations. I question whether or not he has such discretion, but if he has, I wish to state that in my opinion he is abusing this discretionary power, not only in our case, but in many others, to the detriment of the public and the radio industry.

The present chaos and congestion in the air which makes it almost impossible for the listener with the average radio set of limited selectivity to separate one broadcasting station from the other, is not due to the great number of broadcasting stations in the United States, but is the result of the abuse of the discretionary power which the Secretary of Commerce claims to have in the division of wavelengths and operating time, and in spite of this chaotic condition for which the Secretary of Commerce is responsible, he is today asking Congress to pass legislation which will confer upon him even broader powers of discretion than those which he now claims to have.

As a further indication of the extent of this abuse of this alleged discretionary power, I want to point out the fact that the Secretary of Commerce, has licensed 27 broadcasting station on one particular wavelength, yet permits other stations to enjoy an exclusive wavelength, with no time limit. It is obvious that 27 stations cannot operate simultaneously, on one wavelength, and be heard. In our particular case he has licensed us to operate only two hours per week and has licensed another station to operate on our wavelength the remaining 166 hours each week, and even our little two hours is subject to cancellation at the request of the General Electric Company. The public is justly complaining about the congestion, yet if there were an equal division of time and wave bands, and no favoritism shown, all could be heard and the public would receive real service without interference.

In the litigation which according to newspaper accounts the Government is about to institute, there will be involved necessarily the right of citizens of this country to use the air and have a fair division of it, but there will also be presented the question, (if the Government has this right) shall it regulate in favor of monopoly and against the independent interests and the public generally?

The radio public today is fully aware of the fact that certain interests now claim to have what virtually amounts to a monopoly of many exclusive wave bands.

In my opinion any institution other than one whose business is to disseminate news should have nothing which approaches an exclusive right to any wave band. News agencies are in the nature of public utilities, and their use of the air is of vital interest to the public generally. Such broadcasting should necessarily be given preference over music and other entertainment, but I say that none other than such should be given preference.

With the idea of settling one of the greatest questions presented by the development of modern science, Zenith Radio Corporation intends to litigate in every way possible the questions involved. We naturally desire a reasonable division of time for our own broadcasting station, but if we can by litigation settle the question of freedom of the air and a fair and equitable division of time in the interests of the public and the broadcasters is obtained, Zenith will consider its efforts well worth the sacrifice, even though it might in itself be unsuccessful in obtaining a reasonable share of the time for its own use.

Our action has been referred to in the press as "Piracy of wave band not in use by any broadcasting station in the United States." With reference to this I am reminded of the statement by one of the most eminent leaders in England's politics, when in a discussion of the land laws of his country said "What finger wrote the law that made us trespassers in the land of our birth?" With apologies to the Honorable Lloyd George I say, "What finger wrote the law that makes us pirates in the free air of America?"

In conclusion I wish to state that our position is that we fight for principle rather than for personal gain.[63]

The reports on the interference caused by operation of WJAZ were used in the bill of criminal information. Dance music from the Opera Club was heard on Saturday evenings from 8:30 P.M. to 1 A.M. A new schedule was announced for Sundays, 7 to 9 P.M., Wednesdays from 8 P.M. to 2 A.M., Thursdays from 10 to midnight, and Saturdays from 8 P.M. to 2 A.M. on 910 kilocycles.[64] Letters that reported reception of WJAZ were sent on to the U.S. Attorney from a number of states. The Department of Marine and Fisheries of Canada reported WJAZ interfered with five Canadian stations.[65]

United States versus Zenith Radio Corporation and E. F. McDonald was filed on January 20, 1926 in Chicago. The Department was anxious for quick action. Two days later Davis went to Chicago to speak with the supervisor of radio and assistant U.S. attorney John Elliot Byrne, who had been assigned the case.[66] The Department of Commerce issued a statement a day later. Its main theme was that, "Freedom on the part of broadcasting stations to use wavelengths and hours of operation uncontrolled and in accordance only with their desires, would plainly result in the destruction of our broadcasting system."[67]

In preparation, District Attorney Olson asked whether any other broadcasting stations licensed as Class D had limited hours of operation or were required to divide time with others. Carson answered:

You are informed that Department has issued broadcasting licenses to Crosley and Kodel, Cincinnati; Westinghouse, Chicago; Grebe, New York; Radio Corporation of America, New York; and General Electric, Schenectady, all manufacturing and developing companies. Limitations as to hours of operation and division of time not on face of licenses except in case Westinghouse. In other cases limitation of hours of operation and division of time was by collateral agreements on file in Bureau which agreements were conditions precedent to issuing licenses.[68]

Taking pride in their public notoriety and to bring public attention to the suit against them, Zenith dressed its personnel as pirates on February 5, 1926, to pose for promotional pictures and presented the operetta *The Pirate*. They sent photos and a short story to newspapers to publicize the stunt.[69]

The Department of Commerce became concerned over press reaction and issued a statement on what it thought would happen should WJAZ win in court.

The Department said it learned of the intention of more than 24 broadcasting stations to operate on wavelengths of their own choice if the government lost its case against Zenith. Department officials predicted that "complete and utter chaos in the ether would result from an unfavorable decision in the McDonald case, at least until legislation is enacted granting authority to some agency to regulate radio."

> The action against Mr. McDonald, who is president of the Zenith Radio Corporation and owner of "WJAZ" is for operating his station in a wavelength which he was not licensed to use. Believing that the 1912 radio law provides the authority, officials of the Department of Commerce requested the Department of Justice to take legal action against Mr. McDonald.
>
> It is also believed by Department of Commerce officials that if the government loses its case about one or two hundred disappointed applicants for licenses for broadcasting stations will go ahead anyway with the construction of their stations and operate them on any wavelength they see fit.
>
> Members of Congress acquainted with the situation assert that immediate radio legislation will be imperative in the event the Department of Commerce loses its case.[70]

The case opened before Federal Judge James H. Wilkerson on February 15, 1926. The opening statement by defense attorney Lem E. Hart quoted a statement made by Davis in a congressional hearing:

> We do not say to one "You go until 12 o'clock tonight" and to another "You can go until 10 o'clock tomorrow." In the case of disagreement between broadcasters we would have authority to enforce such a time division. We would give them licenses which would allow them to operate at a certain limited time. The situation, however, has not arisen.[71]

The Zenith counsel pointed out that their station had been restricted prior to that testimony. Judge Wilkerson was quoted after these preliminary statements that the Act of 1912 was "a poor piece of work."[72]

The next day Irving Herriott, Zenith's attorney, argued that certain stations authorized by the Secretary of Commerce operate without time limits or on a particular wavelength and that six of the companies controlling those stations have "agreements between themselves forming a sort of trust." Davis denied that WJAZ had been treated unfairly and there had not been discrimination to stop its efforts to experiment in radio. He said the department had to consider the needs of the country. The argument ended that afternoon and the judge took the case under advisement.[73]

Various editorials, cartoons and articles on the case appeared before the final decision was announced. An editorial in the *New York Herald-Tribune* stated that "the old law may have sharper teeth than WJAZ believes, but the rebellion of that station emphasizes the need for new legislation to cover definitely the field of broadcasting."[74] A cartoon in the *Springfield Illinois Republican*, entitled "A Battle on the High Seas," showed two ships, one smaller than the other. The small vessel is labeled, "U.S. Dept. of Justice," and the larger is labeled, "Broadcasting Pirates." They are both firing furiously at each other as they sail upon the "Ether Waves" before a country crowded with radio antenna.[75]

The Bureau of Navigation instructed their radio inspectors to discontinue monitoring WJAZ on March 11, 1926.[76]

On April 16, 1926, Judge Wilkerson announced his decision. It read, in part:

> The material facts are not in dispute. It is agreed that defendant corporation, on the dates charged in the information, operated its station on a wavelength and at times which were not authorized....
>
> There is no express grant of power in the Act to the Secretary of Commerce to establish regulations. The regulations, subject to which the license is granted are contained in the fourth section of the Act....
>
> The Secretary of Commerce is required to issue the license subject to the regulations in the Act. The Congress has withheld from him the power to prescribe additional regulations. If there is a conflict between a provision in the license and the regulations established by Congress, the latter must control....
>
> No language is more worthy of frequent and thoughtful consideration than these words of Justice Matthews, speaking for the Supreme Court in *Yick Wo v. Hopkins*, 118 U.S. 356, 369:
>
>> "When we consider the nature of the theory of our institutions of government, the principles upon which they are supposed to rest, and to review the history of their development, we are constrained to conclude that they do not mean to leave room for the play and action of purely personal and arbitrary power."
>
> Congress cannot delegate its power to make a law, but it can make a law to delegate a power to determine some fact or state of facts upon which the law makes or intends to make its own action depend. Has Congress prescribed the rule or standard which is to control the Secretary of Commerce in the exercise of his discretion with the degree of certainty required in Criminal Statutes? It is axiomatic that statutes creating and defining crimes cannot be extended by intendment, and that no act, however wrongful, can be punished under such a statute, unless clearly within its terms....
>
> My conclusion is that, under the rules applicable to criminal statutes, Sections one and two cannot be construed to cover the act of the

defendant upon which this prosecution is based. Other questions have been argued which it is unnecessary to decide.[77]

Later, McDonald's lawyer, Irving Herriott, attempted to explain from Zenith's point of view what led to the court case, which ended in their favor. It was an attempt to rewrite history.

> [Hoover] placed a limitation in the license which had never been placed in any license before and so far as I know, has never been put in one since; to the effect that the station could be operated only on Thursday nights and then only between the hours of ten P.M. and midnight. That means two hours a week! But I have not told you all of this limitation. The right to operate on that two hours a week was subject to cancellation at any time by the General Electric Company which owns and operates several broadcasting stations, if at any time it desired to use that two hours for its Denver station, to which station the Secretary of Commerce had granted the exclusive right to operate twenty-four hours a day, seven days of the week.
>
> Repeated efforts were made by Commander McDonald and by myself, both before and after this practically worthless license had been issued to secure some additional time; the corporation agreeing to make any fair equitable division of time with any other station in order to avoid having to go to court to insist on its legal rights, but this was of no avail and no other license was forthcoming....
>
> Mr. Davis said to me in his office in Washington that he would welcome a decision of the courts on this question; that the present radio law was not satisfactory and that he would not object if the courts should hold that the Secretary of Commerce had no authority whatsoever over radio. He indicated he would be glad if Zenith Radio Corporation would start court proceedings, but in the exercise of my judgment as Commander McDonald's attorney, I advised him not to file a suit, but to select some wavelength which was not being used by another station in the United States.... The corporation might have selected any wavelength regardless if it were being used by other stations, but being engaged in the radio industry it naturally was interested in doing nothing which would upset the programs from other stations.[78]

Department of Commerce Reaction. Secretary Hoover was in New York City attending a meeting when the WJAZ decision was pronounced. In his absence, Stephen Davis stated:

While I have not seen the text of the decision and therefore cannot have any final opinion on it, it seems from the reports to be a definite holding that the 1912 Radio Act confers no authority upon anyone to assign either wavelengths or time to radio stations. If this is a view of the law, it means that neither broadcasting nor other forms of radio communication are subject to any Federal regulation, but that station operators may select wavelengths and time at their wish. The Court of Appeals of the District of Columbia has decided precisely the opposite, so that apparently we have two opinions which are in hopeless conflict. Secretary Hoover has always realized, and frequently expressed, the insufficiency of the 1912 law, and largely for that reason has dealt with the entire subject through annual conferences of all persons interested in radio communication, whether as transmitters or listeners. The conclusion of these conferences have almost universally been put into practice, so that radio has been largely a self-regulated industry.

The future would seem to depend entirely upon the attitude of Congress towards legislation and its determination as to whether or not Federal control of the situation shall be continued.[79]

Twelve of Chicago's radio station owners adopted a resolution urging Congress to pass the White Bill as an emergency measure to protect the public interest.[80]

Secretary Hoover issued a statement in Washington on April 20.

The court has refused to impose a penalty upon a concern which admittedly was operating at a time and upon a wavelength not authorized under its license. While the holding is in conflict with an earlier ruling in the District of Columbia, it is apparent that under the law of 1912, as now construed, no one has authority to protect the listening public against utter chaos in the service upon which it has come to rely. The Chicago decision denies the authority of the Secretary of Commerce to assign either wavelengths or time of operation. It does not affect broadcasting alone, but is equally applicable to the amateurs and any of these services are open to incursion by the others, and any station may be attacked by its neighbor. If stations proceed to select their own wavelengths and choose their own time, considering only their selfish advantage, effective public service will be at an end.[81]

Subsequent statements by Secretary Hoover reiterated that nothing could be done to prevent a person from broadcasting at any time he pleased, that this would cause chaos on the air and render useless and valueless some six-hundred million dollars worth of radio receiving sets in the country.

In a broadcast on WJAZ, Herriott said remarks by Hoover and his assistants were "wholly unwarranted and are not justified."[82] Herriott based his belief upon his personal legal interpretation of the Act of 1912, which still controlled broadcasting.

The great majority, I say at least 95 percent of the broadcasting stations in the United States today, are not engaged in either bona fide commercial business by radio communication or in experimentation in connection with the development and manufacture of radio apparatus for commercial purposes. The Zenith Radio Corporation is engaged in experimentation in connection with the development and manufacture and sale of radio apparatus for commercial purposes and therefore comes within the special restricted class which has the right to use any wavelength under these regulations (of the Act of 1912), provided it does not exceed six hundred meters. No other type of broadcasting station has the right to use a wavelength in excess of two hundred meters (1499 kHz) unless the Secretary of Commerce specifically and specially authorizes such station to use a higher wavelength. It is only by reason of special authority granted by the Secretary of Commerce that the great majority of broadcasting stations are today authorized to transmit on a wavelength in excess of two hundred meters. The Secretary of Commerce, in his discretion, has seen fit to license broadcasting stations without regard to the nature of their business to operate on such higher wavelengths by special authority. He has the right to do this and we are all very glad that he has done so, but I take issue with him when he says that having by special authority authorized a great number of broadcasting stations to use a higher wavelength than that authorized by the regulations, he now has no control over them and that they may use whatever wavelength they desire. If any station which is specifically authorized under the statute to use one not specifically authorized by the Secretary of Commerce such person is guilty of a violation of the regulations.[83]

Herriott's theory was that the only stations not subject to the Act of 1912 were those owned and operated by radio industry concerns which experimented or developed equipment. He argued that they could operate on any wavelength of their choice but all other stations could operate only on wavelengths under 1500 kHz which the Secretary of Commerce had the right to specify. Herriott interpreted the decision on WJAZ as:

The Court did not say that a license is unnecessary before a station may be operated nor did the Court hold that the Secretary may not revoke licenses for violations of the regulations of the Act. The simple fact is that the Zenith Radio Corporation had a license which contained void restrictions and the court held it was not violating any of the regulations.[84]

Therefore, Herriott stated, Secretary Hoover could cancel all the current licenses and then re-issue licenses specifying that stations operate below 1499 kHz on specifically designated wavelengths. This would allow Hoover to retain control of broadcasting. What Herriott did not take into account was that most radio receivers could not operate below 550 kHz and the distress frequency of 500 kHz had to be protected. This restriction of the broadcast spectrum would make it impossible for all the operating stations to find space in that limited spectrum. The situation Herriott proposed was basically unworkable, but he was attempting to justify the disastrous results of their lawsuit.

> Why has the Secretary, since the decision in the case, made the unwarranted statements as to the effect of the decision? He and his lawyers know that the law is still in force and yet they publicly invite violations of it and say, in effect, that the Government is powerless. I believe I understand why. There is pending in Congress a bill to regulate radio known as the White Bill. This bill effectively places in the hands of Mr. Hoover, a single individual, the sole and arbitrary power to regulate this great new factor in our daily life. It gives him the power to say to one man, "I do not approve of you and you cannot operate a station and use the free air" and to another "you may operate without restrictions." It may very well be that certain persons should have the right to use the air and that others should not, but I say to you fellow citizens of this country, it is contrary to the principles of our Government to place such unlimited dictatorial powers in the hands of one man. The Secretary evidently wants that power.[85]

Herriott wrote Davis a couple of months later:

> I am still of the opinion, however, that broadcasting as we know it today is not commercial within the meaning of the Radio Act of 1912 and I believe you could successfully prevent the great majority of stations using a wavelength above two hundred meters unless specifically authorized to do so.[86]

Commissioner of Navigation Carson wrote to the Deputy Commissioner of the Department of Marine and Fisheries in Canada to express his displeasure with the action of the Zenith Radio Corporation. He called attention to the fact that the company's action "was wholly without any permission or approval by the Government, and that the Government by appropriate legal proceedings attempted to terminate it."[87]

Opinion of the Attorney General. The Intercity Radio Company case of 1923 had concluded that the Secretary could not refuse to license a station, but he could assign a wavelength for the station to prevent interference. The Zenith WJAZ case took away even that power and "left the Secretary of Commerce without judicial guidance."[88]

Congress was still finding it difficult to compromise on a law for radio communication and Hoover now found it almost impossible to control the situation.[89] In an effort to spur action the Department of Commerce began to refuse to consider routine, daily issues. To obtain a final definitive ruling on exactly what the power of the Department of Commerce was under the

Act of 1912, Hoover requested an opinion from the Attorney General on the whole question of Departmental authority.

Specifically, Secretary Hoover asked Attorney General Donovan to answer five key questions:

> (1) Does the 1912 Act require broadcasting stations to obtain licenses, and is the operation of such a station without a license an offense under that Act?
>
> (2) Has the Secretary of Commerce authority under the 1912 Act to assign wavelengths and times of operation and limit the power of stations?
>
> (3) Has a station, whose license stipulates a wavelength for its use, the right to use any other wavelength, and if it does operate on a different wavelength, is it in violation of the law and does it become subject to the penalties of the Act?
>
> (4) If a station, whose license stipulates a period during which only the station may operate and limits its power, transmits at different times, or with excessive power, is it in violation of the Act and does it become subject to the penalties of the Act?
>
> (5) Has the Secretary of Commerce power to fix the duration of the licenses which he issues or should they be indeterminate, continuing in effect until revoked or until Congress otherwise provides?[90]

The Attorney General replied that "radio communication is a proper subject for federal regulation under the commerce clause of the Constitution … And it may be noticed in passing that even purely intrastate transmission of radio waves may fall within the scope of federal power when it disturbs the air in such a manner as to interfere with interstate communication."[91]

In specific answer to the questions, the Attorney General stated that "a license must be obtained before a broadcasting station may be lawfully operated."[92] The second question involved three separate problems:

> (a) The assignment of wavelengths
> (b) The assignment of hours of operation
> (c) The limitation of power

On the assignment of wavelengths the Attorney General cited the Intercity Radio Case of 1923 and told Hoover, "you have assumed that you had discretionary authority in assigning wavelengths for the use of particular stations, and have made such assignments to the individual broadcasting stations."[93] He went on:

> However, in my opinion, these remarks of the Court of Appeals are to be construed as applying only to the *normal* sending and receiving wavelength which every station is required to designate under the first regulation. But under the second regulation, any station is at liberty to use "other wavelengths" at will, provided only that they do not trespass

upon the band from 600 to 1600 meters…. Broadcasting stations, therefore, do not fall within the scope of the fifteenth regulation; and the Secretary is without power to impose on them the restrictions provided therein.

From the foregoing considerations I am forced to conclude that you have no general authority under the Act to assign wavelengths to broadcasting stations, except for the purpose of designating normal wavelengths under Regulation One.[94]

He also concluded that the Secretary of Commerce had no right to determine which or the number of hours broadcasting stations could operate and that it did not appear that he was given the right to determine the minimum amount of power which could be used under the Act of 1912.[95]

Secretary Hoover's Reaction to the Attorney General Ruling. Hoover was greatly disappointed in the Attorney General's ruling that stripped him of most of his assumed authority to assign and regulate wavelengths. Hoover's statement of July 9 sums up his disappointment:

Since 1923 the Department has been making … assignments. In doing so it has followed the decision of the Court of Appeals of the District of Columbia, rendered in that year (the Intercity Company Case). That Court directly held that the Secretary was, by the law of 1912, under the duty to make such assignments for the purpose of preventing interference. Until April of this year this was the only Court ruling on the subject.

The recent decision of the Chicago Court, however, cast doubt on this authority, since it adopted a construction of the 1912 Act directly contrary in this respect to the view taken by the Court of the District of Columbia.

The Attorney General now likewise disagrees with the construction of the District Court of Appeals and advises that while under the law each applicant for a license must designate a definite wavelength, outside the band of 600 to 1600 meters, yet he is at liberty to use other wavelengths at his will.

The Department will, therefore, in accordance with the opinion, not assign wavelengths, but will merely recite on the face of the license the wavelength selected by the applicant as the normal wavelength of the station. Under the Attorney General's opinion, no authority exists in the Department, or elsewhere, to compel adherence to this wavelength, and the Department must issue licenses to each applicant.

The general effect of this opinion is that regulation has broken down and stations are under no effective restriction as to wavelength or power used. The 1912 Act under these various constructions has failed to confer authority for the prevention of interference which was its obvious intent.

Persons desiring to construct stations must determine for themselves whether there will be wavelengths available for their use without interference from other stations. They must proceed entirely at their own risk.

There have always been the most cordial relations between the radio administrations in Canada and the United States. The Department has refrained from assigning to American stations the wavelengths in use in Canada and the Canadian authorities have reciprocated by avoiding the wavelength assigned to our stations. A continuance of this policy is a necessity if international confusion is to be avoided. The Department most earnestly hopes, whatever may ensue, that the sense of fair play, as well as interest in the protection of the situation as a whole will prevent any American station from trespassing upon the Canadian assignments.

The orderly conduct of radio communication and the interest of the listener in broadcasting has been possible largely because of voluntary self-regulation by the industry itself, frequently necessitating some individual sacrifice for general good. The Department trusts that this spirit will continue in the future as in the past.

The legislation which has been long sought from Congress to perfect the 1912 Act reached the stage of passage by both houses, but insufficient time remained in the session in which to compose conflicts between the House and Senate Bills. The legislation will undoubtedly be perfected early in the session which meets in December. Both bills, however, carry explicit authority to the Government to assign wavelengths, limit power and time, and they both establish in the Government the fundamental property in the air channels. These authorities will undoubtedly be confirmed. While any confusion which may arise pending the next session will certainly be eliminated by the passage of legislation, it will be minimized by just as much as broadcasters avoid interference with other stations.[96]

Attorney General Donovan had summed up his analysis of the Act of 1912 with the statement:

It is apparent from the answers contained in this opinion that the present legislation is inadequate to cover the art of broadcasting, which has been almost entirely developed since the passage of the Act of 1912. If the present situation requires control, I can only suggest that it be sought in new legislation, carefully adapted to meet the needs of both the present and the future.[97]

II. The Chaos

Although Secretary Hoover had to relax his control of radio, all supervisors were instructed to observe and report to the Washington staff any cases of willful or malicious interference. This order, based on part of the 1912 Act, was considered to still be in effect.

The Department was using various means to keep track of the radio situation. One innovation was the use of a radio test car to locate interference sources. During the final month of 1925 and up to January 25, 1926, this car was in operation in the Detroit area. The radio supervisor manning the truck located 30 sources of serious interference. This interference was then called to the attention of the parties involved. During this experimental period, 53 cities in five states were visited; 48 amateur, 15 broadcasting, 11 commercial, and 14 ship stations were found to be causing interference.

The Bureau of the Budget was asked for funds to provide three more such vehicles, one to be stationed in New York, one in Chicago, and one on the Pacific Coast.[98]

During 1926 all supervisors sent in a monthly report of complaints they received of interference.[99] Out of a possible 108 reports, one a month from nine supervisors, only 21 could be located in the files.[100] But those 21 are very interesting for what they reveal.

Source	*Number of Complaints*
Electric Light and Power Line Interference	1044
Commercial and Naval Code Interference	262
Amateur Interference	348
Electrical Equipment Interference	203
Broadcast Station Interference	1118*
Oscillating Receiver Interference	74
Msc., Trolley Lines, Telephone, Cable	135

800 of the Broadcast Station Interference complaints were apparently due to the Westinghouse experiments when WBZ and WBZA were operating simultaneously on 900 kHz and interfering with each other. This particular series of Westinghouse experiments were performed three days in May 1926.

When new station applications were received, the Bureau of Navigation now replied with a form letter:

> In view of the recent decision of the Attorney General the Department does not consider it has authority to assign wavelengths.
>
> Therefore, each station is at liberty to use any wavelengths they may desire, from which it would appear in the case in question the Bureau cannot exercise jurisdiction.[101]

The Department of Commerce also decided not to attempt any further actions toward broadcasting stations who changed their frequencies until its authority would be clarified with pending legislation. The Department hoped Congress "will definitely and clearly establish some form of Federal authority."[102]

Broadcast Wavelength "Pirates." Radio Station WAMD in Minneapolis "pirated" the wavelength of 294 meters (1020 kHz) in July 1926. The station owner, Stanley Hubbard, said that they "were trying to speed this radio business up so that we can get out of this congestion."[103] This station caused Secretary Hoover some public embarrassment. He had pleaded that month with stations to stay on their assigned wavelengths.

On July 20, 1926, Secretary Hoover gave a speech before the opening session of the United States League of Local Building and Loan Associations Convention in Minneapolis. The address was broadcast by WAMD ([W]here [A]ll [M]innesota [D]ances), on the "pirated" wavelength which received the front page headline in the *Minneapolis Journal*. Hubbard claimed, "Hoover knew before he broadcast his speech that we were using a wavelength other than the one assigned to us by the Department of Commerce." Hoover's secretary protested that this was not true.[104]

Hoover was quoted in the *Minneapolis Journal*:

> The radio situation is in a chaotic stage. It will remain there until Congress enacts the legislation that has been before it for the last two years. Meanwhile, our Department is powerless to do anything to regulate the use of wavelengths.
>
> Under this condition it is up to the trade to cooperate and avoid confusion as much as possible. When one or two radio stations in a district shift their position it disturbs all the rest.[105]

After only one week of operating on the pirated higher wavelength, WAMD returned to its assigned 244 meters (1230 kHz). The station had received a telegram from the management of station KPRC ([P]ost [R]adio [C]ompany), Houston, Texas, threatening court action against WAMD if they continued to interfere with KPRC's signal.

Hubbard then issued a statement listing five disadvantages that could confront a station if it left its frequency for another:

> (1) The loss of right by priority to 244 meters in case some other station adopts this wavelength which, incidentally, is one of the best in the country.
>
> (2) Possibility of an injunction or damage suit on account of interference caused by WAMD being on their wavelength.
>
> (3) Possible criminal prosecution by the government in case of malicious interference, which could take place immediately after the government notified the station that it was causing interference by not being on its own wavelength.
>
> (4) The possibility of breaking down rather than building up of good will which is possible throughout continuous broadcasting on other than the assigned wavelength.
>
> (5) The desire of the station management to cooperate not only with other large broadcasting stations but trade and listeners' associations as well.[106]

In Missouri, radio stations KLDS, Independence, and WOS, Jefferson City, were licensed to operate on the same wavelength, sharing the available time. The Missouri State Marketing Commissioner, in charge of WOS, a state station, rejected the schedule that had been arranged between the two stations. Judge Albert L. Reeves held in District Court in Kansas City that a radio station having accepted a license from the government was bound to observe the terms of that license. He ruled in this instance that having accepted a division of time, both stations had recognized the federal government's power to regulate and license radio stations.[107]

Officials of the Department of Commerce tentatively expressed the belief that the decision would have no general value except for stations having written agreements between themselves regarding broadcasting hours and sharing of a wavelength.[108]

Secretary Hoover wrote to President Coolidge's secretary:

> Immediately after the breakdown of authority there was, as expected, an outburst of "pirate" stations, both in change of wavelength and new stations, but there was a much less number than we had expected. However, as the result of threats of action in the courts between station and of active organization of listeners in various localities, and of the denunciation by the press of "pirate" stations, *all offending stations have gone back to their original positions except ten or twelve, and of the new stations all but two had reduced their power and thus their carrying area as to practically eliminate serious interference by them, at least during the summer months* [emphasis added]. In these cases we shall probably see a temporary solution.[109]

Hoover was overly optimistic because the situation worsened. Arthur Batcheller reported problems in the Second District. "I have to advise that as a result of the recent changes in wavelength made by a number of stations in the Second District, conditions are unsatisfactory." He warned that when cold weather set in, the static would clear and signal ranges would increase, causing a considerably aggravated interference situation.[110]

Scattered reports of stations jumping frequencies continued to arrive at the Bureau of Navigation but there was public disagreement as to how much interference and actual "chaos" there was. Hugo Gernsback reported in *Radio News*, October 1926:

> While it is true that, up to this writing, a small number of stations have changed their wavelengths, no such thing as *chaos*, nor anything resembling it has resulted for very simple and fundamental reasons. The few stations which did actually change their wavelengths, did so probably because they had a grievance. In practically every instance they were stations which had been assigned crowded low wavelengths.[111]
>
> Fortunately, nine out of ten broadcasters have realized the serious consequences arising from a destruction of the delicate wavelength structure which Secretary Hoover and his able assistants have built up

during the last few years. At this writing, confusion has been limited to one or two highly congested areas.[112]

There were reports that about 48 stations had attempted to revise their wavelengths upward before the summer ended, and 65 new stations were to begin broadcasting. When Carson was asked if the department should respond, he replied that the Bureau felt this article was not "worthy of any further attention."[113]

The Oak Leaves Station, WGES, in Oak Park, a suburb of Chicago, was assigned the frequency of 1330 kHz. But it "pirated" 1200 kHz and moved to 950 kHz which was 40 kHz from the *Chicago Tribune's* WGN. The department was attempting to maintain a standard separation of 50 kHz. The *Tribune* Company argued listeners tuning to WGN might end up listening to WGES by mistake. A temporary injunction was secured by *Tribune*, enjoining WGES from interfering with their signal. After a hearing on November 17, 1926, Judge Frances Wilson upheld the "priority principle" between broadcasting stations in the absence of a workable communications law. His reasoning was, since WGN had been using 990 kHz for a considerable length of time and had built up a large listening audience, "priority of time creates a superiority in right."[114] Wilson did not prevent WGES from using any other particular wavelength but enjoined them from using any wavelength that cause material interference to WGN. [115]

This case was without precedent, so Judge Wilson had to draw analogies from trade name, copyright, water rights and electrical interference cases. If this decision had been applied as a precedent, the common-law principles of equity and property rights might have somewhat negated the need for further legislation. But, station owners did not want to spend money to legally defend their frequencies and the listening public was demanding some action on the part of Congress because of interference problems.

On December 18, 1926, Tyrer sent a telegram to the Churchill Evangelistic Association radio station in Buffalo, New York, berating the station for causing "serious interference" in Canada.

> Canadian Administration again complain serious interference to Canadian stations caused by your station. Canadian listeners bitterly complaining. Have wired Canadian Administration Department without authority remedy but has notified you.[116]

Tyrer reported to Canadian Radio Administrator Johnston:

> It is very much regretted that the owners of broadcasting stations in the United States have ignored the wishes of Secretary Hoover and are operating on the wavelengths which were formerly used exclusively by your stations.
>
> Since the first of July, when the Attorney General rendered his opinion … the Department has granted *126 licenses for new stations* [emphasis added].

This makes a total of 642 broadcasting stations licensed in this country. *During this period 91 stations have changed their wavelengths and about 132 stations have increased their power* [emphasis added]. New applications are being received very day and the situation is therefore getting worse daily.[117]

A Department of Commerce report issued early in December revealed that since July 1, when governmental radio control began to fail, 102 new stations had taken to the air by simply applying for licenses, which had to be granted. This was an average of approximately five a week, and brought the total number of stations at the end of 1926 to 620.

The report emphasized the fact that the interference that was becoming more prevalent daily would not be cleared even if stations stopped changing wavelengths. It showed that from July 1 to December 1, 1926, 94 reports of wavelength changes had been received, most of them in the higher wavelengths. During November alone, 27 stations were licensed to broadcast, and there were 20 wavelength changes. While all new stations still had to receive licenses from the Bureau of Navigation, they were not required to report changes in their wavelengths. Those who reported did so voluntarily, so the real number that may have switched wavelengths without informing the Department of Commerce cannot be determined.[118]

Other Regulatory Difficulties. The many new stations broadcasting in the already crowded broadcast spectrum contributed as much interference as the established stations did by changing their wavelengths. By February of 1927 over 210 new broadcasting stations were licensed, bringing the total number to 733.[119]

Stations were still finding it difficult to remain on frequency with any degree of accuracy. Westinghouse was experimenting with piezo-electric crystal control. They found that KDKA's transmitter shifted for some unknown reason. The Bureau of Standards tested the crystal on January 7, 1926 and found that it was accurate to within two percent. Supervisor Edwards visited KDKA and learned from Dr. Frank Conrad that the crystal Westinghouse was using was also transmitting periodically on a frequency very close to the one the crystal was adjusted for and this caused the transmitter to slip off the base frequency of 970 kHz to the close harmonic thus causing a fluctuation.[120]

The Bureau of Standards determined that a piezo-oscillator quartz plate had to be grounded so that one of its fundamentals or harmonics was either the exact licensed frequency of the broadcasting station or a frequency which differed from the station's frequency by only a small amount, such as 200 or 300 cycles.[121]

In 1927 there was extensive adoption of piezo-electric crystal control which made the Federal Radio Commission's task easier. Improvements were achieved by keeping the crystal at a constant temperature in a heated container (oven). The Federal Radio Commission was then able to order all stations to maintain frequency within one-half of a kilocycle.[122]

Receivers that could not reject signals from nearby sources also caused problems. One of many typical reports:

> The Bureau is informed that Notley resides within two blocks of F. K. Bridgeman's station [WFKB] and it is but natural that on any other receiver but the most selective set that interference would be created over a fairly broad wave band when the receiving apparatus is located within five blocks of a 500 watt transmitter.[123]

In another case the Department of Commerce found that a station license held by *The Principal*, a Missouri church school, was not actually operating its own radio station but was sharing equipment and frequency with another. They operated, under the call letters KFQA, a studio connected by land lines to KMOX ([K]irkwood, [MO] [X]mas). The church wanted to use distinctive call letters so as to not lose their identity:

> Moreover, the management of KMOX is equally desirous of having us use our own call letters in sponsoring our programs, since they often consist of church services and KMOX, being owned by many organizations, cannot well afford to sponsor any one church or religious program. Therefore, it is to our mutual interest to retain the respective identities of the two stations, with separate staff, call letters and announcers.[124]

The Department of Commerce allowed the KFQA call letters to be used in this manner pending further consideration.[125]

Increases in power created interference problems as much as the unauthorized switching of frequencies. A few stations were authorized an increase in power following the Zenith case. These occurred only because a supervisor had begun the approval process prior to the WJAZ decision. Permission to change facilities would not have been granted, "had this indication not been made by the Supervisor...."[126] RCA's WJZ (New Jersey) had been given permission to perform experiments with "high" power up to 50 kilowatts but it caused a great deal of interference over a wide area. RCA officials attempted to overcome the public's anger and "they were satisfied a great many of the complaints had been settled and that they were actively engaged with a large force of experts in visiting each party who filed a complaint for the purpose of overcoming their difficulty."[127] Nevertheless, on February 16, 1926, the New Jersey State Senate adopted a resolution directed specifically at WJZ's operations, asking Congress to empower the Secretary of Commerce to control radio stations and to control nuisances.[128] The Department of Commerce did not order WJZ's power to be reduced because the Zenith case had convinced them that they had no right to regulate power increases after April 1926.

III. The Passage of Legislation

H. R. 5589. Many, including Hoover, felt that the only way to prevent chaos was for Congress to immediately pass one of the bills it had under consideration. January 18, 1926, had been tentatively set as the date for hearings in the House on the White Bill (H. R. 5589). Senators Dill and Howell were scheduling their hearings for January 8. When Rep. White heard of this, he had his hearing advanced to January 6. He hoped this move would allow time for the passage of his bill and its transfer to the Senate before the Senate could pass its own bill sending that to the House. Rep. White's anxieties seemed unwarranted because the majority of the senators expressed little interest in the bills. Senate discussion devoted to broadcasting was primarily concerned with the question of monopoly. In contrast, action in the House came quickly.[129]

At the House hearings Secretary Hoover said:

> The primary condition that makes legislation necessary is the congestion in broadcasting. This situation has existed for some time. I have hoped that natural laws, working with scientific and mechanical advance, would themselves solve the problem without legislative intervention. But such has not been the case. Inventive genius has not been able yet to furnish us with more broadcasting channels. The desire to broadcast daily becomes more widespread, the demand for licenses steadily increases, we have today more powerful stations in operation and more applications that cannot be granted than ever before. The law has imposed the duty of providing for every applicant so far as possible, with the result that we now have too much crowding together, unscientific geographical distribution, overlapping confusion. The interference between stations has become so great as to greatly minimize their public service....
>
> I think, therefore, that in discussing this bill, we may take three facts as settled: first, radio legislation is absolutely and immediately essential if we wish to prevent chaos in radio communication, especially broadcasting; second, the bill now proposed has already received substantial approval and third, the principles declared in this bill have received the approbation of both the radio industry and the radio public.
>
> The distinctive features of this draft, which I consider of the greatest importance, are as follows:
>
> First: The bill affirmatively asserts and assumes jurisdiction in the Federal Government over all phases of radio communication in so far as such communication constitutes or affects interstate or foreign commerce. I believe that Federal supremacy is absolutely essential if this system of communication is to be preserved and advanced. There can be little question of the interstate character of this service. Every word broadcasted traverses state lines.

Second: It provides an administrative organization by which Federal control is to be exercised. It requires a Federal license as a prerequisite to the operation of a transmitting station. This licensing system has been in effect since the passage of the Act of 1912, and has demonstrated its soundness in spite of other deficiencies in that law.

Third: It retains complete control in the Federal Government of all channels of radio communications. It declares that there shall be no ownership or vested right in wavelengths and that the period of use allowed under the license shall be limited to five years, subject to renewals. In doing so, the bill carries into law the system which now exists by Department practice. While the law of 1912 contains no limitations whatever on the license period, so that long time privileges or perpetual franchises might have been granted, the Department has been heedful to prevent any such situation....

Fourth: It recognizes that the public interest is paramount in all forms of radio activity. To that extent, the bill adopts as to this service the principle which has been found so effective in state regulation of public utilities. It recognizes that the interest of the public as a whole supersedes the desire of any individual.

Fifth: It vests in the Secretary of Commerce the power to grant or refuse licenses, but this power is so limited as to obviate the possibility of its arbitrary exercise. The Secretary is required to make his determination with public benefit as the test and standard. There is a complete check upon either arbitrary, unjust or erroneous action by an appeal to the courts, by which any controverted question is determined independently and de novo. I have always taken the position that unlimited authority to control the granting of radio privileges was too great a power to be placed in the hands of any one administrative officer, and I am glad to see the checks and reviews which are imposed upon that power under this bill.

Sixth: The bill provides for a national commission of nine members to which may be referred any question upon which the Secretary of Commerce desires their judgment. There are many purely administrative questions in the detail of administrative regulation, such, for instance, as the assignment of a particular wavelength to a given station, which may properly be left to the judgment of a single official. But there are other broader and more important matters such, for instance, as the determination of the persons who are to exercise radio privileges under the rule of public interest, which involves a large element of discretion and in which it is wise to have the consensus of several minds. Such decisions, especially where the questions become controversial, should properly be made by a board rather than an individual. To draw a legislative line between these two classes of function is difficult. It seems to me that line lies at the point of controversy over privileges. The judgment of the board is made final and binding, subject only to the appeal of the courts. I consider this a highly important question.

Seventh: Applicants desiring to engage in broadcasting or commercial communications are required to obtain a permit in advance of the construction of the station.

Eighth: The bill authorizes the revocation of station licenses for failure to operate or for violation of the law. This is another step in the recognition of the sound principle that public service is the basis for the license privilege. The exercise of this power is likewise subject to court review.[130]

H. R. 5589 was referred to a subcommittee for discussion and revisions. A revised bill (H. R. 9108) was then sent back to the House.

H. R. 9108. The revised White Bill would give the Secretary of Commerce substantial authority to deal with the radio situation because he would be granted the power to revoke or refuse a license. His decisions would be subject to court review upon the request of the aggrieved.

A Federal Radio Commission would be established to whom the Secretary might go for advice and which would have an important part in settling public disputes concerning radio. The commission would be composed of five members, one from each geographical zone. The first zone would embrace the East; the second, the Great Lakes Region; the third, the South; the fourth, the Middle West; and, the fifth, the Far West including Hawaii and Alaska. Each commissioner would be appointed by the President for a term of seven years. Their compensation was set at $25 dollars a day, and they would not be in session more than 120 days a year.

The proposed bill dealt stringently with monopolistic practices. The Secretary of Commerce was directed to refuse a license or a construction permit to anyone found guilty by a federal court of monopolizing radio communication through the control of the manufacture or sale of radio apparatus. A further clause to restrict monopoly would prevent the interstate transportation of vacuum tubes or other radio apparatus carrying any prohibitions or restrictions on their use or bearing any fixed sale price. All stations would be licensed for five years, and the license would in no way constitute ownership of the airwaves.

The attempt to modify the language of the clause dealing with advertising was not successful, and, if anything, it was strengthened. The revised section required radio stations that received any service or money, directly or indirectly, to announce the person or firm paying for the service.

An added provision made it necessary for at least one concern in each state to be allowed the privilege to operate one or more radio stations.[131]

Secretary Hoover was not completely happy with the monopoly provision. He was aware that if a company like the Radio Corporation of America was found guilty of a small offense, all international communications by the United States would be placed in jeopardy. Boyd B. Jones, an attorney suing for infringement of the Canadian inventor Fessenden's patents against the big three radio manufacturers, wrote the President to support the monopoly part of the legislation. Hoover responded to the President's inquiry on the matter by writing to Coolidge's secretary:

> So far as Jones' letter relates to the radio legislation now pending in Congress I know that it is much the same type of representation as he has made before the Committee now considering this legislation. The proposals which he makes in respect to radio legislation in effect would make the Secretary of Commerce a prosecuting official of the Government to determine and prohibit combinations in restraint of trade, a position which I have consistently opposed as it is my belief that these matters must be left to the Courts, and that no Administrative official should be substituted for the Courts in these matters. The radio bill now before Congress does provide for the denial and the revocation of a license to any concern which has been found guilty by a court of illegal practices in violation of the anti-trust laws. This itself is a very drastic provision, for if applied to the Radio Corporation of America, against whom Jones' action lies, it would mean the destruction of the international and transoceanic radio services which it now carries on with many parts of the world and upon which our people rely for valuable public service. It is indeed the only competition for the cables. To destroy it would leave the cable in undisputed possession of the field. Obviously a punishment as drastic as this and with such far-reaching public effect should not be involved except in the most extreme case and then only after a proper judicial ascertainment of guilt. Substitution of the Secretary of Commerce to make these determinations would be a violation of the whole administration of justice.[132]

The National Association of Broadcasters, whose president was Eugene F. McDonald of Zenith which had precipitated the current situation, was now becoming concerned about who would be given the control over radio broadcasting. The *NAB Bulletin*, dated February 5, 1926, stated:

> The pivotal point in Radio Legislation seems to rest upon what authorized person or body shall say who shall broadcast and upon what wavelengths and hours of operation. Obviously, there are three logical suggestions, namely:
>
> 1. A government official, such as the Secretary of Commerce.
> 2. A Committee of outstanding citizens.
> 3. A permanently employed commission.
>
> Let us analyze these. Suggestion No. 1 has the disadvantage of placing unusual power in the hands of one person, but has the advantage of undivided authority, supported by the data gathered by an extensive Government organization. Suggestion No. 2 has the disadvantage of placing great responsibility upon citizens who may not be qualified, or whose interest would not be sufficient. If employed in an advisory capacity to

the Secretary of Commerce, it has the advantage of softening any criticism which might arise from decisions by the Secretary of Commerce, or of moderating decisions. Suggestion No. 3 has the disadvantage of establishing another Government commission, and would find objection in the minds of those legislators who are opposed to commissions in general. It has the advantage of requiring a number of minds to meet before rendering decisions, and if organized upon a permanent basis would undoubtedly attract competent men who would give their whole time and attention to the problems which would be submitted to them.

The Department of Commerce is paving the way for a fair and impartial handling of future broadcasting licenses, through adopting the policy of issuing temporary permits for present broadcasting. Therefore, if a radio law is passed, whatever authority is created for handling of radio problems will have a free hand in handling the situation.

The question is, what form shall this authority take.[133]

Judge Stephen B. Davis, Solicitor for the Department of Commerce, replied to an inquiry from a J. C. Cooper on March 8, 1926, on the status of the proposed legislation:

> The White Bill was very thoroughly considered in committee and all of the committee with one exception, joined in the report recommending its passage. Judge [Ewin] Davis of Tennessee, ranking Democratic member on the committee, made a minority report urging the creation of a communications commission with much broader powers than those contemplated in the proposed bill....
>
> The Senate Committee had had rather extensive hearings on the Dill bill, the theory of which is much the same as the White Bill in the House, although the two differ in detail. The Senate Committee has made no report, and, so far as I know, has come to no conclusion. I rather imagine that if the White Bill does pass the House this week, some attempt will probably be made to reconcile its provisions with those of the Dill bill and that we may thus get some legislation. The time, however, is very short and inasmuch as this is the first time that radio legislation has been before the Senate, it requires a considerable amount of study and consideration by the Senate Committee.[134]

The White Bill passed the House on March 15 by a 218 to 124 vote. The measure was then sent on to the Senate Interstate Commerce Committee for consideration.

S. 1 and S. 1754, Howell and Dill Bills. S. 1 and S. 1754 were designed to grant to the Secretary of Commerce the power to issue licenses to "any applicant who will render a public benefit, is needed in the public interest or convenience, or is contributing, or will contribute to the development of the art of radio."[135]

Davis testified on the censorship provision:

> Frankly, I do not think there is anything in the act which will give the power of censorship. I fully agree that there should be nothing to give the Secretary the power of censorship, and it is perhaps wise to give this formal declaration of that policy. Anyway, that is the purpose of this section.[136]

Zenith's and NAB president McDonald, whose WJAZ was on an unauthorized wavelength for two months, testified before the Senate committee on March 2. He stated that WJAZ had defied the government only for the purpose of bringing to the attention of Congress the need for legislation. His attorney, Irving Herriott, then stated that any proposed legislation that might be enacted into law would be unenforceable unless Congress first confiscated the air, or the ground, for the purpose of radio. He thought the Constitution would have to be amended. Herriott pointed out that it would be particularly "unAmerican" to vest in any one man, or officers of the government, the right and power to control the air. He supported the formation of a commission.[137]

Sen. James E. Watson, a Republican from Indiana and chairman of the Interstate Commerce Commission, said that he expected a radio bill would soon be offered to the Senate for a vote. However, the pressure of other legislation and further argument on the form of the legislation kept the various radio bills from being expedited. During this lag it was rumored the Senate committee handling the bill wanted radio jurisdiction placed within the Interstate Commerce Commission and the removal of all control from the Secretary of Commerce.

A letter from Sen. Watson to Herbert A. Luckey of the National Broadcast Listeners League in Indianapolis lent credence to this. The letter made it obvious that Senator Watson was proposing legislation designed to remove all power from Secretary Hoover. He wrote that the suggestion of transferring radio to the Interstate Commerce Commission had been made by several witnesses at the hearings and that a prominent official in the Department of Commerce, referring to Hoover, stated that no one man should have the power over radio as provided in the two bills.[138]

Secretary Hoover came out against the concept of a communications commission. He wrote:

> The suggestion of a general commission, which would license and have regulatory power over all systems of communication, whether by radio or wire, including telephones, telegraphs and cables, raises extensive and serious questions, which have no place in a bill devoted to radio control. It would mean a commission for communications with powers much greater than those of the Interstate Commerce Commission over railroads and introspective of merits, it would be impossible to obtain for it the necessary consideration at the present session of Congress.

The White Bill makes no attempt to regulate the internal affairs of the radio stations. It is confined almost entirely to the providing and control of air channels and the prevention of interference. To widen its scope to the general regulatory field might seriously jeopardize its passage.

I believe firmly in an administrative commission such as is created in the White Bill to which could be referred all matters of a controversial nature which arise in the administration of the laws by the Secretary of Commerce. I suggested that this commission be given the power of appellate review and this was included in the bill as it passed the House. A commission of this kind would meet only as occasion demands, probably not over ninety days in any year, would operate at small expense and without cumbersome machinery.[139]

S. 3668, the Borah Bill. After the Zenith decision, the movement to wrest control of radio from the Department of Commerce reached a peak. Sen. Borah introduced a bill, S. 3668, on April 24, 1926. Its introduction came as a complete surprise because, as chairman of the Foreign Relations Committee, Borah had not been known to be concerned with radio. Although Borah was not to be a central figure in the final law's passage his great influence motivated the Senate to definitive action. Borah's involvement stemmed from his opposition to monopoly. Borah's proposed bill contained the strongest anti-monopoly and antitrust provisions ever written into a radio bill. Although never formally considered by the Senate, Borah's bill was the catalyst for discussion and led to the eventual passage of the 1927 Radio Act.[140]

It was reported in the *St. Louis Globe-Democrat* on April 25 that the Borah effort was an anti-administration bill, inasmuch as the White Bill lodged the power with Hoover and a suggested advisory commission. Borah's bill would have formed an independent commission of three members, each of whom would receive a salary of $10,000 a year, and be required to devote their full time to the work.

Some of Borah's opponents said he had given so little time to the subject that he himself could never have written the bill. This bill seemed to serve notice to the Senate that he would block any measure which did not meet with his approval. The Borah bill supported the Commission issue, forcing the Senate and administration to reconsider their opposition.[141]

In some quarters it was considered a coincidence that Borah's bill took power away from Secretary Hoover during the period when there was some talk of Hoover's so-called presidential hopes. However, Borah's effort was just too late and his bill had to give way to the legislative debates of July and December 1926.

Sen. Dill was also preparing another bill designed to take the power over radio away from the Secretary of Commerce. The White Bill was spoken of as an administration bill.[142]

Herriott, Zenith's attorney, went on the attack against Hoover's possible control of radio in a broadcast on WJAZ:

> There is pending in Congress a bill to regulate radio known as the White Bill. The bill effectively places in the hands of Hoover, a single individual, the sole and arbitrary power to regulate this great new factor in our daily life. It gives him the power to say to one man, "I do not approve of you and you cannot operate a station and use the free air" and to another "you may operate without restrictions." It may very well be that certain persons should have the right to use the air and that others should not, but I say to your fellow citizens of this country, it is contrary to the principles of our Government to place such unlimited dictatorial powers in the hands of one man. The Secretary evidently wants that power.... We should have a Commission and we can have one immediately. The Secretary of Commerce will say the White Bill provides for a Commission. Yes, that is true, but the commission provided for in the White Bill is a mere makeshift and is subject to the domination and by the terms of the bill will be practically dominated by the Secretary of Commerce. The sort of law we want and should have is one which will take away entirely from the Department of Commerce the right to regulate radio and place it in the hands of a Commission functioning after the manner of the Interstate Commerce Commission which regulates our railroads. By misinterpreting the decision in our case the Secretary of Commerce is apparently endeavoring to excite the members of Congress to the point where they will pass the White Bill as an emergency measure, when in truth and in fact there is no emergency.... The best way to safeguard our rights is to place the power to regulate radio in the hands of an independent commission and I urge all of you ... to write to your representatives and senators and impress upon them the importance of seriously considering the vesting of this power in a commission in preference to putting it irrevocably in the hands of the Secretary of Commerce or any other single officer of the Government. I trust that the Congress will not and I believe it will not allow itself to become excited over Hoover's ridiculous assertions of his loss of power, and hurriedly and ill advisedly pass the White Bill....
>
> In closing I want to publicly ask this question of Hoover: "Why do you object to giving up your authority over radio, and having that authority rested in an independent commission?"[143]

White Bill Versus the Commission Bills. President Calvin Coolidge had gone on record in 1925 as disapproving the creation of any more independent commissions. His statement restated a letter Hoover had sent to him. Coolidge's strong opposition against an independent commission also came about because of grievances he had with some independent agencies in his administration.

Hoover's and Coolidge's position was strongly opposed by the Senate Interstate Committee considering radio legislation. Sen. Joseph Robinson charged that executive control of radio would mean "full publicity for Coolidge speeches, while political opposition would be deprived of the right to speak through the ether to voters."[144]

Secretary Hoover reiterated his opposition to an independent commission:

> Congress has full power to confer the needed authority. The White Bill now before the Senate, which has passed the House, gives the power. There have been suggestions that this authority should be administered entirely outside of the Department of Commerce by a special commission set up for the purpose.
>
> There are three separate functions which must be performed by some Government agency. The first is the determination of who may broadcast. This is a discretionary or semi-judicial authority. I have continually advocated that the use of wavelengths is the use of public property, and that the determination of who should have use should not be in the hands of any one person but should be placed in the hands of a Commission, representative of the different sections of the United States, wholly independent of the Department. Such a commission, to be appointed by the President with the approval of the Senate, is provided for in the White Bill. This board will not need to be in continuous session and will imply but little expense.
>
> The second important function lies in the administration to the decisions of this commission and the minimizing of interference from many causes outside wave conflict. The third is the furthering of development of the art in the interest of the listeners and of the industry. These last two functions are essentially administrative, and in my view should rest in one of the executive departments rather than by creating a new and additional government agency, which would imply considerable additional expense. Moreover, boards and commissions, by their divided authority have always been a failure in administration; they are desirable for discretionary or judicial determinations. The tendency to create in the government independent agencies whose administrative functions are outside the control of the President, is, I believe thoroughly bad.[145]

Attacks on the future role of the Department of Commerce continued unabated and Zenith's McDonald continued to apply pressure with letters to various Congressmen. A form letter passed on by Congressman Rowbottom stated:

> Hoover will control the most potent and far-reaching instrumentality for the molding of public and political opinion that the world has ever known if the White Bill becomes a law!
>
> Before the advent of radio, public opinion was molded and dominated by the newspapers and magazines. Radio today is as powerful a factor in this respect as either. Any large broadcasting station has a greater

circulation than the combined newspapers in the State of Illinois.... Radio reaches into the family circle with the spoken word, and the message is not only delivered to those who can read, but to those who cannot do so. Newspapers realize the power of this new molder of public opinion, and they are acquiring today as many stations as they can, either by direct purchase, or indirect control. Hoover very apparently also realizes the enormous power of the radio.

It would be just as dangerous to vest in one man, control over newspapers and magazines, as to give such power to an individual to control free speech over the radio. If the White Bill becomes a law, Hoover will absolutely control and dominate broadcasting in the United States. As indicative of his power, let me cite to you an example which has come to my attention. The manager of one of the largest and best known broadcasting stations in the United States wrote me under date of April 16th and complimented me upon my stand in my controversy with Hoover, and my support of a radio commission. In spite of this gentleman's opinion privately expressed to me, an appeal was made over his broadcasting station last evening to the people to write their Senators and Representatives, to support Hoover and the White Bill. I have talked with many other broadcasters, most of whom I know because of the fact I organized and was the first President of the National Association of Broadcasters, and almost without exception they have advised me that they were heartily in favor of an independent radio commission, as opposed to the White Bill, but that they did not dare to openly oppose Hoover.

If the Secretary of Commerce is able to exercise such control over the policies of broadcasting stations today, how much greater influence will he have if the White Bill becomes a law and he is vested with the authority which that bill proposes to give to him?...

From the standpoint of the radio industry, one man control is not desirable, and from a political standpoint—most dangerous and contrary to the principles of our Republican form of Government. Even though we may all have implicit confidence in Hoover, he will not always be Secretary of Commerce.[146]

Sen. Dill's second bill (S. 4156), similar to that introduced earlier by Senator Borah, provided for the establishment of an independent commission of five members, and was introduced on May 2, 1926. Four days later the committee sent the bill to the Senate. Speaking on behalf of his bill, Dill explained on the floor of the Senate that the independent commission was being proposed because:

The committee decided that the importance of radio and particularly the probable influence it will develop to be, in the social, political, and economic life of the American people, and the many new and complex problems its administration presents, demand that Congress establish an entirely independent body to take charge of the regulations of radio communication in all its forms.

The exercise of this power is fraught with such great possibilities that it should not be entrusted to any one man nor to any administrative department of the Government. This regulatory power should be as free from political influence or arbitrary control as possible. A commission which would meet only occasionally would gain only a cursory and impotent knowledge of radio problems. It would necessarily be largely dependent on the administrative authority, namely the Secretary of Commerce, for the expert knowledge it would require.[147]

Sen. Dill, like McDonald, felt that 1) radio was enormously powerful and influential, and 2) too dangerous to have under the control of one man (who would be an appointee of the sitting administration). Sen. Dill therefore proposed an independent commission to control radio.

Davis noted that the Senate had substituted other legislation for the White Bill. "It is at least doubtful whether any radio legislation will be passed at this session."[148] But National Association of Broadcasters secretary Paul B. Klugh differed. He estimated, "our guess is that the chances are 90 out of 100 that a Radio Control Bill will be passed before Congress adjourns."[149] He questioned whether "President Coolidge will veto the final bill remains to be seen, and it depends entirely upon what Congress finally passes."[150]

Although the Dill Bill was given to the Senate in May, it did not come up for discussion until the last week (June-July 1926) of the congressional session. It was believed the measure could be passed quickly in the Senate, and the differences between it and the House bill settled in conference in time for the bill to be enacted before adjournment. The plan might have been successful if objections had not been raised by Senator Cole Blease, a Democrat from South Carolina. Asserting he would "want to know the religion of the commission" and whether "they would favor the teaching of evolution by radio" before he would consent, Sen. Blease forced a delay of one day, which prevented the bill from reaching conference until late in the day before adjournment.[151] The Dill Bill was passed in the Senate on July 2, but several members expressed unfavorable opinions about some provisions and hoped they would be made more agreeable in conference with the House. With only a few hours left to work, the conference agreed to disagree and a futile attempt was made to pass an emergency resolution to limit the period of broadcast licenses to 90 days until the enactment of a new radio law. This attempt failed because the Vice President did not have time to sign the measure.

The political ramifications were explained in the *Providence Journal*:

> There is small room to doubt that the action of the Senate committee is tinged with politics. Senator Watson, of Indiana, chairman of the Committee, is a prospective candidate for the Republican nomination for President, and must look upon Secretary Hoover as a possible rival. Senator Borah, of Idaho, whose bill to create an independent radio commission is now before the Committee, like Senator Watson, has no love

for Secretary Hoover. Senator Couzens, of Michigan, a member of the Committee, who was active in securing the Committee vote, is regarded as an anti-administration and anti–Hoover senator. The same is to be said of Senator Howell, of Nebraska, another member of the Committee.

Briefly stated, the anti-administration forces in the committee have taken this method of striking at the President and Secretary Hoover.[152]

President Coolidge made his famous statement, "I do not choose to run for President in 1928" on August 2, 1927.[153] The Republican senators mentioned above did not believe that prosperity would continue and were leading an attack on the administration. W. W. Jermane, of the *Seattle Times,* wrote: "They, therefore, are making plans for an opening that may possibly come, and do not want Hoover, with his genius for straightening out difficult solutions, to have a chance, by settling all radio troubles...."[154]

Hoover applied pressure in the other direction when he asked for an opinion on his regulatory power from Attorney General Donovan. Hoover was serving notice on Congress that they could not hold him responsible for the deteriorating situation in radio, and the broadcast control issue was due to Congress' lack of ability to pass legislation.

More than a few people were unhappy with Hoover's action. Senator C. C. Dill stated:

> When Congress adjourned without legislation, Hoover refused to try to maintain his control of the radio situation until December, although the broadcasters were almost unanimous in supporting such control. Instead, he secured an opinion from the Attorney General declaring he had practically no power and announced he would no longer attempt to restrain broadcasters as he had previously.
>
> This seemed almost an invitation to broadcasters to do their worst.[155]

The *New York Times* editorialized:

> The question is being asked why Secretary Hoover who has worried along with the hoary old 1912 radio control law since coming in to the Cabinet five years ago and still maintained his authority for three months following the Chicago Zenith decision, should have so suddenly called for a showdown from the Attorney General now instead of bluffing it through a little while longer?
>
> It is doubtful if the Government ever so completely reversed its policy or at a critical time more quickly removed its stabilizing influence from a great and growing industry as it did in so precipitately divesting itself of radio control. And this in view of the fact that Congressional relief is assuredly only five or six months away, and that such decisive action as the Government has taken may jeopardize the whole industry.
>
> According to radio men in Washington no one has advanced a plausible reason why the Government should have forced the issue at this

particular time or who could point to any good which might come out of it.[156]

Radio Broadcast magazine presented its explanation for Secretary Hoover's actions:

> There is no doubt in the minds of a number of people in a position to know, that the Department of Commerce might have been able to "carry on" during the summer despite the decision of the Chicago court.
>
> But, smarting from the criticisms of Congress and a number of broadcasters, Hoover did not feel justified in attempting to shoulder the burden any longer. Therefore, he asked the Department of Justice for a ruling on the matter, realizing as he must have, what the decision would be....
>
> There was another factor—one that cannot be found in the record, and which is received with a fine display of scorn by Hoover and his staff of assistants. It is the keen disappointments of Herbert Hoover over the failure of Congress to extend to him a vote of confidence in appreciation of his efforts in bringing broadcasting through its swaddling clothes and teething periods.
>
> Equally disappointing to Hoover was the failure of broadcasters to rally to the defense of the principles to which they unanimously committed themselves at the Fourth National Radio Conference.[157]

Secretary Hoover stated:

> One of our troubles in getting legislation was the very success of the voluntary system we had created. Members of the Congressional committee kept saying, "It is working well, so why bother."[158]

Political considerations obviously had some bearing on Hoover's decision to force the issue between himself and Congress.

Compromise and Legislative Action. President Coolidge's secretary asked Hoover if there was anything the President could do to help obtain the necessary legislation as suggested by Orrin Dunlap, radio editor for the *New York Times*. Hoover replied:

> I do not believe any action is called for from the President at the present time. When we announced the breakdown of control due to the failure of Congress to complete legislation and the decision of the courts I also strongly urged all radio stations to stick to their wavelengths, together with a warning against opening new stations. Furthermore, I have sent word to the stations that they should in case of interference by "pirate" stations try out their common law rights. And, in addition, I have had the departmental agencies urge the various associations of broadcasters, manufacturers, and listeners to organize against "pirate" stations.

Immediately after the breakdown of authority there was, as expected, an outburst of "pirate" stations, both in change of wavelength and new stations, but there was a much less number than we had expected. However, as a result of threats of action in the courts between stations and of active organization of listeners in various localities, and of the denunciation by the press of "pirate" stations, all offending stations have gone back to their original positions except ten or twelve, and of the new stations all but two have so reduced their power and thus their carrying area as to practically eliminate serious interference by them, at least during the summer months. In these cases we shall probably see a temporary solution.

I have thought all along that with a little encouragement the development of public opinion will settle this whole question, and I believe that worst stage of it is gone by. Of course one cannot be certain of anything.

I do not like to see the President make a request which I believe will be at once repudiated by certain stations which are very anti-administration, and which will only result in bitter attacks upon him. And I am sure this will be the case in the particular stations that have not so far indicated their intention to correct their activities. It is much better to let public opinion in their own localities settle these questions than to involve the President in it, and in fact it might even dull the activities of the agencies that are at work at present if he took on the burden of these disputes.[159]

The Department of Commerce received a favorable review in *Radio Broadcast* magazine:

The Department of Commerce, under its present head, has demonstrated its ability to cope with the problem of the regulation of broadcasting. The dictatorial powers lately assumed by the Department are the outcome of the failure of Congress to enact a radio law and do not, in themselves, constitute an argument against future regulation by the Department. We do not favor a commission similar to the Interstate Commerce Commission for the regulation of radio because radio is *not* a public utility, being non-exclusive and non-essential; and second, because a commission consisting of political appointees is both expensive and inefficient.[160]

However, the situation was worsening because some 100 stations changed wavelengths and over 150 raised their power. President Coolidge requested some suggestions for inclusion in his fourth annual address and Secretary Hoover submitted the following letter to Coolidge:

The Department of Commerce has for some time urgently presented the necessity for further legislation in order to protect radio listeners from the interference between broadcasting stations and to carry out other regulatory functions. Both branches of Congress at the last session passed enactments intended to effect such regulation but the two bills yet remain to be brought into agreement and final passage.

Due to the decisions of the courts, the authority of the Department under the law of 1912 has broken down; many more stations have been operating than can be accommodated within the limited number of wavelengths available; further stations are in course of construction; many stations have departed from the scheme of allocation set down by the Department and the whole service of this most important public function has drifted into such chaos as seems likely, if not remedied, to destroy its great value. I most urgently recommend that legislation should be early completed.

I do not believe it is desirable to set up further independent agencies in the Government. Rather I believe it advisable to entrust the important functions of deciding who shall exercise the privilege of radio transmission and under what conditions, the assigning of wavelengths and determination of power, to a board to be assembled whenever action on such questions becomes necessary. There should be right of appeal to the Courts from the decisions of such a Board. The administration of the decisions of the Board and the other features of regulation and promotion of radio in the public interest, together with scientific research should remain in the Department of Commerce. Such an arrangement makes for more expert, more efficient and more economical administration than an independent agency or board, whose duties, after initial stages, require but little attention, in which administrative functions are confused with semi-judicial functions and from which of necessity there must be greatly increased personnel and expenditure.[161]

A portion of this statement was used word for word by the President in his speech on December 7, 1926.

When the second session of the 69th Congress began in December, the proposed bill was expected to be ready for immediate action. The meeting of the House and Senate conferees was postponed until after Congress convened. Some observers interpreted this to mean that Congress was convinced that enactment of new radio laws would be impossible during the session because of the wide differences of opinion. Rep. White stated: "Chances are not good for radio legislation to pass this session."[162] He believed the marked difference between the Dill Bill and his own would halt the advancement of regulation in the conference sessions.

Rep. White then prepared an emergency resolution to try to bring some relief. Sen. Dill also prepared a similar resolution. White sought to restrict all licenses until legislation was passed. Dill's resolution (Senate Joint Resolution 125) provided that licenses were to be restricted to 90-day renewals and that broadcasters had to sign a waiver giving up any claim "to any wavelength or to the use of the ether in radio transmission because of previous license to use the same or because of the use thereof."[163] Hoover approved of the resolution submitted by Dill and it passed Congress on December 8, 1926.[164]

The conferees from the House and Senate met to try to work out a solution to the impasse. With only two months remaining in the short session of Congress, radio legislation seemed unlikely.

The public was aroused by the thought of another summer without legislation and an avalanche of mail descended on Congress. Sen. David I. Walsch of Massachusetts expressed on the Senate floor: "My daily mail is being amazingly inflated by complaints from all sections of Massachusetts, and from other New England States as well, in regard to the present chaos in the radio situation."[165]

Some state legislatures got involved on the grounds that radio had become recognized as an instrument through which general information and educational matters were broadcast. The Vermont Senate adopted a resolution asking that the Vermont congressmen do all in their power to obtain the prompt passage of a measure to protect the owners and users of radio apparatus. Rep. Charles L. Underhill, a Republican, introduced an entirely new bill (H. R. 15909) in the House. It was short, and simply stated that no one should operate any radio transmission apparatus without a license granted by the Secretary of Commerce.[166]

On December 21 the conferees sought the advice of Hoover on a compromise proposal by Sen. Dill that for one year the commission provided for in White's House bill should be given all the functions of the regulatory commission as passed in the Senate. What Hoover advised was not fully disclosed, but it departed from the White Bill's provisions, in which the commission would take a hand *only* on appeal by a dissatisfied applicant from the ruling of the Department of Commerce.

One newspaper commented that "Hoover had cut the ground from under the house conferees by declaring in favor of the essential principle of the senate bill, although he had helped to draft the house bill and had been instrumental in committing the President to support of it."[167]

In the ensuing meeting of the congressional committee, one of the House members was reported to have remarked that "Hoover has run out on us."[168]

Hoover stressed that his position from the start had been that wavelengths should be allocated and licenses assigned by a commission instead of the Secretary of Commerce. There should be a division of functions between administration and judicial considerations. However, Hoover said he was still not in favor of committing the entire regulation of radio to a commission as provided by the Senate bill.

With Hoover favoring one feature of the Senate bill, Sen. Dill pressed the House conferees to agree to his compromise proposal. Rep. White refused to agree to this compromise and advocated reporting an impasse to the House, but was dissuaded by Sen. Watson, who urged negotiations.[169]

On January 14, 1927, President Coolidge met again with the House conferees and was told that agreement was not far away. After a few more sessions, Sen. Dill and Rep. White formed a subcommittee to write a compromise bill for radio control. Eight days later a tentative bill was agreed upon and both White and Dill were assured of its enactment in that session.[170]

Rep. White submitted the Dill-White Bill (H. R. 9971) to the House on January 28, where it was adopted as it came from the subcommittee. The measure was then sent to the Senate where it was subjected to a debate. Sen. Heflin said that the language used in the original Senate bill had been lost.[171]

Sen. Key Pittman of Nevada further delayed action on February 5 by moving to recommit the bill with instructions to the Senate conference to revise its provisions. He insisted that a provision be written into the bill to restrict any claims for vested rights to the airwaves and that the bill be limited to a year, after which Congress could make new laws if desired. Sen. Pittman further charged that the Senate had surrendered to the House when it agreed to allow the Secretary of Commerce to control radio instead of placing a commission perpetually in control as the Senate had originally specified. Senators Dill and Watson argued that the commission would be supreme although the Commerce Secretary was in technical control.[172]

Efforts to get a vote on the radio bill failed on February 7 and the Pittman effort to get the bill recommitted was not successful. Focus on an upcoming McNary-Haugen Farm Bill forced abandonment of attempts for immediate passage of the radio bill. Senators Pittman and Howell stated that they were not filibustering and only desired to convince the Senate of the bill's defects.[173]

Sen. Dill was becoming apprehensive when he predicted that within five months there would be more than 1,200 broadcasting stations on the air making ordinary receiving sets worthless except for local programs.[174]

By February 17 the measure was back on the floor, but there was no vote because of other business, and opposition was mounting.[175]

Attacks were again mounted on the bill by Senators Pittman, Howell and Blease. Arguing that there was nothing in the measure to prevent monopolies or broadcasting stations from charging for programs, Sen. Pittman suggested a temporary control requiring the Secretary of Commerce to cease issuing licenses to stations and to refuse modification of wavelengths. Sen. Howell predicted a monopoly of the air, and Sen. Blease said, "In less than two years the air will be controlled for political and partisan purposes."

However, late on the afternoon of February 18, Sen. Dill was able to call for the vote. The Dill-White Bill passed the Senate without a recorded vote and without a change in its wording.[176] The bill was signed by President Coolidge on February 24, 1927, making the Radio Act of 1927 the official radio law.[177]

Each of the influential broadcast entities lobbying for their interests received their share of broadcasting in proportion to their political influence. The major broadcast players ended up better off than they would have been under some other possible alternative arrangements.[178]

The day of the signing Hoover issued a statement on the procedures to be followed by station licensees until the Commission was formally appointed. He said, "The completion of the radio legislation makes it possible to eventually clear up the chaos of interference and howls in radio reception."[179]

"President Coolidge ... asked me [Hoover] to select its [the Commission's] members, which I did. They were all men of technical and legal experience in the art, and none of them were politicians."[180] Hoover had his personal secretary, George Akerson, write to people who asked to be considered as Commissioners. Akerson sent the following response to one such candidate, a William Shaforth:

> Some time ago the Chief [as Hoover was called by his friends and staff] received a letter from you regarding a possible appointment to the Radio Commission. At that time the make-up of the Commission had practically been decided upon. Moreover, the Chief thought that you would not find the work particularly pleasing because of the situation which was then developing in Congress. As you perhaps noticed, the Deficiency Bill failed to pass and the Commission has no money to work with. Only three of the five members appointed by the President were confirmed by the Senate and can, therefore, be assured of getting their back salaries next December. The other two can only take chances of getting back pay, since if they are not confirmed it has been ruled they cannot get any money.
>
> The Chief wants me to tell you that he appreciates very much your desire to be of public service, and he hopes that some one of these days something will come along to which he can recommend you.[181]

IV. The End of Broadcast Regulation by the Department of Commerce

Congress adjourned on March 3, 1927, without acting on the finance bill which was to have provided $155,000 in operating funds for the Federal Radio Commission.[182]

An angry Hoover issued a statement a few days later:

> The whole sub-current of the fight over radio legislation during the past two years has been to prevent the radio listeners being dominated by politics, or any other selfish interest in control of broadcasting.
>
> Three years ago the Department of Commerce stated there must be Federal regulation owing to the limited number of wavelengths and therefore the inability of all persons to broadcast without mutual destruction of all service; that this limitation on stations would result directly in a privilege; that the public interest was therefore involved; that the determination of who should exercise this privilege would result in a discretionary or semi-judicial authority which should not rest in any one person or under the control of any political group, region, or otherwise;

that there should be a maintenance of a full representation of local stations distributed throughout the whole of the cities and towns of the country in order that radio should be the agent of distribution of local as well as national talent; that multiplicity of stations is the only guarantee for freedom from control and freedom of expression. In order to attain these objects the Department recommended legislation providing that the determination of who should use the wavelengths and the power that should be applied should be exercised by an entirely independent non-political commission chosen from different sections of the country; that its decisions should be based upon public interest; that there should be an appeal to the courts from decisions of the commission; that the large administration job of putting into effect the decisions of this commission should be vested in one of the existing administrative departments and thus avoid the creation of more duplicating agencies in the Government. The radio industry and radio listeners have consistently supported these views.

All this has at last been accomplished and it is sealed through the appointment by the president of the commission of five absolutely independent men, having no political activities, representing the different sections of the country, each of whom contributes essential expert skill and expertise to the work of the commission.

I am confident that this commission will act at once in the interest of the listeners to energetically clear up the chaos of howls which arise through interference of stations and is the result of the long delay in securing this legislation. As the decisions of who shall use wavelengths must be based on public interest, I have no fear that those many radio stations which have developed high skill and sense of service to their listeners will be fully protected.

The failure of the Deficiency Bill in the Senate deprives the Commission of funds with which to either pay its salaries or other expenses of the Commission. It has been suggested that as the law provides that the Secretary of Commerce shall exercise the powers of the commission in its absence, that the Commission should, owing to this lack of funds, merely assemble and adjourn. As this would defeat the purpose we have all sought, I am inviting the members of the Commission to assemble in Washington, and, if the commission desires, the Department of Commerce will cooperate to the best of its ability in finding some way of enabling it to function through the loan of clerical staff and otherwise.[183]

The Radio Service was separated from the Bureau of Navigation in late March, and placed "under the Secretary's immediate supervision." The administrative duties performed by David B. Carson, Commissioner of Navigation, were turned over to William D. Terrell, who became the Chief of the new division.[184]

The Radio Division of the Department of Commerce. In the first annual report of the Federal Radio Commission, Chairman William Hannah Grubb Bullard stated:

When the commission began its work less than six weeks ago, it was apparent that the first requisite was complete and accurate information as to the actual broadcasting situation. The license applications on file with the Department of Commerce merely showed what the applicants asked for; they did not give any adequate information as to just what power and time each station was actually using, and in some cases they did not even indicate whether the station was actually in operation.[185]

Under the Act of 1927 the Secretary of Commerce still had substantial administrative powers vested in the Radio Division, formerly the Radio Service:

To prescribe the qualifications of station operators and to issue licenses to operators.

To suspend licenses of operators for violation of any law or treaty or of any regulation of the Commission or the Secretary.

To inspect all transmitting apparatus to determine whether it conforms to the law, the regulations, and the license.

To report to the Commission violations of the law, the regulations, or the provisions of the license.

To designate call letters.

To publish lists of call letters and other desirable information.[186]

Thus, administrative authority was still in the hands of the Department of Commerce, while the Federal Radio Commission had the regulatory and licensing authority. The Secretary could refer any matter he felt necessary to the Commission for its consideration.

In addition, the act "provided that one year after the first meeting of the Commission all of the powers and authority vested in the Commission (except as to revocation of licenses) should be vested in and exercised by the Secretary of Commerce." The powers of the Commission were extended twice for periods of one year and finally extended indefinitely in December of 1929. Thus, regulation of broadcasting permanently passed from the Department of Commerce to the Federal Radio Commission.[187]

During the 71st Congress, 1929-30, several radio-related bills passed either the House or the Senate, but none was enacted. H. R. 11635, which passed the House on April 30, 1930, dealt originally with matters of procedure and was amended in the Senate to provide for the transfer of the Radio Division to the Radio Commission. The bill passed the Senate in February of 1931 but the amended bill was not acted upon by the House, and consequently failed to pass.[188]

Senate Joint Resolution 176, which passed the Senate in May 1930, proposed the transfer of the Radio Division of the Department of Commerce to the Federal Radio Commission five months after the FRC was given indefinite tenure. The bill did not pass the House.[189]

The Radio Division became an adjunct of the Federal Radio Commission in 1927. On July 20, 1932, the Radio Division was transferred to the FRC. When the Federal Communications Commission was formed in 1934, the Radio Division became the field staff of the FCC. William D. Terrell became the chief supervisor under the Federal Communication Commission, the same position he had held in the Radio Division.

Secretary Hoover's involvement diminished, which he acidly noted in a letter to a newspaper which sought his assistance in obtaining a license from the Federal Radio Commission:

> I will do what I can in the matter of the radio station, but you know that the Radio Board has no more to do with the Department of Commerce than the United States Supreme Court. They are naturally very jealous that their authority shall not be interfered with by government departments. You must not, therefore, place any anticipation on what can be done except by direct approach to the Board.[190]

The *New York Times* reported that on March 15, 1927, the one-year term of the Federal Radio Commission would end and its powers officially revert to the Secretary of Commerce, "but instead of taking over control of the matters pending before the Commission, Mr. Hoover, in view of the fact that legislation was pending to extend the Commission's existence as a control body ... asked the Commission to continue to function as before."[191]

Secretary Hoover entered his name in the Ohio presidential primary.

The International Radio Telegraph Convention. An invitation by the State Department drew representatives from 79 countries to Washington in October 1927 for a month of conferences to revise the outdated 1912 International Radio Telegraph Conference of London. This conference had been delayed throughout the early 1920s because little agreement could be reached while the radio industry and its development, both technical and economic, kept conditions unstable.

Secretary Hoover, as chairman, gave the opening address. A portion of his statement indicates his general stance on regulation had not changed.

> Regulation of traffic upon the channels of the ether is as essential as the regulation of traffic upon our crowded streets, but equally in both cases the purpose must be to expedite movement, to stimulate progress, not to retard it. Let us see to it, therefore, that we put no harness upon freedom, that regulation does not confine its use and purpose.[192]

Hoover closed the conference by summarizing what had been accomplished.

> In realization of the limited number of channels or wavelengths for communication you will all recollect that at one time it was proposed that

the use of these channels through the ether should be divided among the different countries of the world. That would have been equal to an assignment of different lanes across the seas upon which the vessels of a particular nationality should travel exclusively. It soon became apparent that this solution would lead only to greater confusion, to international jealousies, and to injustice. This conference has found a basic solution by dividing the channels into groups, each group being used for a particular variety in communication....

Of course, in a large sense many of the problems of the conference could be expressed as a reduction of interference. Aside from the broad provisions for the orderly arrangement of traffic, detailed regulations to this end have been developed through the requirements as to technical operation of stations, which shall result in learning the amount of present interference, and above all, assure development of the art itself. It will be of interest to the general public to know of the provisions of the Convention as to spark sets, whose interference is so fatal to the broadcast listener. It provides that 12 months after adoption, no more spark sets are to be installed in the world, and that existing sets, within a definite period of years, shall be replaced by continuous wave sets or other more modern equipment, and thereby interference will be greatly minimized.[193]

The conference agreement was submitted to President Coolidge in December, and went into effect January 1, 1929. It standardized the spectrum allocations of radio throughout the world. The radio frequency spectrum from ten to 60,000 kilocycles was allocated to mobile, fixed, broadcasting, special and other services. All nations agreed to use the same bands of frequencies for corresponding services, eliminating interference between different services. The standard of frequency agreed upon was the standard of time, the mean solar second.

The frequency allocations adopted:[194]

Kilocycles (later kHz)	*Services*
10 — 100	Fixed services
100 — 110	Fixed services and mobile services
110 — 125	Mobile services
125 — 150	Maritime mobile for public
150 — 160	Mobile services
	(a) Broadcasting
	(b) Fixed services
	(c) Mobile services
160 — 194	Regional differences allowed for all services within this range

Kilocycles (later kHz)	*Services*
194 — 285	Europe: Air mobile services
	Air fixed services

Kilocycles (later kHz)	*Services*
	Fixed services
	Broadcasting
	Other: Mobile services
285 — 315	Radio beacons
315 — 350	Air mobile
350 — 360	Mobile
360 — 390	Radio Compass
390 — 460	Mobile
460 — 485	Mobile, except radio-telephony
485 — 515	Distress call and mobile
515 — 1,500	Broadcasting
1,500 — 1,715	Mobile
1,715 — 60,000	Mobile, amateur, experimental

V. Summary

The Department of Commerce in 1926 was refusing to license additional radio stations, creating pressure upon itself from individuals and corporations who wished to enter the growing field. The Fourth National Radio Conference, which approved the restrictions on licensing, was composed of established broadcasters. Those who wanted to become broadcasters did not feel this regulation was binding on them.

The Zenith Radio Corporation, which obtained a license in 1925, was restricted by the lack of frequency space to two hours of operation a week and promised satisfaction with the arrangement. Zenith then pressed for increases in broadcast time or another frequency. After applying for Canadian frequencies and being denied, the company's station, WJAZ, began to operate on a Canadian frequency without permission. The Department of Commerce initiated court action in April of 1926. The Court found that the Department of Commerce had no right to enact regulations other than those prescribed in the Act of 1912 and could not, therefore, limit a license as to frequency.

Because Congress failed to act upon the radio regulation bills that were before it, and because of the attacks on the administration throughout the debates, Secretary Hoover surrendered all semblance of radio control. This was an effort to get Congress to act. But there was no action and the attacks upon administration measures continued unabated. Hoover forced the issue by requesting an opinion on his powers from the Attorney General. The

Attorney General's opinion supported the WJAZ Zenith Company decision and reduced the powers the Department of Commerce had exercised to the issuance of licenses.

With this decision, at least 100 stations changed frequencies and more than 200 were issued licenses even though there was no room on the crowded airwaves. This created chaos.

The main difficulty in achieving legislation was the question of which agency should control radio regulation. Secretary Hoover compromised his stand of keeping the control within the Department of Commerce. He agreed to an understanding which placed some administrative control in the Radio Service and left regulatory and licensing control with an independent commission. This brought about the passage of the Radio Act of 1927.

The Radio Service became a separate division within the Department of Commerce and worked closely with the Federal Radio Commission. Control was never completely returned to the Department of Commerce as specified in the Act of 1927. Eventually, the Radio Division became an adjunct of the FRC. The FRC became the Federal Communications Commission in 1934.

The final chapter will review the six years of broadcast regulatory development as it evolved through the Department of Commerce. Individuals and companies had experienced a period of comparative freedom for growth, but now broadcasting was under the complete regulatory control of an independent agency. The legal authority of the government had been clearly established. The outline for regulating the broadcasting industry had developed and been tested in six years of effort by the Department of Commerce and Herbert Clark Hoover.

Chapter V

REGULATION UNDER
THE ACT OF 1927

When broadcasting burst on the scene in the 1920s, the industry had to be invented. The Department of Commerce throughout this period was regulating radio broadcasting under the provisions of the Radio Act of 1912. Because of the limited use of wireless prior to the advent of radio broadcasting, there had been no pressing need for further legislation.

The flood of transmitters (licensing had been pro forma), growing signal interference, swelling complaints, pleas to preserve self-regulation through a series of conferences, expedients like the voluntary rotation of some stations' broadcasting hours and, finally, chaos, culminated in a new radio law.

There has been a lack of in-depth analysis and a great deal of misinterpretation of the events surrounding the development of broadcast regulation in the 20th century. Through this study of the regulatory activities of the Department of Commerce we have discerned its influence and established how the government's regulation of broadcasting evolved. The Radio Act of 1927 was based upon tried and tested conditions and expectations based on six years' experience of regulatory control by the Department of Commerce.

With the advent of broadcasting, the Department of Commerce selected two frequencies (750 and 833 kHz) and licensed all broadcast stations to operate on one or the other of these channels. This limitation soon resulted in those who sought broadcast licenses not being able to transmit without interfering with others. Action had to be taken at the federal level to change this situation.

The Department of Commerce sought to adapt its authority while at the same time working toward a new law that would take into account a different use of the radio spectrum. Twenty bills were placed before the 67th

Congress (1921-23), 13 proposed laws were submitted to the 68th Congress (1923-25) and 18 bills were introduced to the 69th Congress (1925-27), all to regulate radio communication. Secretary Hoover called the various segments of the radio industry together for a series of conferences to try to formulate a consensus in the fledgling industry to establish operational rules and to offer recommendations to Congress for legislation. Hoover and his Department of Commerce personnel laid the technical and legal foundation for commercial broadcasting. They made policy decisions during this period of regulatory development by giving attention to and favoring large, well-funded companies that resulted in the development of corporate capitalistic broadcasting.[1]

The U.S. system of broadcasting was to be built on competition rather than consensus, so any semblance of unanimous industry support was impossible to obtain. The legislative suggestions of the Department of Commerce were not acted upon by Congress until both private and public pressures came together to make it imperative to pass the Radio Act of 1927. Of 51 bills proposed between 1921 and 1926, only the Radio Act of 1927 was to pass both houses of Congress.

While legislation was being either ignored or argued in Congress, the Department of Commerce had to do all it could to regulate broadcasting. The controversy and debate surrounding the form that future regulation was to take was directly influenced by the controls the Department put into effect during the long period of legislative inaction.

We now know that because of the Department of Commerce's excellent work and expertise, the Radio Act of 1927 was able to spell out precisely what the Federal Radio Commission was and what the commission was to do to regulate radio.

I. The Power to Regulate

The Radio Act of 1912 specified that the Department of Commerce would license any form of interstate or foreign communication by radio. The United States Attorney General held in 1912 that the Secretary of Commerce had no authority to refuse to license any station. This interpretation was upheld in the Intercity Radio Company case of 1923. While he had no right to withhold a license, he did have discretionary authority to assign a wavelength for the station's use "to prevent interference." The Department of Commerce began to regulate wavelength assignments and added further regulations specifying hours of operation and limiting the power of stations by adding them to the licenses.

The Radio Act of 1927 specified that the Federal Radio Commission, by licensing, regulated all forms of interstate and foreign radio transmissions and communications within the United States. The commission was given the power to make "regulations not inconsistent with the law as it may deem necessary to prevent interference between stations and to carry out the provisions of this Act: Provided, however, ... such changes will promote public convenience or interest or will serve public necessity...."[2]

The first conviction under the Radio Act of 1927 for operating a broadcasting station without a license and illegally transmitting in interstate commerce was against George W. Fellowes in St. Louis. Fellowes argued that "the air is free for anybody to use." The court understood that radio could not be properly useful "unless some regulation of this sort were enforced to stop every Tom, Dick, and Harry from getting on the air." Sentenced to one year and a day, Fellowes was instead deported because of irregularities in his citizenship.[3] The U.S. courts have continually reaffirmed the federal government's authority to require a license before any person can use the public airwaves. These opinions upheld the constitutionality of the licensing procedures developed by the Department of Commerce.[4]

When he first took office, five years before Congress asserted control of the United States over all channels, Secretary of Commerce Hoover spoke of radio as a "national resource." At the first industry-government conference called in 1922 Hoover stated:

> There is involved, however, in all of this regulation the necessity to so establish public right over the ether roads that there may be no national regret we have parted with a great national asset into uncontrolled hands.[5]

Broadcasting was being considered as analogous to the field of public utilities. Public utilities had traditionally needed regulation because of their unique relationships to the public and the monopolistic character of their operations. The phrases "public interest," "convenience," and "necessity" are found separately in the Transportation Act of 1920, which amended Title IV of the Interstate Commerce Act of 1887. However, the combined wording of the phrase "public interest, convenience, and necessity" as found in the Radio Act of 1927 does not appear in any earlier legislation.[6]

Secretary Hoover was told when he took office that the demand for broadcast licenses, using the then limited technology, would soon exceed the supply in the spectrum space. The justification for government regulation was to become obvious to all and became known as the "scarcity principle." Some choice would have to be made between competing applicants. Hoover said:

> Because of this situation there is growing up a demand for the limitation of the number of stations in a given area, and that such a limitation would be based on the service needs of the community just as public utilities are generally limited by the

rule of public convenience and necessity. The public interest
of radio broadcasting is rapidly widening.[7]

This is one of the earliest references to what was to become the genesis of the idea of the public interest as the basis for licensing radio stations.
Hoover often used the term "public interest" in reference to radio. He
asserted that radio had become a "public concern impressed with the public
trust" and its use should be considered primarily "from the standpoint of the
public interest to the same extent and on the same basis of the same general principles as our other public utilities."[8] Use of this language by Hoover
and his Department of Commerce staff helped Congress to settle on the
phrase "public interest, convenience, and necessity" in subsequent legislation. The Federal Radio Commission was given broad discretionary authority because of that standard when that legislation was tested in the Supreme
Court. Radio, it was held, devolved from the commerce clause of the Constitution. Intrastate, as well as interstate, control was necessary in the national
interest. The federal government must license stations within state boundaries because radio waves inside a state affect the radio waves crossing state
lines.[9]

II. The Radio Commission

The Radio Act of 1927 created a Federal Radio Commission, which for
a period of one year was to be the original licensing authority. After one year
the Secretary of Commerce was to reclaim the licensing authority and the
commission was to become an advisory and appellate body to the Department of Commerce. This was a compromise between the Republican-dominated House, which supported Hoover's desire to keep regulation in the
hands of the Department, and the Senate, where a coalition of Southern
Democrats and Midwestern Progressives insisted on a new independent regulatory agency.[10]

Within one month of becoming Secretary of Commerce, Hoover stated
in March 1921 that "one of the misfortunes of our present Government structure, and one which needs constructive thought is that we have no bureau or
central organized authority for dealing with the communications question."[11]
It was necessary to develop a bureaucracy as government activities developed.
Eugene T. Chamberlain, Commissioner of Navigation from 1908 to 1921, had
drawn up a bill in 1915-16 that provided for an advisory committee to assist
the Secretary of Commerce on communication issues. When Rep. White
proposed new legislation just prior to the First National Radio Conference,
Hoover suggested the advisory committee be added to its provisions, which
was done. But it was limited to an advisory role:

Experience has shown that there must be complete authority in one department to control all stations both Governmental, and non-Governmental. Without such unified control, radio regulation becomes hopeless....[12]

In 1925 Hoover clarified his position:

I have both before Congressional committees and in at least a half a dozen public addresses stated that no one official should dictate who is to use the radio wavelengths, and I have for years advocated that this being a semi-judicial function it should be placed in the hands of an independent commission.[13]

Secretary Hoover meant that an "independent commission" with regulatory power and making discretionary decisions should still be vested in the Department of Commerce. In testifying on a proposed bill in January 1926, Hoover said:

The bill provides for a national commission of nine members to which may be referred any question upon which the Secretary of Commerce desires their judgment. There are many purely administrative questions in the detail of administrative regulation ... which may properly be left to the judgment of a single official. But there are other broader and more important matters, ... which involves a large element of discretion and in which it is wise to have a consensus of several minds. Such decisions, especially where the questions become controversial, should properly be made by a board rather than an individual. [14]

Hoover's concept would provide political cover for unpopular actions which would be necessary. The move to consider an independent commission that would regulate all communications (wired and wireless) which was to become reality in 1934, did not receive Secretary Hoover's support. He came out strongly against a completely independent commission with total regulatory powers. His opposition appears to have territorial overtones. In March 1926 he said:

The suggestion of a general commission, which would license and have regulatory power over all systems of communication, whether by radio or wire, including telephones, telegraphs and cables, raises extensive and serious questions, which have no place in a bill devoted to radio control.[15]

Hoover felt complete control by another bureaucracy would conflict with the department's ability to handle the problems it faced. He strongly supported the concept of an advisory commission as opposed to one with regulatory powers.

I believe firmly in an administrative commission such as is created in the White bill to which could be referred all matters of a controversial nature which arise in the administration of the laws by the Secretary of Commerce.[16]

Hoover had experience with an advisory commission when he set up the Interdepartmental Radio Advisory Committee (IRAC) in March of 1922 to oversee governmental broadcasting interests. The IRAC extended its activities in 1923 to cover all matters pertaining to governmental radio. In the Radio Act of 1927 the radio stations operated by government agencies were not subject to licensing by the FRC. After he became President, Hoover turned such matters over to the IRAC, which still has that function.

Hoover wrote President Coolidge late in 1926:

> I do not believe it is desirable to set up further independent agencies in the Government. Rather I believe it advisable to entrust the important functions of deciding who shall exercise the privilege of radio transmission and under what conditions, the assigning of wavelengths and determination of power, to a board to be assembled whenever action on such questions becomes necessary. There should be right of appeal to the Courts from the decisions of such a Board.[17]

Secretary Hoover's proposal of an advisory appellate body to the Department of Commerce's regulation of radio was supposed to become a reality. Had the Radio Act of 1927 not been extended by Congress to March 6, 1929, and then again to December 31, 1929, and finally made of indefinite duration later that month, he would have achieved his goal.

The Radio Act of 1927 provided a check on the actions of the commission by allowing appeals to the Court of Appeals of the District of Columbia. During the Department of Commerce's regulation of broadcasting, only two court appeals were made by unhappy applicants. Both were successful in challenging the department's powers: the 1923 Intercity Radio Company case and the 1926 Zenith WJAZ case.

The organizational structure the Department of Commerce had developed to regulate steamboat inspections was adapted for radio station inspections. The Bureau of Navigation had nine offices, located primarily in port cities. After the Second Radio Conference stations were placed into five nationwide zones. The Radio Act of 1927 divided the United States into five zones with a commissioner appointed from each zone. Although not geographically the same, the Department of Commerce used the zoning system for years.

Specific Powers of the Federal Radio Commission. There were a number of specific powers granted to the Federal Radio Commission under the Radio Act of 1927.

To CLASSIFY STATIONS. The Department of Commerce had begun to classify stations when it began to license broadcast stations on two frequencies in 1921. In 1922 the Department no longer would allow amateur stations to "broadcast" weather reports, market reports, music, concerts, speeches, news or similar information or entertainment. So, it instituted a class of stations known as "broadcast" stations to transmit a specific type of programming no longer permitted other stations.[18]

To Prescribe the Nature of the Service to Be Rendered. The classification of stations was to be by the type of service rendered. John F. Dillon, radio inspector from California and later one of the first members of the Federal Radio Commission, suggested in 1922 further classification within the broad designation of "broadcast" stations. He proposed that stations be further defined according "to the character of the matter which it is engaged in broadcasting,"[19] and that better class stations be given another frequency other than 360 meters. David B. Carson, Commissioner of Navigation, supported this plan and Class B stations were authorized to operate on 400 meters. The Class B station was specifically regulated as to programming and mechanical reproduction.

To Assign Frequencies to Stations or Classes of Stations, to Determine Power and to Allocate Time of Operation. Dillon's early suggestion that a new class of station be given another wavelength and higher power was implemented by the department. This was necessary because the time-sharing requirements being enforced by the Department of Commerce on the available two frequencies were becoming intolerable. Class B station proliferation on 400 meters quickly made time-sharing for that class necessary as well. [20]

The Department of Commerce answer to the congestion problem was to clear a complete band of frequencies from other use (such as the Navy) and assign specific wavelengths within that band to broadcast stations. This band was then divided into classes with specific frequencies for each class and a maximum designated power. Should there be more stations than frequencies in any locality, stations were required to share time.

To Determine the Location of Classes of Stations or Individual Stations and to Establish Zones to Be Served by Stations. The Department of Commerce assigned specific frequencies to localities or zones. An effort was made to have no more than two stations for each frequency within a geographic area. However, without the ability to refuse licenses the Department of Commerce was forced to require time-sharing when more than one station sought to use an available frequency. Experimentation by high-powered stations was permitted by the Department of Commerce only when those stations were constructed outside of metropolitan areas.[21]

To Regulate the Apparatus to Be Used with Reference to Its External Effects and the Purity and Sharpness of Emissions. Class B stations were required to use specific types of apparatus, signaling systems and antenna structures. The Bureau of Standards also worked on technology to measure wavelengths accurately and to keep stations on frequency by narrowing transmissions. Class D stations (developmental) were even more stringently controlled technically. The department worked with the radio industry on other technical problems, such as controlling interference caused by regenerative receivers and piezo-electric crystal control of transmitters.

TO MAKE REGULATIONS TO PREVENT INTERFERENCE. The Radio Act of 1912 specified that the Department of Commerce was responsible for "preventing or minimizing interference."[22] The Department of Commerce used this clause as the legal justification to impose its regulations.

TO MAKE SPECIAL REGULATIONS APPLICABLE TO CHAIN BROADCASTING. Although "chain" (network) broadcasting on a regular basis was still a novelty during most of the 1920–1927 period, Hoover was persuaded to support the concept. By allowing experimentation with radio relay, wire interconnection and rebroadcasting, the Department of Commerce saw such activities as hopefully diminishing the need for many stations and demand for licenses. Hoover saw little danger in networks, so little specific control over their operations was given to the Federal Radio Commission.

Specific Limitations on the Commission. The Radio Act of 1927 limited the commission on certain issues. Congress also gave the commission some options in areas it felt had not been effectively addressed during the Department of Commerce's attempt at regulation by consensus.

MUST PROVIDE EQUAL SERVICE TO ALL PARTS OF THE COUNTRY. The Department of Commerce had established zones for certain localities limiting the number of frequencies available in major cities. They refused to license stations on any wavelength that was in use in a nearby community. Time-sharing increased the number of stations which could go on the air, but it was an unsatisfactory solution. Congressmen from sparsely populated areas of the country wanted their constituents to have access to as many stations as were licensed in or near heavily populated communities. This political demand was found unworkable by the subsequent regulatory bodies.

COULD MAKE REGULATIONS ONLY WITH CONSENT. Congress bowed to the concept of consensus by legislating that changes in wavelengths, authorized power, the character of emitted signals or the times of operation of a station could not be made without the consent of the station licensee. Consensus and voluntary cooperation came from the many industry-wide and individual conferences called by the Department of Commerce. This impractical precondition was nullified by a qualification strongly supported by the Department, "unless in the judgment of the commission, such changes will promote public convenience or interest or will serve public necessity...." This escape hatch gave the FRC the ability to regulate when it was obvious that giving licensees a veto power was not practicable.

COULD NOT LICENSE ANTITRUST VIOLATORS. Hoover had stated strong opposition to the concept of "monopoly control" and pledged "broadcasting will not cease and neither will our public policy allow it to become monopolized."[23] He felt current antitrust law was sufficient and opposed stronger antitrust provisions in the radio law. United States companies would be at a disadvantage in international communications if they could lose their licenses for some minor violation which did not apply to foreign businesses. Even if individuals or corporations through patent control could monopolize the equipment, Hoover knew in 1924, "the Government can prevent them from using the ether, and thus destroy the value of the apparatus if it chooses."[24] To discourage potential monopolies, the Department of Commerce under Hoover limited the license period to 90 days. There were few practical impediments placed in the path of ever larger communication enterprises. The Department of Commerce was able to control the threat of monopoly in the broadcast industry no better than the succeeding regulatory agencies.

CENSORSHIP BY THE COMMISSION FORBIDDEN. The Department of Commerce took the stance that it had "no power to regulate the matter being broadcast."[25] It was felt that the station owner had the responsibility to program with the audience in mind. However, certain types of programming, notably contests and phonograph record use, were closely regulated. Some radio inspectors applied standards to Class B stations which went beyond those specified by the Bureau of Navigation. Secretary Hoover said:

> The very moment that the Government begins to determine what can be sent out, it establishes a censorship, and almost immediately it will be called upon to discriminate between opera and jazz, fundamentalist and modernist sermons, and so on throughout the whole field of clashing ideas.[26]

Early Federal Radio Commission decisions were based on program content as well as technical matters. The FRC's *2nd Annual Report* noted that program service would be taken into account in the granting or withholding of a license.[27] Stations were required to carry diverse and balanced programming to serve the tastes, needs and desires of the general public.[28] Examples: a licensee who used his station to campaign for public office, attack personal enemies, express personal views and used defamatory language had his license revoked.[29] A licensee was held responsible for the content of sponsored programs when a political candidate during and after a political campaign used profanity in vitriolic attacks on his opponents.[30] In the first judicial affirmation of the FRC's right to revoke a broadcast license on the basis of past performance, Dr. John R. Brinkley's license was not renewed for undesirable programs: Person-to-person communication which ran counter to the definition of Broadcasting in §3(o) when he gave medical advice in response to letters and for advertising a goat gland cure for impotence.[31] The FRC also denied a renewal on the basis of defamatory attacks, undesirable program content and advertising a cancer cure.[32] "Battling Bob" Shuler's license renewal was denied because of attacks on the Catholic and the Jewish religions, the Salvation Army, Christian Science, the courts and a local Chamber of Commerce. The Court of Appeals upheld the FRC's actions as not violating the §109 "no censorship clause" (also §326—*Act of 1934*), because this was not prior censorship but action that came after offending material was broadcast.[33]

CONSTRUCTION PERMITS NECESSARY PRIOR TO BUILDING. The Department of Commerce did not have the right to reserve a frequency for any station. However, Secretary Hoover wrote Senator Kellogg in 1921 that "such permits have some merits as I do not believe any great expansion of the wireless facilities would arise unless there was assurance of the license."[34] The fact that the Department of Commerce did not issue such permits did not prevent certain inspectors from promising frequency space. When licensing was ceased temporarily in 1925, the Department of Commerce still had to issue licenses to those people who had been promised a frequency.

III. Powers Retained by the Department of Commerce

The Department of Commerce involvement with broadcast regulation diminished, but by no means ceased with the passage of the Radio Act of 1927. This law combined a semi-independent agency with the Department of Commerce's newly named Radio Division. Other individuals in the department also continued their involvement with broadcast regulation when they joined the newly formed Federal Radio Commission.

The Radio Act of 1927 created the Federal Radio Commission of five members, appointed by the President with the advice and consent of the Senate. Certain administrative duties were left in the hands of the Secretary of Commerce. The Radio Division of the Department of Commerce was to accept applications for station licenses, renewals or changes. These were then to be referred to the Commission for concluding action. The Secretary of Commerce could refer to the Commission any matter on which he desired judgment. An appeal could be made to the Commission on any decision or regulation made by the Radio Division or the Secretary of Commerce.

The commerce secretary was to license and fix the qualifications of station operator-engineers. He could also suspend those licenses for cause. The Radio Division would inspect transmitting equipment, designate call letters and conduct investigations designed to uncover violations of the Act or the terms of the licenses.

The FRC and later the FCC were given the power to revoke licenses. The FRC in 1927 eliminated stations that were no longer operating, moved station frequencies and required reduced power to lessen interference.

This division of labor was legislated for one year only. The Secretary of Commerce was then to take over all the powers and duties of the Federal Radio Commission, except its power to revoke licenses and its appellate powers. The Commission would become merely an appellate and advisory body of the Department of Commerce.[35]

In the Commerce Department's appropriations request for 1928 the Bureau of Navigation's budget was reduced at its own request. A proposal for ten sub-offices, 28 additional inspectors and other help was not resubmitted. It was expected that the Bureau, because of the founding of the Federal Radio Commission, could return to the Treasury "somewhere between ninety-thousand and a hundred-thousand dollars" from the 1927 allocation.[36]

This structure was a compromise between the views of the Senate and the House. After one year the complexity of the problem made it apparent that only the worst cases of radio interference had been eliminated, so for the next two years Congress approved a year-by-year renewal of the Radio Commission's status.

In December of 1929 the Radio Commission was finally placed on indefinite tenure. It was argued periodically before Congress that the Commission should be abolished and the regulatory powers over radio be returned to the Department of Commerce. Federal Radio Commissioner O. H. Caldwell stated that the Radio Division of the Department of Commerce should be given the Commission's power because it was a more efficient administrative agency than the Commission could possibly be. He rebutted the argument that the Department was not equipped to handle the technical work involved:

> Some questions have been asked as to just what the radio division of the Department of Commerce is. That radio division at present [1929] consists of 135 people, in comparison with the Radio Commission's present staff of 82 people. The staff of the radio division of the Department of Commerce includes 75 trained radio men, who are competent radio experts, scattered over the country. The radio Commission at this time has only four trained radio men outside of the two officers who have been loaned it by the Army and Navy.... Those men supervise the operation of all of the radio stations of the country, including the ships, the land stations, the broadcasting stations, and 16,000 amateurs.[37]

The Radio Division, under the authority of the Wireless Act of 1910, and as amended in 1912, continued its inspection work of all American and foreign vessels departing from United States ports. The Radio Division also continued its many activities in the field, which included examination and licensing of radio operators; inspection of transmitting stations; making field strength measurements; monitoring radio stations; making investigations of violations of radio laws and regulations; investigating reports of interference or unsatisfactory service; undertaking engineering surveys of applicants' stations; furnishing technical information on radio subjects; and designating call letters.[38]

Other provisions of the Radio Act of 1927 related to requirements for ships at sea, messages between ship and shore stations, time arrangements to prevent interference with government stations, the confidential character of private messages, prohibitions against interception of messages and sending of false distress signals.

The Radio Service of the Bureau of Navigation had been made a separate Radio Division in March of 1927, following the passage of the Radio Act of 1927 which formed the Federal Radio Commission. It was not until nearly five years after the Act of 1927 was passed that the Radio Division was officially made the field staff of the Federal Radio Commission in July 1932.

A combination engineer and administrator was needed to guide the initial efforts of the five-man Commission set up for the task of bringing order out of chaos. Someone was needed who could command attention and respect and who loved radio. From Hoover's recommendation, President Coolidge appointed Ret. Adm. William Hannah Grubb Bullard for a six-year term on the Commission as a representative from the second zone of the five created under the new law. His home was in Media, Pennsylvania.

Admiral Bullard, perhaps more than any other individual, was responsible for establishing the radio industry in the United States on a firm basis. His greatest contributions were from 1912 through 1916 as Superintendent of the Naval Radio Service, and from 1919 through 1921 as Director of Naval Communications.

The dependence of this country on foreign-controlled radio patents became apparent to Admiral Bullard and to other high naval officers during World War I. The Marconi Wireless Telegraph Company of America, a British-controlled subsidiary of the worldwide British Marconi interests, was the leading factor in wireless transmission and reception in this country.

General Electric held key patents adaptable to radio. For several years it had been trying to develop a machine capable of transmitting continuous waves suitable for sending messages across the Atlantic. In 1915 one of its radio engineers, Dr. E. F. W. Alexanderson, perfected his Alexanderson alternator, a machine for generating a powerful high frequency current. Its value was immediately recognized by the British Marconi Company, which sent Marconi himself to the U.S. to try to obtain exclusive rights to the device. A tentative arrangement was made to purchase several of the machines, and the rights to thousands of other radio patents controlled by

General Electric, but before the arrangements could be concluded World War I sidelined the deal.

In 1917 General Electric negotiated with American Marconi for the installation of an Alexanderson 50-kilowatt machine in its high power station at New Brunswick, New Jersey, where this and related devices were to be demonstrated. About this time the Navy Department took over the New Brunswick station for war use and, working with General Electric engineers, installed the Alexanderson apparatus and raised its power to 200 kilowatts.

In 1919 representatives of British Marconi offered to buy 24 of the transmitters for $127,000 each—14 for the American Marconi Company's use and ten for the British Marconi Company. General Electric was unwilling to sell outright and insisted upon a lease arrangement and royalty for the rights, causing some delay in the negotiations.

Commander S. C. Hooper, chief of the Radio Division of the Navy Bureau of Engineering, who understood the value of the Alexanderson alternator, went to Director of Naval Communications Admiral Bullard and voiced his objections to the negotiations between General Electric and British Marconi. Admiral Bullard laid the situation before officers of the General Electric Company.

General Electric officials broke off their negotiations with British Marconi and worked with the Navy Department on an agreement for the formation of a company controlled entirely by American citizens. Bullard was the Navy's key man in those discussions and in the events that followed. While there was some doubt expressed by Secretary of the Navy Josephus Daniels that the execution of such a contract could not be effected without consent of Congress, officers of General Electric went forward with the plan.[39]

The first step toward the formation of the new American radio company was to purchase American Marconi. General Electric also agreed to contribute more than $3,000,000 to the enterprise and to turn over its radio patents and those that might be developed in the next 25 years. In order to expedite the formation of the new American company it was decided to use the American Marconi stations and personnel as a nucleus.

Thus, the Radio Corporation of America was established by General Electric in October 1919. Admiral Bullard, who was so instrumental in its founding, was named the government representative to the board of the Radio Corporation of America (RCA). He retired from the Navy in 1922.

Some six months after he assumed his post as chairman of the Federal Radio Commission, Admiral Bullard died on November 24, 1927.

IV. Radio Commission Becomes Federal Communication Commission

In 1933 President Roosevelt requested his Secretary of Commerce, Daniel C. Roper, to conduct a study of the radio situation. A bill was introduced proposing placing all communications industries, including wire and wireless, under one independent commission. A similar proposal failed in 1926 due to the opposition of AT&T. The Federal Communication Commission came into being with the passage of the Communications Act of 1934.

A comparison of the Radio Act of 1927 with the Communications Act of 1934 shows no substantive changes.[40] The Communication Act of 1934, as amended, has been the major communication law for the last two-thirds of the 20th century.

Some of the members of the Department of Commerce staff continued their involvement with broadcast regulation in the successor agencies.

William D. Terrell, the first radio inspector of shipboard wireless was appointed to the fledgling Bureau of Navigation Radio Service in 1911. He was the chief radio inspector in 1915 and became the chief of field activities of the Federal Radio Commission in 1927. When the Federal Radio Commission became the Federal Communications Commission in 1934, Terrell was named field supervisor. He retired in 1941, but at the request of President Franklin D. Roosevelt he returned to the FCC for two more years of service. He retired again at the age of 72. Terrell died March 24, 1965.[41]

Dr. J. Howard Dellinger of the Bureau of Standards became the first chief engineer of the Federal Radio Commission. Dr. Charles Joliffe, head of the Bureau of Standards from 1922, succeeded to the chief engineer's post when Dr. Dellinger returned to the Bureau of Standards in 1930. Jolliffe moved on to the RCA Laboratories in 1935, later becoming executive vice president and technical director of the company and its laboratories.[42]

George Sterling had lived radio since 1908 when he built his first amateur radio receiver.[43] He served with the Army Signal Corps in France during World War I where he assisted in setting up a radio intelligence service. He became a radio inspector for the Merchant Marines and for RCA. In 1923 he became a radio inspector for the Department of Commerce. He stayed on at the Federal Radio Commission and then the Federal Communications Commission. As a charter member of the FCC staff, he had field responsibilities for the enforcement of radio regulations.[44] In World War II he held the post of Chief of the Radio Intelligence Division. In 1947 he was Chief Engineer of the FCC and in 1948, as a Truman appointee, was confirmed as commissioner.[45] He was probably the last commissioner who could take a radio apart and put it back together. On September 13, 1954, the Eisenhower administration needed to free up a seat on the FCC so he could appoint a Republican as chairman. Sterling unhappily resigned with three years remaining on his second term. He retired to his home at Peaks Island, Maine.[46]

John F. Dillon, radio inspector from San Francisco, was one of the first members of the Federal Radio Commission to be confirmed, but died shortly afterwards. Arthur J. Batcheller, former radio inspector in New York, was then appointed to replace Dillon, but did not pass the confirmation process.[47]

V. Summary

The general impression of historians about the entire beginning of the regulation of broadcasting was that there was both industry and regulatory "chaos." But the Department of Commerce methodically and with great foresight developed, applied and influenced from 1912 to 1927 almost everything that led to the composition and passage of the Radio Act of 1927. Through trial and error the essential ingredients of the regulatory scheme embodied in the Act were refined during the daily operations of the Bureaus of Navigation and Standards of the Department of Commerce and were greatly influenced by the philosophy expressed and promoted by Secretary of Commerce, Herbert C. Hoover.

Some give credence to the "great man" theory of historical study by assigning Hoover the major role in the implementation of the concepts finally adopted by Congress. Others imply that the pressures exerted by the broadcast industry were most influential on congressional deliberations, and there are those who perceive Congress alone being totally responsible for the Radio Act of 1927. Let's explore the three views:

The Role of Herbert C. Hoover.

> Herbert Hoover defined, explained and advocated certain fundamental principles of public policy which are today the accepted foundation upon which our American system of free broadcasting has been built....
> If any man should be called the Father of the American System of Free Broadcasting it is the Honorable Herbert Hoover.[48]

From his experiences in public life Herbert Hoover had developed a personal philosophy of the relationship between government and business. His well-publicized philosophy of individual striving greatly influenced the concepts that were developing about possible regulation. Hoover's role was anything but passive.[49]

The expertise of his staff played a major role in influencing Hoover. The staff of the Bureau of Navigation Radio Service supplied Secretary Hoover with specific suggestions and recommendations on the direction regulation should take. Almost immediately after becoming Secretary of Commerce, Hoover was made aware of the challenges he faced planning for broadcast development. The staff perceived the primary difficulties to be the determination of who was to broadcast, what was to be broadcast, and under what conditions.

Hoover effectively used his position to focus attention on the issues placed on the agenda by the Bureau of Navigation staff, the radio industry and other interests at annual conferences. Hoover spoke out consistently that broadcast regulation must: a) establish service to the public as its paramount characteristic; b) avoid monopoly in the control of facilities but not restrict necessary growth; c) prohibit censorship by both private parties or groups or by the government; d) sustain broadcasting as an area for free and full development by private enterprise; but e) be subject to the degree of regulation necessary to protect the public against abuses.

These concerns are equally relevant for the 21st century. "Radio's early history foretells the Internet's regulatory future. No medium is an island, and certain communications issues are universal: privacy, copyrights, defamation, pornography, fraud, commercialism, anti-trust and parents' prerogatives over what passes home portals."[50]

The Radio Corporation of America conceived of broadcasting as similar to a public utility invested with the public interest and suggested this concept at the First National Radio Conference.[51] Hoover took this concept and developed it further. Hoover had a vast array of concerns to deal with as Secretary of Commerce, including radio. He was able to digest information provided by his capable staff and develop plans and policies that gained him national respect. That Secretary Hoover's thoughts and concepts were so influential reflected his general influence in government and the respect with which he was viewed during the 1921-1927 period.

The Role of the Radio Industry.

> The Radio Act of 1927, the first United States legislation to reflect the existence of broadcasting, was to a large extent the product of the radio industry itself.[52]

Secretary Hoover had the uncanny ability to blend the best of industry into government policy and proposals. That a government official such as Secretary Hoover should "turn for counsel to the most successful elements in the [radio] industry was taken for granted."[53] The Department of Commerce staff observed the industry closely, talked with members of that industry and accepted research conducted by the industry. There were not sufficient funds or staff to conduct a complete clearing of frequencies within the various zones, nor was the Bureau of Standards interested in applied research as much as pure research. Therefore, the Department of Commerce and Secretary Hoover, of necessity, relied upon the industry to assist in determining its direction.

Some scholars mistakenly treat the recommendations of the various radio conferences (composed of members of the industry being regulated) as having developed the actual rules and regulations implemented "in toto" by the Department of Commerce. An example of the misunderstanding of events and mistiming of the elements is illustrated by Laurence F. Schmeckebier who wrote: "The recommendations of the Second Conference promptly received the approval of the Secretary of Commerce, and a new classification of stations was announced April 4, 1923, to be effective on May 15."[54] In actual fact, the Department of Commerce conceived of the classification prior to the Second Conference and asked for the approval of the industry, not the other way around.

The department drafted the agendas for the conferences. Most of the recommendations of the conferences were first suggested by the Department of Commerce. They were then placed on the agenda for discussion, modification and to seek consensus, if possible. The Bureau of Navigation implemented those recommendations it felt they were necessary to prevent interference and provide proper service to the public and ignored those that ran counter to their positions. Because the conference memberships were familiar with the proposed regulations and were unsure of the direction in which broadcasting would develop, the majority accepted regulation by the department with little opposition. The industry insisted on a law only when interference and piracy of frequencies became a strong possibility. The Department of Commerce worked with congressmen and continually called for, revised and developed the legislation upon which Congress finally acted. The department reacted to situations as it devised its regulation.

There was comparative freedom for broadcasting to develop as the Department of Commerce made valiant efforts to handle the problems faced by the industry. The Department of Commerce staff was under pressure as various constituencies demanded help with their immediate problems. Stretching their limits, the department attempted to apply structure to the evolving industry. The serious players generally realized there had to be an enlargement of government power. The 1923 Intercity case had put the department on notice and the 1926 Zenith case provided the final impetus to structure control by the government. It was the industry, as it grew, and the Department of Commerce, as it reacted to this growth, that produced the essential elements that made up the Radio Act of 1927.

Gleason Archer states in commenting on the First National Radio Conference, that:

> Secretary Hoover wittily observed that "this is one of the few instances where the country is unanimous in its desire for more regulation."[55]

The Role of Congress. Walter Emery writes:

> It was definitely established in the Act that the radio spectrum belonged to the public and that a broadcaster acquired no ownership rights in a frequency when granted a license.[56]

Certainly, the Radio Act of 1927 codified this concept. However, the Department of Commerce established this concept, and Hoover had publicly stressed public ownership throughout the Department of Commerce regulation of radio. Hoover stated that there was a necessity to establish "the public right over the ether roads." By keeping license renewals to 90 days the Department of Commerce kept this public ownership at the forefront of its regulatory efforts.

The fundamental hypotheses of the Act were 1) The radio waves or channels belong to the public; 2) Broadcasting is a unique service; 3) Not everyone is eligible to use a channel; 4) Radio broadcasting is a form of expression protected by the First Amendment; 5) The government has discretionary regulatory powers; and 6) The government's powers are not absolute.[57]

All of these elements existed in the Department of Commerce regulations prior to the passage of the Act.

Broadcasting was defined as a "unique service" by the Commerce Department when it was first assigned two frequencies on September 15, 1921. Further classifications also stressed its unique aspects.

Hoover and his staff realized that the greatest problem they faced was determining who would be allowed to broadcast. An advisory commission was created to deal with this problem.

The Department of Commerce always maintained that it had no right to dictate what material should be broadcast and left this to the owners of the facilities.

The Bureau of Navigation assumed discretionary powers over broadcasting when the first wavelengths were allocated. These powers ended in 1925 with the cessation of broadcast station licensing and were legally placed in question with the Zenith case of 1926. For some five years the Department of Commerce had acted with expediency and forethought.

The government's powers were limited. The powers assumed by the Department of Commerce in the actions they took and the powers they sought finally ceased with court action. With the passage of the Radio Act of 1927, Congress codified the Department's powers.

Burning issues of the day—conservation, monopoly and censorship— influenced the Radio Act of 1927 because Congress was dealing with these issues in other legislative acts.[58] These same issues were of central importance in the many other areas the Department of Commerce was responsible for. Congress had as background all the testimony and activities on these issues when it was formulating the Radio Act of 1927. By stressing these particular social concerns, Secretary Hoover focused the attention of Congress on these issues.

Who influenced whom?

The roles of the Department of Commerce, Secretary Hoover, the radio industry and Congress in the regulation of broadcasting were so intertwined that assigning specific cause and effect relationships is too simplistic. However, it has been proven that it was the Department of Commerce staff which discussed, devised and implemented regulation prior to any legislative consideration. Therefore, the Department of Commerce's role must be given more weight than it is generally assigned.

There are examples of insufficient credit being given to the Department. Sydney Head, for example, noted: "In its second year the FRC set up the classification system providing for local, regional and clear channels."[59]

Walter Emery stated: "The Federal Radio Commission established the regular broadcasting band from 550 to 1500 kilocycles, and provided for a 10 kilocycle separation between stations."[60] While these statements are essentially true, the classification of stations and providing them with shared and cleared channels were Department of Commerce accomplishments. The broadcast band was cleared by the Department of Commerce. The Department of Commerce experimented with a five, seven and ten kilocycle separation before settling on the only workable solution: a ten kilocycle separation. This was later formally adopted by the FRC.

The Federal Radio Commission's power to regulate was predated by Department of Commerce's practical application.

Edgar E. Willis wrote:

> In addition to the development of station and network facilities, there were two other requirements for putting broadcasting on a firm foundation. One was the establishment of a system of regulation that would permit the kind of development appropriate to a free enterprise system and which at the same time would protect the public's interest in the use of air channels. This compromise was fashioned in the Radio Act of 1927 and in its revision, the Federal Communications Act of 1934. The second was financial stability.[61]

Between 1921 and 1927 the Department of Commerce established a system of regulation appropriate to a free enterprise system, at the same time protecting the public's interest.

The courts, in reviewing the Federal Radio Commission's powers established in the 1927 Act, held that under the "commerce clause powers" the FRC had the authority to limit or prohibit access, to prohibit transfer of license ownership and to preempt state and municipal regulation of intrastate, as well as interstate, broadcasters. Under "due process standards" the judiciary addressed such issues as public hearings, rules of evidence and appeals process details. The federal courts were supportive of the FRC's authority and willing to define and broaden the somewhat vague wording of the Radio Act of 1927, ultimately enhancing the FRC's ability to regulate broadcasters.[62]

Hoover became the 31st President of the United States in 1928 and served one term in office. His triumphs came to an end with the Great Depression, which began in October 1929, and for which he was hardly responsible, although critics attacked his methods of dealing with the crisis. In 1932 he ran against Franklin D. Roosevelt. By 1932, bank failures, 14,000,000 unemployed and farm distress worked against him, and Roosevelt won the presidency.

In his post-presidential years Hoover continued to be active in public service, most significantly as the leader of the Commission on the Organization of the Executive Branch of Government. Known as the Hoover Commission, two reports were issued (1947-49, 1953-55). The commission made many recommendations dealing with the structure of government, and most were adopted. Some involved broadcasting regulation. The opinion of the Hoover Commission was that:

> The outstanding attribute of the [Federal Communications] Commission today is its lack of a comprehensive regulatory program.[63]

The Hoover Commission of 1955 reported that the FCC had taken corrective action, as suggested, to cut down the amount of paperwork required of broadcasters.

In 1960 Hoover's advocacy of a free broadcast system caused him to testify when Congress was considering revisions of Section 315 of the Communications Act of 1934. One proposal was to require the three television networks to set aside eight hours of prime time for presidential candidates. Hoover opposed this legislation, saying, "My own opinion is that if we are to avoid government censorship of free speech we had better continue the practice of candidates providing their own television and radio programs."[64] This is still a very current issue.

In his later years Hoover received numerous honors from the many facets of the broadcast industry which recognized his role in the development of the American system of broadcasting. Herbert C. Hoover, former Secretary of Commerce and President of the United States, died on October 20, 1964, at the age of 90.[65]

The United States, unlike other nations, viewed the broadcast spectrum in the 1920s as a public domain that all citizens should have access to, much like federal lands and mineral rights. However, unlike federal lands and mineral rights which citizens could access, claim and privatize, the public and political sentiment of the 1920s strongly opposed privatization of the radio spectrum for a variety of reasons. There was a desire to guarantee equal access for all citizens. Ironically, commercialization of the radio spectrum occurred more drastically and thoroughly than with any other public resource. Private ownership of a public resource was enabled by the Radio Act of 1927 and later the Communication Act of 1934 through the licensing system. Licenses allowed the commercial exploitation of the spectrum while simultaneously holding to the concept that the spectrum would never become private property, and therefore would remain "accessible" to all. Changes in technology and ideology have made the concept of property rights, instead of public domain, much more viable in the public and political arena in recent years. This has enabled the government to profit from spectrum auctions and the charging of fees for the use of frequencies. The early fears about protecting equal access to the spectrum have come full circle. The understanding of the spectrum as a "special" resource due to its unique effects on society has led to its continued unique regulation.[66]

Originally, the idea of property linked to broadcasting implied limited government regulation, through which the issuance of licenses and fair market practices, competition would be encouraged. A much more competitive commercial broadcast industry has developed. [67]

It is time not just to amend the current law which came about at the beginning of the 20th century, but because of the changes in technology and ownership, to devise a complete revision.

However, as we have seen through the lens of history, if consensus is required among the competing interests, then such revision may never occur.

NOTES

Chapter I

1. U.S., Federal Communications Commission, *Television Network Program Procurement, Part II*, Docket No. 12782 (Washington, D.C.: U.S. Government Printing Office, 1965), p. 59.

2. Frances Chase, Jr., *Sound and Fury: An Informal History of Braodcasting* (New York: Harper & Row, 1942), p. 4.

3. Orrin E. Dunlap, Jr., *Radio and Television Almanac* (New York: Harper & Brothers, 1951), p. 37.

4. Rexmond C. Cochrane, *Measures for Progress: A History of the National Bureau of Standards* (Washington, D.C.: U.S. Department of Commerce, 1966), p. 68.

5. Elliot N. Sivowitch, "A History of Radio Spectrum Allocation in the United States, 1912–1926" (unpublished master's thesis, History Department, Syracuse University, 1954), p. 6–7.

6. Christopher H. Sterling and John M. Kittross, *Stay Tuned: A Concise History of American Broadcasting*, second ed. (Belmont, California: Wadsworth Publishing, 1990), p. 37.

7. U.S. Department of Commerce, Bureau of Navigation, *Radio Service Bulletin*, no. 117 (December 31, 1926), p. 26.

8. Cochrane, p. 138.

9. *Ibid.*, p. 140.

10. Linwood S. Howeth, *History of Communications—Electronics in the United States Navy* (Washington D.C.: U.S. Government Printing Office, 1963), p. 76–77.

11. Howeth, pp. 118–120. The abbreviation "kHz" has been used for some time in other countries and was adopted by the U.S. National Bureau of Standards, The Institute of Electrical and Electronics Engineers (IEEE), and other American organizations. The *hertz* is the unit of measurement of frequency. One hertz is the equivalent of one cycle per second. Hertz is abbreviated Hz (no period). In accordance with standard procedure, the first letter of the unit abbreviation is capitalized. The usual prefixes can be added to the abbreviation; thus, kHz means the same as kilocycles per second, and mHz means the same thing as megacycles per second. The prime reason for adopting the hertz as the unit of frequency measurement is that it

is a more precisely defined unit less subject to misuse than its predecessor. The hertz, defined as one cycle per second includes the period of time the cycles occur, whereas kilocycles would need the additional statement of "per second" to inform one of the period covered.

The hertz commemorates Heinrich Rudolph Hertz, a German physicist (1857–1894). He discovered radio waves scientifically and devised the Hertz antenna. We know it today as the simple dipole, an antenna not depending on the presence of ground for operation, fed at the center, where current is maximum. The older designation as kilocycles is occasionally used here as well. Of course, sources quoted prior to the use of kHz are unchanged. Also, SOS (Save Our Ship) was discontinued at the end of the century as automated equipment became standard.

12. Sterling and Kittross, p. 37.
13. *Ibid.*
14. Howeth, p. 153.
15. *Ibid.*, p. 154.
16. *Ibid.*, p. 126.
17. Sterling and Kittross, p. 37.
18. Dunlap, p. 39.
19. *Ibid.*, p. 158.
20. Cochrane, p. 140.
21. *Ibid.*
22. *Ibid.*
23. Gleason Leonard Archer, *History of Radio to 1926* (New York: American Historical Society, 1938), pp. 64–65.
24. Walter Lord, *A Night to Remember* (New York: Henry Holt, 1955), pp. 36–38, 171–172.
25. Howeth, p. 163.
26. Sivowitch, p. 8.
27. Howeth, pp. 158–159.
28. U.S. Congress, House, Subcommittee of House Committee on Appropriations, *Hearings on Legislative, Executive, Judicial Appropriation Bill, 1922,* December 20, 1920, p. 1218.
29. Stephen B. Davis, *The Law of Radio Communication* (New York: McGraw-Hill Book Company, 1927), p. 35 (as cited from *Report on Bill 698* to accompany S. 6412, 62nd Congress, 2nd Session, pp. 7–8).
30. *Ibid.*
31. *Ibid.*, p. 36.
32. U.S. Department of Justice, *Radio Communication—Issuance of Licenses*, Opinions of the Attorney General (vol. 29, November 22, 1912), pp. 579–583.
33. Sivowitch, p. 21.
34. Howeth, p. 217.
35. Dunlap, p. 50.
36. *Ibid.*, p. 58.
37. Cochrane, p. 191.
38. For an account of the litigation involving de Forest's audion tube, the British and American Marconi Companies' Fleming valve, the General Electric audion of 1913, and Western Electric's audion of 1917, see Paul Schubert, *The Electric Word: The Rise of Radio* (New York: Macmillan, 1928), pp. 212–214; and W. Rupert Maclaurin, *Invention and Innovation in the Radio Industry* (New York: Macmillan, 1949).
39. Cochrane, p. 192.

40. Erik Barnouw, *A Tower in Babel: A History of Broadcasting in the United States to 1933*, vol. 1. (New York: Oxford University Press, 1966), pp. 39–41, 61.

41. Howeth, pp. 208–255.

42. Cochrane, p. 192.

43. *Ibid.*, p. 194.

44. *Ibid.*

45. *Ibid.*, p. 197.

46. *Ibid.*

47. Barnouw, pp. 52–55.

48. Archer, pp. 165–181.

49. Lee de Forest, *Father of Radio* (Chicago: Wilcox-Follett, 1950), p. 351. This book is occasionally susceptible to some exaggeration.

50. Louise M. Benjamin, "In Search of the Sarnoff 'Radio Music Box' Memo." *Journal of Broadcasting and Electronic Media* (vol. 37, no. 3, Summer 1993), pp. 325–335.

51. *History of Broadcasting and KDKA Radio* (Pittsburgh: Westinghouse Public Relations Department, KDKA Radio, 1966), pp. 4, 10.

52. Susan J. Douglas, *Inventing American Broadcasting, 1899–1922* (Baltimore: Johns Hopkins University Press, 1987).

53. Sydney W. Head, *Broadcasting in America* (Boston: Houghton Mifflin, 1956), p. 108.

54. Cochrane, p. 290.

55. *Ibid.* A photograph dated September 1920 purportedly shows this "broadcasting" station.

56. Cochrane, p. 221.

57. *Ibid.*, p. 225.

58. Herbert C. Hoover, *Memoirs; Volumes I and II* (New York: Macmillan, 1951–52), vol. II, p. 42.

59. *New York Times*, February 25, 1921, pp. 2, 10. This editorial also spoke of Hoover's "dictatorial temper."

60. *Memoirs*, vol. II, p. 42.

61. Cochrane, p. 230.

62. *Memoirs*, vol. II, p. 43.

63. *New York Times*, March 11, 1921, p. 3.

64. *Memoirs*, vol. II, p. 61.

65. *Ibid.*, p. 62.

66. *Time*, January 13, 1967, p. 16.

67. Oswald Garrison Villard, *Prophets: True and False* (New York: Alfred A. Knopf, 1928), p. 28. Highly critical of Hoover.

68. *Memoirs*, Vol. II, p. 42.

69. *Ibid.*, p. 62.

70. *Ibid.*, p. 71.

71. Villard, p. 28.

72. Carl N. Degler, "The Ordeal of Herbert Hoover" (Bobbs-Merrill reprint series) History, no. H-52; from *The Yale Review*, vol. LII, no. 4, Summer, 1963, pp. 563–564.

73. *Ibid.*, p. 564.

74. *Ibid.*

75. Herbert C. Hoover, *American Individualism* (Garden City, N.Y.: Doubleday, Doran and Company, 1922), p. 24.

76. *Ibid.*, pp. 9–10.

77. Lyons, p. 206.

78. Degler, p. 565.

79. *Ibid.*, p. 567.

80. Hoover, *American Individualism*, p. 53.

81. Degler, p. 576.

82. *Ibid.*

83. Villard, p. 25.

84. *Ibid.*

85. Memorandum from Christian A. Herter to Commerce staff, National Archives Record Group 40, March 7, 1921. Hereafter National Archives will be designated NA, Record Group as RG.

86. Memorandum from Walter J. Drake to David B. Carson, NA RG 173, December 15, 1924.

87. U.S. Congress, *Appropriation Bill, 1922*, December 20, 1920, p. 1218.

88. U.S. Congress, House, Subcommittee of House Committee on Appropriations, *Miscellaneous Hearings on Appropriations, 1921*, April 22, 1921, p. 3.

89. U.S. Congress, *Appropriation Bill, 1922*, December 20, 1920, p. 1220.

90. Personal interview with George Turner, April 11, 1968.

91. Letter from David B. Carson to *Radio Broadcast Magazine*, NA RG 40, February 20, 1923.

92. Telephone interview with Charles C. Kolster, May 25, 1968.

93. U.S. Government Printing Office, *Official Register of the United States*, 1926, p. 91.

94. U.S. Congress, House, Committee on Appropriations, *Department of Commerce, 1927*, January 25, 1926, p. 35.

95. *Ibid.*

96. U.S. Congress, House, Subcommittee of House Committee on Appropriations, *Appropriations, Department of Commerce, 1928*, 1927, p. 39.

97. Telephone interview with George Turner, April 11, 1968.

98. Interview, Charles C. Kolster.

99. U.S. Congress, Senate, Committee on Interstate Commerce, *Nomination of C. M. Jansky, Jr., and Arthur Batcheller as Members of the Federal Radio Commission*, February 18, 1929, p. 28.

100. U.S. Department of Commerce, Bureau of Navigation, *Radio Service Bulletin*, no. 69 (January 2, 1923), p. 15.

101. *Ibid.*

102. Interview, George Turner.

103. U.S. Congress, House, Subcommittee of House Committee on Appropriations, *Second Deficiency Appropriation Bill, 1925*, February 10, 1925, p. 199.

104. Interview, George Turner.

105. U.S. Congress, Committee on Interstate Commerce, *Nomination*, pp. 5, 28.

106. U.S. Congress, *Second Deficiency Bill, 1925*, 1925, p. 201.

107. Letter from William D. Terrell to *Radio Broadcast Magazine*, NA RG 40, July 10, 1924.

108. U.S. Congress, *Appropriations, 1928*, p. 74.

109. Letter from Herbert Hoover to Charles G. Dawes, director of the budget, Herbert C. Hoover Presidential Library, West Branch, Iowa, Container No. 1-I/538, March 3, 1922. Hereafter the Hoover Presidential Library shall be designated as HHPL, followed by file or container identification.

110. U.S. Congress, *Hearings on Appropriations, 1921*, p. 4.

111. U.S. Congress, *Hearings on Appropriations, 1922*, p. 3.

112. U.S. Congress, *Hearings on Appropriations, 1926*, p. 39.

113. *Ibid.*
114. *Ibid.*
115. Cochrane, p. 289.
116. *Ibid.*, p. 286.
117. *Ibid.*, p. 289.
118. *Ibid.*, p. 292.
119. U.S. Congress, *Hearings on Appropriations, 1924*, p. 277.
120. Cochrane, p. 242.
121. *Ibid.*, p. 157.
122. U.S. Congress, *Hearings on Appropriations, 1926*, p. 74.

Chapter II

1. Letter from William Downey to Kenneth Gapen, National Archives Record Group 40, May 8, 1932. Hereafter National Archives shall be abbreviated as NA, Record Group as RG, followed by appropriate number designation and date.

2. Erik Barnouw, *A Tower in Babel: A History of Broadcasting in the United States to 1933* (New York: Oxford University Press, 1966), p. 91.

3. The figures for 1921 differ between Gleason L. Archer, *History of Radio to 1926* (New York American Historical Society, Inc., 1938), p. 216; and Hiram L. Jome, *Economics of the Radio Industry* (New York: A.W. Shaw Company, 1925), p. 70. Archer reports 32 total stations for 1921 when they are added up and Jome reports 23. As the Commerce Department itself reports 28 total for January 1922, it seems like Jome's figures are more accurate; however, no complete record for 1921 is extant in National Archives files.

4. Robert W. McChesney, "The Battle for the U.S. Airwaves, 1928–1935," *Journal of Communication* (vol. 40, no. 4, Autumn 1990), p. 30.

5. _____, "Free Speech and Democracy! Louis G. Caldwell, the American Bar Association and the Debate Over the Free Speech Implications of Broadcast Regulation, 1928–1938," *The American Journal of Legal History* (vol. 35, 1991), p. 354.

6. Linwood S. Howeth, *History of Communications—Electronics in the United States Navy* (Washington, D.C.: U.S. Government Printing Office, 1963), p. 382.

7. Census of Manufacturers, NA RG 40, October 9, 1924.

8. *Memoirs*, vol. II, p. 40.

9. *Ibid.*

10. Letter from Herbert Hoover, Jr. to Bensman, April 11, 1966.

11. Report of the Bureau of Navigation, March 1921, NA RG 40.

12. *Ibid.*

13. U.S. Congress, House, Subcommittee of House Committee on Appropriations, *Miscellaneous Hearings on Appropriations, 1921*, April 22, 1921, p. 3.

14. Report of the Bureau of Navigation, March 1921, NA RG 40.

15. Letter from Hoover to Ludwig Hesse, NA RG 173, March 23, 1921.

16. Memorandum from Nagle to Hoover, NA RG 40, May 12, 1921.

17. Letter from Senator Kellogg to Hoover, Herbert C. Hoover Presidential Library, West Branch, Iowa, Container No. 1-I/538, April 9, 1921. Hereafter the Hoover Presidential Library shall be designated as HHPL, followed by file or container identification.

18. Memorandum from Hoover to Dr. Stratton, HHPL 1-I/538, April 9, 1921.

19. Letter from Hoover to Senator Kellogg, HHPL 1-I/274, April 9, 1921.

20. Memorandum from F. C. Brown to Hoover, HHPL 1-I/538, September 21, 1921.

21. Memorandum from Dr. Stratton and Chamberlain to Hoover, HHPL, 1-I/541, April 13, 1921.

22. *Ibid.*

23. *Ibid.*

24. *Ibid.*

25. Letter from Hoover to Senator Kellogg, HHPL 1-I/538, April 23, 1921.

26. *Ibid.*

27. Letter from Richard Emmet to Chamberlain, HHPL 1-I/81, April 13, 1921.

28. Memorandum from Dr. Stratton and Chamberlain to Hoover, HHPL 1-I/541, April 13, 1921.

29. *Ibid.*

30. *Ibid.*

31. *New York Times*, April 19, 1921, 23:4.

32. U.S. Congress, House, *Hearings on H.R. 11964: To Amend the Radio Act of 1912*, Committee on the Merchant Marine and Fisheries, 67th Congress, 4th Session, January 2–3, 1923, p. 18.

33. Letter from Christian Herter to Cooper, NA RG 40, October 8, 1921.

34. *Ibid.*

35. *Ibid.*

36. Letter from Postmaster General Hubert Work to Hoover, NA RG 40, May 3, 1922.

37. *Ibid.*

38. Letter from Hoover to Work, NA RG 40, May 11, 1922.

39. Memorandum from F. C. Brown to Hoover, NA RG 40, September 21, 1921.

40. *Ibid.*

41. Memorandum from Terrell to Hoover, NA RG 40, September 30, 1921.

42. Letter from Paul Drake to Herter, HHPL 1-I/539, August 13, 1921.

43. Letter from Drs. Kennelly and Dellinger to Hoover, NA RG 40, August 22, 1921. See also *Radio Service Bulletin*, November 1, 1921, no. 55, pp. 8–11.

44. *Ibid.*

45. *Ninth Annual Report of the Secretary of Commerce*, Washington, D.C.: U.S. Government Printing Office, 1921, p. 140.

46. *Ibid.*

47. Letter from Chief Signal Office, U.S. Navy to Carson, NA RG 70, November 12, 1921.

48. Letter from Edwards to Carson, NA RG 70, November 17, 1921.

49. *Ibid.*

50. Cited in letter from L. R. Trimm to Arthur Tyrer, NA RG 173, January 27, 1922.

51. U.S. Department of Commerce Bureau of Navigation, *Radio Service Bulletin*, no. 55, November 1, 1921, p. 3.

52. Telegram from Hoover to Maxim, HHPL B-171, August 20, 1921.

53. Letter from Trimm, January 27, 1922.

54. U.S. Department of Commerce Bureau of Navigation, *Radio Service Bulletin*, no. 58, February 1, 1922.

55. Minutes of the First National Radio-Telephone Conference (mimeographed), Washington, D.C.: U.S. Government Printing Office, 1922, p. 106.

56. Memorandum from Carson to Assistant Secretary Huston, NA RG 173, January 27, 1922.

57. Memorandum from Carson to Hoover, NA RG 40, February 13, 1922.

58. Memorandum from Carson to Hoover, NA RG 40, February 20, 1922.

59. *Ibid.*

60. Letter from Huston to Radio Inspectors, NA RG 40, January 11, 1922.

61. "Popularizing Radio—A Double Barreled Scheme," *Radio News,* vol. 4, no. 10 (December 1922), p. 49. In 1928 the forward seeing Gernsback started the magazine, *All About Television.* He also invented the genre of science fiction.

62. Daniel Stashower, "A Dreamer Who Made Us Fall in Love with the Future," *Smithsonian* (August 1990), pp. 45–55.

63. Letter from Gernsback to Terrell, NA RG 40, December 4, 1922.

64. Letter from Carson to Gernsback, NA RG 40, December 5, 1922.

65. Letter from Gernsback to Carson, NA RG 40, December 6, 1922.

66. Letter from Tyrer to Gernsback, NA RG 40, December 8, 1922.

67. Letter from Henry P. Joy, President of Packard Motors, to Hoover, NA RG 40, December 1, 1922.

68. Letter from Hoover to Joy, NA RG 40, December 10, 1922.

69. Letter from Edwards to Carson, NA RG 40, December 10, 1922.

70. Letter from Joy to Hoover, NA RG 40, December 20, 1922.

71. Archer, p. 291.

72. Memorandum filed by the *New York Times* on Intercity Conflict, from file Intercity Case, NA RG 40, May 11, 1921.

73. Hearst's German sympathies are noted in W. A. Swanberg, *Citizen Hearst* (New York: Scribner & Sons, 1961), pp. 298–304.

74. *New York Times,* May 18, 1921, 4:3.

75. Letter from U.S. Attorney Caffey to Hoover, NA RG 40, May 19, 1921.

76. U.S. Department of Commerce Bureau of Navigation, *Radio Service Bulletin,* no. 36, April 1, 1920, as cited in letter to Hoover from Caffey, NA RG 60, May 24, 1921.

77. *Ibid.*

78. Letter from Huston to Dr. Stratton, NA RG 40, November 7, 1921.

79. *New York Times,* November 17, 1921, 9:2.

80. Letter from Hoover to Versfelt, NA RG 40, November 22, 1921.

81. *New York Times,* November 19, 1921, 10:1.

82. *Ibid.*

83. *Ibid.*

84. Letter from Hoover to Versfelt, NA RG 40, November 22, 1921.

85. *New York Times,* November 24, 1921, 27:1.

86. Letter from Solicitor General Beck to Hoover, NA RG 60, February 12, 1923.

87. Letter from Terrell to Hoover, NA RG 40, February 1, 1922.

88. *New York Times,* February 8, 1922, pp. 6–7.

89. *New York Times,* December 22, 1922, 1:4.

90. *New York Times,* April 2, 1922, XX, 2:1.

91. *New York Times,* February 10, 1922, 9:3.

92. Memorandum from Carson to Hoover, NA RG 40, February 20, 1922.

93. *New York Times,* February 13, 1922, 11:1.

94. Letters to Conference participants, HHPL 1-I/539, February 21, 1922.

95. Louise Benjamin, "Working It Out Together: Radio Policy from Hoover to the Radio Act of 1927," *Journal of Broadcasting and Electronic Media* (vol. 42, no. 2 Spring 1998), p. 224.

96. "Minutes of Open Meetings of the Department of Commerce Conference on Radio Telephony" (mimeographed), February 27, 1922, p. 105. Wisconsin State Historical Library, Madison, Wisconsin.

97. *Ibid.*

98. U.S. Department of Commerce Bureau of Navigation, *Radio Service Bulletin*, no. 61, May 1, 1922, p. 26.

99. *Ibid.*, pp. 24–25.

100. Minutes of First Conference, p. 96.

101. Memorandum from Carson to Hoover, HHPL 1-I 538, March 2, 1922.

102. Elliot N. Sivowitch, "A History of Radio Spectrum Allocation in the United States, 1912–1926" (unpublished master's thesis, Syracuse University, 1954), p. 51.

103. *New York Times*, February 28, 1922, p. 16.

104. *Ibid.*

105. U.S. Department of Commerce Bureau of Navigation, *Radio Service Bulletin*, no. 61, p. 29.

106. *Memoirs*, vol. II p. 141.

107. Memorandum of RCA on First Radio Conference, HHPL 1-I/53, April 17, 1922, p. 3.

108. See "The Origin of 'Public Interest' in Broadcasting," by Darrell Holt, *Educational Broadcasting Review* (October 1967), p. 17.

109. RCA memorandum, p. 2.

110. Herbert C. Hoover, *The Address Upon the American Road* (New York: D. Van Nostrand Company, 1948), vol. IV, pp. 142–143.

111. "Value of Radio Phones—Hoover Sums Up Uses of Air Communication," HHPL, vol. IX, no. 221A, May 4, 1922.

112. Memorandum from Tyrer to Kruesi, NA RG 40, June 10, 1922.

113. Memorandum from Kruesi to Tyrer NA RG 40, June 10, 1922.

114. Memorandum from Carson to Kruesi, NA RG 40, June 16, 1922.

115. Letter from Kruesi to Carson, NA RG 40, June 23, 1922.

116. Letter from Kruesi to O'Hara, NA RG 40, June 23, 1922.

117. Memorandum from Kruesi to Hoover, NA RG 40, June 30, 1922.

118. Letter from Hoover to Congressman White, NA RG 40, August 12, 1922.

119. Letter from Congressman White to Terrell, NA RG 40, May 19, 1922.

120. Telegram from Terrell to *Detroit News*, NA RG 173, May 19, 1922.

121. Clipping in NA RG 40 from *Washington Times*, May 2, 1922.

122. Telegram from Tyrer to Horn, NA RG 173, June 12, 1922.

123. "Policing the Ether," HHPL, vol. XI, no. 151, August, 1922.

124. Letter from Carson to Kolster, NA RG 40, August 3, 1922.

125. Report from Arthur Batcheller to Carson, NA RG 40, November 18, 1922.

126. *Ibid.*, p. 2. Also stated in U.S. Congress, *Hearings on Bill to Amend Act of 1912*, p. 40.

127. *Ibid.*

128. Letter from Crosley to Congressman Longworth, NA RG 40, October 28, 1922.

129. Report from Batcheller, p. 3.

130. Memorandum from Nagle to Carson, NA RG 40, November 27, 1922.

131. Letter from Batcheller to Carson, NA RG 40, December 18, 1922, p. 3.

132. Memorandum "To accompany House Bill, H. R. 11964," NA RG 40, December 30, 1922, p. 3.

133. *Ibid.*

134. *Ibid.*, p. 5.

135. *Ibid.*, pp. 6–8

136. *Ibid.*, p. 9.

137. "Report on Radio Broadcasting Stations for 1922," NA RG 40, January 1923.

138. *10th Annual Report of the Secretary of Commerce*, 1922, p. 35.

139. U.S. Congress, *Hearings on Bill to Amend Act of 1912*, p. 39.

140. *Ibid.*, p. 40.

141. Letter from Hoover to Secretary of State Hughes, NA RG 40, March 12, 1923.

142. *Ibid.*

143. Memorandum from Nagle to Carson, NA RG 40, November 27, 1922.

144. U.S. Congress, *Hearings on Bill to Amend Act of 1912*, p. 41.

145. Letter from Nagle to Carson, NA RG 40, January 6, 1923.

146. Letter from Batcheller to Carson, NA RG 40, January 9, 1923.

147. *Ibid.*

148. Letter from Carson to Hoover, NA RG 40, January 10, 1923.

149. Letter from Hoover to White, NA RG 40, January 15, 1923.

150. Letter from Carson to Edwards, NA RG 40, January 10, 1923.

151. Letter from Comptroller General to Hoover, NA RG 40, January 22, 1923.

152. "The Urgent Need for Radio Legislation," HHPL, B-276, January 1923.

153. Letter from Hoover to Secretary of the President, NA RG 40, February 1, 1923.

154. Letter from Walter S. Rogers to Senator Kellogg, NA RG 40, February 7, 1923.

155. U.S. Congress, House, *Report of the Federal Trade Commission on the Radio Industry*, in response to House Resolution 548, 67th Congress, 4th Session, submitted December 1, 1923.

156. Memorandum from Herter to Tyrer, HHPL 1-I/538, February 12, 1923.

157. Recommendations of the First National Radio Conference, reprinted in *Hearings on Bill to Amend Act of 1912*, p. 37.

158. *New York Times*, April 6, 1921, p. 14.

159. *Ibid.*

160. *Ibid.*

161. *Recommendations on Governmental Radio Broadcasting*, NA RG 40, April 17, 1922.

162. Letter to various government departments from Hoover, NA RG 40, April 22, 1922.

163. Memorandum from Stephen B. Davis to Hoover, NA RG 60, March 16, 1927.

164. E. M. Webster, "The Interdepartmental Radio Advisory Committee," Proceedings of the Institute of Radio Engineers (I.R.E.), August 1945, p. 495.

165. Letter from Dr. Stratton to Hoover, HHPL 1-I/541, November 24, 1922.

166. Letter from Carson to Hoover, NA RG 40, November 14, 1922.

167. Letter from Dr. Stratton to Hoover, NA RG 40, December 16, 1922.

168. Letter from Hoover to Smithers, Chief Coordinator, HHPL 1-I/539, May 24, 1922.

169. Letter from Carson to Edwards, NA RG 173, May 5, 1922.

170. Letter from Terrell to Huston, NA RG 40, March 15, 1922.

171. *Ibid.*

172. Letter from Tyrer to Edwards, NA RG 173, December 16, 1921.

173. *Ibid.*

174. *Ibid.*

175. Barnouw, p. 100.

176. Letter from Tyrer to Edwards, NA RG 173, December 16, 1921.

177. Letter from Dillon to Hoover, HHPL 1-I/539, March 27, 1922.

178. *Ibid.*

179. Letter from Carson to Hoover, HHPL 1-I/539, March 31, 1922.

180. Letter from S. J. Woodhue to Kolster, NA RG 173, March 4, 1922.

181. Letter from Kolster to Terrell, NA RG 173, March 4, 1922.

182. Letter from Carson to Kolster, NA RG 173, May 10, 1922.

183. Letter from Senator Charles Townsend to Hoover, NA RG 173, March 29, 1922.

184. Letter from Carson to Hoover, NA RG 173, March 29, 1922.

185. Memorandum by Huston for files, NA RG 173, April 21, 1922.

186. Letter from *Detroit Free Press* to Huston, NA RG 173, May 17, 1922.

187. Letter from Carson to Ross, NA RG 173, April 13, 1922.

188. Memorandum for files, NA RG 173, April 21, 1922.

189. *New York Times*, July 30, 1922, II, 1:4.

190. Memorandum, "Second District Radio Committee Meeting," NA RG 173, May 15, 1922.

191. *New York Times*, July 30, 1922, II, 1:4.

192. *Ibid.*, see also July 23, 1922, 21:1, and July 25, 1922, 5:2.

193. Letter from McLean to Edwards, NA RG 173, July 27, 1922.

194. Letter from Carson to Westinghouse, NA RG 173, August 2, 1922.

195. Letter from Westinghouse to Carson, NA RG 173, August 2, 1922.

196. Letter from Kolster to Carson, NA RG 173, August 2, 1922.

197. Letter from Carson to Kolster, NA RG 173, August 3, 1922.

198. Memorandum from Edwards, NA RG 173, October 2, 1922.

199. Memorandum from Carson to Hoover, NA RG 40, January 6, 1923.

200. Memorandum from Hoover to Carson, NA RG 40, August 5, 1922.

201. U.S. Department of Commerce Bureau of Navigation, *Radio Service Bulletin*, no. 65, September 1, 1922, p. 11.

202. *Ibid.*

203. U.S. Congress, Senate, *Hearings Before the Committee on Interstate Commerce*, 71st Congress, 1st Session, May 24, 1929, p. 1071.

204. Letter from Carson to Westinghouse, NA RG 173, August 29, 1922.

205. Inspection Report by Edwards, NA RG 173, October 2, 1922.

206. Letter from Carson to Dillon, NA RG 173, October 26, 1922.

207. Letter from Horn to Carson, NA RG 173, October 17, 1922.

208. Letter from Crosley to Congressman Longworth, NA RG 40, October 28, 1922.

209. Letter from Edwards to Carson, NA RG 173, October 21, 1922.

210. Letter from Dillon to Carson, NA RG 173, January 18, 1923.

211. *Ibid.*

212. Letter from Carson to Dillon, NA RG 173, January 30, 1923.

213. Memorandum from Carson to Hoover, NA RG 40, November 3, 1922.

214. Memorandum from Carson to Hoover, NA RG 173, November 3, 1922.

215. Letter from Edwards to Carson, NA RG 173, November 20, 1922.

216. *Ibid.*

217. Memorandum from Carson to Hoover, NA RG 40, December 19, 1922.

218. Memorandum from Herter to Tyrer, HHPL 1-I/538, February 21, 1923.

219. Telegram from Hoover to Terrell, HHPL 1-I/538, February 21, 1923.

220. Telegram from Hoover to Griswold, NA RG 40, March 6, 1923.

221. *Ibid.*

222. Admiral Hooper statement, dictated to G. H. Clark, Smithsonian Institution Library, Division of Electricity, Washington, D.C., February 1923.

223. Howeth, p. 384.

224. *Supra.*

225. *Ibid.*

226. Howeth, p. 383.

227. Sivowitch, p. 65.

228. U.S. Department of Commerce Bureau of Navigation, *Radio Service Bulletin*, no. 72, April 2, 1923, pp. 10–11.

229. *Ibid.*, p. 13.

230. Report of the Bureau of Navigation, March 1923, NA RG 40.

231. Press release of the Department of Commerce, HHPL B-301, April 2, 1923.

232. *Ibid.*

233. Report of the Bureau of Navigation, March 1923, NA RG 40.

234. *Ibid.*, April 1923, NA RG 40.

235. Letter from Carson to Edwards, NA RG 173, April 12, 1923.

236. Letter from Edwards to *Detroit News*, NA RG 173, March 3, 1920.

237. Letter from Carson to Kolster, NA RG 173, April 18, 1922.

238. Letter from Carson to Kolster, April 20, 1922.

239. U.S. Department of Commerce Bureau of Navigation, *Radio Service Bulletin*, no. 69, January 2, 1923, p. 8.

240. Letter from Huston to Edward, NA RG 173, May 2, 1923.

241. U.S. Department of Commerce Bureau of Navigation, *Radio Service Bulletin*, no. 72, April 2, 1923, p. 12.

242. Letter from Beane to Carson, NA RG 173, October 22, 1923.

243. Letter from Horn to Carson, NA RG 173, October 22, 1923.

244. Report on the Bureau of Navigation, October 23, 1923, NA RG 40.

245. Letter from Hoover to *Detroit News*, NA RG 173, May 15, 1923.

246. *Ibid.*

247. Issued April 7, 1923. Letter from Parkhurst to Edwards, NA RG 173, May 17, 1923.

248. *Ibid.*

249. *Ibid.*

250. Letter from Edwards to Carson, NA RG 173, November 8, 1923.

251. Report of the Bureau of Navigation, December 1923, NA RG 40.

252. *Ibid.*

253. *Eleventh Annual Report of the Secretary of Commerce*, 1923, p. 22.

254. Letter from Davis to Terrell, NA RG 40, April 9, 1923.

255. *Ibid.*

256. Memorandum of April 11, 1923, NA RG 40.

257. *Ibid.*

258. *Ibid.*

259. Memorandum submitted by Samuel Kintner, NA RG 40, April 20, 1923.

260. *Ibid.*

261. Memorandum for files, Hoover, NA RG 40, May 1, 1923.

262. Letter from Carson to Edwards, NA RG 40, May 15, 1923.

263. Benjamin, "Working It Out Together," p. 228.

264. Sterling and Kittross, p. 88.

265. Rexmond C. Cochrane, *Measures for Progress: A History of the National Bureau of Standards* (Washington, D.C.: U.S. Department of Commerce, 1966), p. 286.

266. *Ibid.*

267. *Ibid.*

268. *Ibid.*

269. *Ibid.*

270. *Ibid.*

271. *Ibid.*

272. Memorandum from Emmet to Dr. Stratton, NA RG 60, February 29, 1922.

273. Cochrane, p. 286.

274. *Ibid.*

275. See appropriations reports for lists of publications.

276. Cochrane, p. 287.

277. "Recommendations of the First National Radio Conference," U.S. Department of Commerce Bureau of Navigation, *Radio Service Bulletin*, no. 61, May 1, 1922, pp. 29–30.

278. Cochrane, p. 289.

279. U.S. Department of Commerce Bureau of Navigation, *Radio Service Bulletin*, no. 68, December 1, 1922.

280. Cochrane, p. 348.

281. *Ibid.*

282. *Ibid.*

283. "Transmission of Music" (mimeographed), Bureau of Standards report, NA RG 40, May 1923.

Chapter III

1. Report of the Bureau of Navigation, January 1924, NA RG 40.

2. Report of the Bureau of Navigation, months indicated, NA RG 40.

3. Report of the Bureau of Navigation, June 1924, NA RG 40.

4. Report of the Bureau of Navigation, September 1924, NA RG 40.

5. Report of the Bureau of Navigation, November 1924, NA RG 40.

6. Report of the Bureau of Navigation, December 1924, NA RG 40.

7. Report of the Bureau of Navigation, March 1925, NA RG 40.

8. Report of the Bureau of Navigation, December 1925, NA RG 40.

9. Report of the Bureau of Navigation, December 1925, NA RG 40.

10. J. H. Dellinger, "Radio Communication," from file, Dellinger Papers, records of the National Bureau of Standards, NA RG 167.

11. Isabel Leighton (ed.), *The Aspirin Age: 1919–1941* (New York: Simon and Shuster, 1949), p. 145.

12. Dellinger paper, "Radio Communication."

13. Duane G. Straub, "The Role of Secretary of Commerce Herbert Hoover in the Development of Early Radio Regulation" (unpublished master's thesis, Michigan State University, 1964), p. 51.

14. Letter from Beck to Hoover, NA RG 60, January 10, 1924.

15. Letter from Beck to Hoover, NA RG 60, August 16, 1924.

16. Letter from Scofield to Beck, NA RG 60, August 25, 1924.

17. Joel Rosenbloom, "Authority of the Federal Communications Commission with Respect to the Programming of Radio and Television Stations," FCC memo no. 49935, September 27, 1957, p. 12.

18. *Ibid.*

19. Melvin R. White, "History of Radio Regulation Affecting Program Policy" (unpublished Ph.D. dissertation, University of Wisconsin, 1948), p. 86.

20. U.S. Congress, House, *Hearings Before the Committee on the Merchant Marine and Fisheries, on H. R. 7357, to Regulate Radio Communication*, 68th Congress, 1st Session, March 11–14, 1924, pp. 8–11.

21. Elliot N. Sivowitch, "A History of Radio Spectrum Allocation in the United States, 1912–1926" (unpublished master's thesis, Syracuse University, 1954), p. 77.

22. *Memoirs*, vol. II, p. 139.

23. Sivowitch, p. 79.

24. Rosenbloom, p. 13.

25. *Ibid.*

26. Report of the Bureau of Navigation, May 1924, NA RG 40.

27. *Ibid.*

28. *Ibid.*

29. Report of the Bureau of Navigation, July 1924, NA RG 40.

30. *Ibid.*

31. Letter from Arthur Batcheller to Carson, NA RG 60, August 26, 1924.

32. Letter from Edwards to Carson, NA RG 60, August 26, 1924.

33. U.S. Department of Commerce Bureau of Navigation, *Radio Service Bulletin*, no. 89, September 2, 1924, p. 6.

34. Report of the Bureau of Navigation, September 1924, NA RG 40.

35. Letter from Hoover to Charles E. Hughes, NA RG 60.

36. U.S. Department of Commerce Bureau of Navigation, *Radio Service Bulletin*, no. 89, September 2, 1924, p. 6.

37. Letter from Beane to Carson, NA RG 173, September 20, 1924.

38. *Ibid.*

39. Letter from William Wirt Milles to Bogadus, NA RG 40, September 26, 1924.

40. *Ibid.*

41. Letter from Carson to Ohio Insulator Company, NA RG 40, October 2, 1924.

42. C. M. Jansky, Jr., "Herbert Hoover's Contribution to Broadcasting," *Journal of Broadcasting* (vol. I, Summer 1956-57), p. 243.

43. U.S. Department of Commerce, *Proceedings of the Third National Radio Conference*, October 6–10, 1924 (Washington, D.C.: U.S. Government Printing Office, 1924), p. 1.

44. Letter from J. R. Wade to Hoover, Herbert C. Hoover Presidential Library, West Branch, Iowa, Container No. 1-I/539. Hereafter noted as HHPL.

45. *Third Conference Proceedings*, p. 1–9.

46. Sivowitch, p. 87. This material was found by Sivowitch in a Washington government warehouse in an unfiled section, according to an interview I had with him. Subsequent correspondence with the National Archives indicated that this material was no longer available, as they could not locate it.

47. *Ibid.*

48. "Radio Problems—Address before California Radio Exposition, San Francisco," HHPL, vol. XVI, no. 396, August 16, 1924.

49. Sivowitch, p. 91.

50. *Ibid.*, p. 92.

51. *New York Times*, October 9, 1924, p. 21.

52. *Ibid.*

53. Sivowitch, p. 95.

54. *Ibid.*

55. *Ibid.*

56. *Ibid.*

57. *Ibid.*, p. 98.

58. *Ibid.*, p. 99.

59. *Ibid.*

60. *Ibid.*

61. *Ibid.*

62. *Ibid.*, p. 100.

63. *Ibid.*, p. 101.

64. Letter from Carson to Smith, NA RG 40, November. 22, 1926.

65. Sivowitch, pp. 103–104.

66. Louise Benjamin, "Working It Out Together: Radio Policy from Hoover to the Radio Act of 1927, *Journal of Broadcasting and Electronic Media,* vol. 42, no. 2 (Spring 1998), p. 230.

67. Report of the Bureau of Navigation, October 1924, NA RG 40.

68. *Ibid.*

69. *Ibid.*

70. *Ibid.*

71. *Ibid.*

72. Report of the Bureau of Navigation, October 1924, NA RG 40.

73. Report of the Bureau of Navigation, December 1924, NA RG 40.

74. *Ibid.*

75. Letter from Hoover to White, HHPL, 1–I/531, December 4, 1924.

76. *Ibid.*

77. Letter from Hoover to Smith, HHPL, 1-I/539, December 4, 1924.

78. Daniel E. Garvey, "Secretary Hoover and the Quest for Broadcast Regulation," *Journalism History,* vol. 3, no. 3 (Autumn 1976), 3:3, p. 69.

79. "The March of Radio: Hoover's Suggestions for New Radio Legislation," *Radio Broadcast,* March 1925, pp. 890–892.

80. *Ibid.*

81. *New York Times,* December 6, 1924, p. 4.

82. Letter from Stokes to *Herald Examiner* editor, HHPL 1-I/541, December 30, 1924, also to *Birmingham Age-Herald* editor, February 6, 1925.

83. "Hoover Battles to Block Special Privilege in Radio," interview with *Cleveland Plain Dealer,* HHPL, vol. XX, no. 490, May 28, 1925.

84. *Ibid.*

85. "Radio: Its Influence and Growth—Address from Washington, D.C. on stations WRC, WJZ and WGY on the Opening of the Fourth Annual Radio Exposition, N.Y.C.," September 12, 1925, HHPL, no. B-510.

86. *Ibid.*

87. Letter from Hoover to Broadley, *Youngstown Telegram* editor, NA RG 40, November 24, 1925.

88. Eric Barnouw, *A Tower in Babel: A History of Broadcasting in the United States to 1933.* (New York: Oxford University Press, 1966), p. 122.

89. Clipping from *Washington Star,* NA RG 173, March 6, 1924.

90. Barnouw, p. 176.

91. "Control of Radio Broadcasting," HHPL, vol. XV, no. 363; also reprinted in *Radio Broadcast Magazine,* June 1924; March 10, 1924.

92. *Ibid.*

93. *Ibid.*

94. *Ibid.*

95. "Hoover Takes Stand on Question," HHPL, no. B-366A, March 22, 1924.

96. "Radio Talk Broadcast from WCAP, Washington, D.C.," HHPL, vol. XV, no. 367, March 26, 1924.

97. *Ibid.*

98. "Radio Problems," August 16, 1924; also interview in *Radio News,* October, 1924, HHPL, vol. XVIIII, no. 401A.

99. "Radio Monopoly and LaFollette," HHPL, vol. XVII, no. 405, October 16, 1924.

100. *Ibid.*

101. *Ibid.*

102. "Hoover Battles to Block Special Privilege in Radio."

103. *Ibid.*

104. *Ibid.*

105. Robert W. McChesney, "Free Speech and Democracy! Louis G. Caldwell, the American Bar Association and the Debate Over the Free Speech Implications of Broadcast Regulation, 1928–1938," *The American Journal of Legal History*, vol. 35 (1991), p. 351.

106. Letter from Pontslor to Edwards, NA RG 40, January 15, 1924.

107. Letter from Carson to Edwards, NA RG 40, January 15, 1924.

108. *National Stockman and Farmer* editor to Carson, NA RG 40, January 29, 1924.

109. Letter from Carson to Bayard, NA RG 40, February 28, 1924.

110. Letter from Bayard to Carson, NA RG 40, March 2, 1924.

111. "The Government's Duty Is to Keep the Ether Open and Free for All, *New York World*, HHPL, B-364, March 16, 1924."

112. "Radio Talk Broadcast from WCAP, Washington, D.C.," March 26, 1924, HHPL, vol XV, no. 367.

113. Letter from McDonald to Carson, NA RG 40, January 15, 1925.

114. Letter from Carson to Eisemann, NA RG 173, January 6, 1925.

115. "Radio: Its Influence and Growth."

116. *Ibid.*

117. U.S. Department of Commerce Bureau of Navigation, *Radio Service Bulletin*, no. 94, February 2, 1925, p. 22.

118. Letter from Freeman to Hoover, NA RG 40, January 21, 1925.

119. Letter from Nathan to Hoover, NA RG 40, March 2, 1925.

120. Letter from Carson to Nathan, NA RG 40, March 17, 1925.

121. Letter from Deiler to Carson, NA RG 60, March 28, 1924.

122. Letter to *New York Mirror* editor from Stokes, dictated by Mr. Hoover, NA RG 40, March 30, 1925.

123. Letter from Hoover to Fox, NA RG 60, December 9, 1925.

124. Letter from Hoover to Secretary of the President, NA RG 40, January 27, 1925.

125. "Radio Problems."

126. *Ibid.*

127. "An Interview with Secretary Hoover," HHPL, vol. XVIII, no. 401A.

128. "Secretary Hoover Reviews Radio Situation," HHPL, B-303; also reprinted in *Radio Broadcast Magazine*, May 1925, pp. 38–39.

129. *Ibid.*

130. Letter from Hoover to Congressman Aswell, NA RG 40, December 14, 1925.

131. "The Government's Duty Is to Keep the Ether Open."

132. *Ibid.*

133. "Radio Talk Broadcast from WCAP."

134. *Ibid.*

135. "Chamber of Commerce of the U.S.—Address at Annual Meeting Cleveland," HHPL, B-378, May 7, 1924.

136. *Ibid.*

137. *Ibid.*

138. *Ibid.*

139. *Ibid.*

140. Charles K. Field, *The Story of Cheerio* (New York: Garden City Publishing Company, 1937), p. 216.

141. "State Regulation of Electric Utilities," Address by Herbert Hoover, HHPL, vol. XV, no. 569, February 3, 1925.

142. "Radio Talk Broadcast from WCAP, Washington, D.C."

143. Letter from Horn to Hoover, NA RG 40, January 15, 1924.

144. *Ibid.*

145. Letter from Carson to Edwards, NA RG 40, January 21, 1924.

146. Letter from Carson to Edwards, NA RG 40,

147. Letter from Carson to Edwards, NA RG 40, February 28, 1924.

148. Letter from Horn to Carson, NA RG 40, April 3, 1924.

149. Letter from Van Frank to Senator Oldfield, forwarded to Hoover, NA RG 40, November 14, 1924.

150. Letter from Terrell to Horn, NA RG 40, January 15, 1925.

151. Letter from Hoover to Dearing, NA RG 40, March 21, 1925.

152. Letter from Edwards to Carson, NA RG 173, April 8, 1925.

153. Letter from Horn to Carson, NA RG 173, June 11, 1925.

154. Letter from Horn to Carson, NA RG 173, August 6, 1925.

155. Letter from Tyrer to Horn, NA RG 173, August 6, 1925.

156. "Public Invited to Join in Unusual Radio Experiment," press release of the Department of Commerce, HHPL, 1-I/539, August 16, 1925.

157. Report of the Bureau of Navigation, November 1925, NA RG 40.

158. Letter from Hoover to Congressman Edge, NA RG 40, December 17, 1925.

159. *Ibid.*

160. U.S. Department of Commerce Bureau of Navigation, *Radio Service Bulletin*, no. 101 (September 1, 1925), p. 18.

161. Sivowitch, pp. 70–71; as cited from Hearings on H. R. 7357.

162. "The Department of Commerce Considers Interference and Other Problems in Radio," *National Magazine*, vol. 52 (March 1924), p. 400.

163. U.S. Department of Commerce Bureau of Navigation, *Radio Service Bulletin*, no. 82 (February 1, 1924), p. 21.

164. *Ibid.*

165. U.S. Congress, *Second Deficiency Bill, 1925*, pp. 200–204.

166. *Ibid.*

167. *Ibid.*

168. *Ibid.*

169. U.S. Congress, *Hearings on Appropriations, 1926*, p. 32.

170. *Ibid.*

171. "A Year of Conferences," *Radio Broadcast*, November 1925, p. 26.

172. Letter from British Embassy to Hughes, NA RG 40, October 1, 1924.

173. Letter from Hoover to Hughes, NA RG 40, October 16, 1924; regulations printed in *Radio Service Bulletin*, June 2, 1924, no. 86, p. 13, and October 1, 1925, no. 101, p. 12.

174. Letter from IRAC to Hoover, NA RG 40, November 20, 1924.

175. Report of the Bureau of Navigation, March 1925, NA RG 40.

176. Report of the Bureau of Navigation, January 1924, NA RG 40.

177. Report of the Bureau of Navigation, February 1924, NA RG 40.

178. "Radio Talk Broadcast from WCAP, Washington, D.C."

179. *Ibid.*

180. Report of the Bureau of Navigation, December 1924, NA RG 40.

181. *Radio Service Bulletin*, no. 90 (October 1, 1924), p. 11.

182. *Radio Service Bulletin*, no. 102 (November 2, 1925), p. 11.

183. Report of the Bureau of Navigation, April 1925, NA RG 40.

184. Letter from Horn to Terrell, NA RG 40, April 27, 1925.

185. Report of the Bureau of Navigation, April 1925, NA RG 40.

186. *Ibid.*

187. *Ibid.*

188. *Ibid.*

189. *Ibid.*

190. Report of the Bureau of Navigation, December 1924, NA RG 40.

191. Gleason L. Archer, *History of Radio to 1926* (New York: American Historical Society, 1938), p. 354.

192. Letter from Edwards to Horn, NA RG 173, February 11, 1925.

193. *Ibid.*

194. *Ibid.*

195. Letter from Horn to Carson, NA RG 173, April 27, 1925.

196. *Memoirs*, vol. II, p. 142.

197. *Ibid.*

198. *Ibid.*, p. 143.

199. Interview of Lewis Weeks with Herbert Hoover, November 3, 1961. This incident is also reported in Leighton, *The Aspirin Age*, previously cited, pp. 50–80.

200. *Ibid.*

201. Court of Appeals upheld the FRC action on appeal as not prior censorship, *Trinity Methodist Church, S. v. FRC*, 62 F. 2d 850 (DC App. 1932).

202. Letter from Hoover to Gernsback, NA RG 40, May 2, 1925.

203. Report of the Bureau of Navigation, December 1925, NA RG 40.

204. Letter from Carson to Deiler, NA RG 173, December 15, 1925.

205. *Ibid.*

206. *Ibid.*

207. *Ibid.*

208. Interview, George Turner.

209. Letter from Davis to Senator Willis, NA RG 40, November 1, 1924.

210. *Ibid.*

211. Letter from Davis to Edwards, NA RG 40, November 10, 1924.

212. "Agreement Covering New Wavelength Allocation—Cincinnati Zone—Eighth District," NA RG 40, November 21, 1924.

213. Lawrence W. Lichty, "The Nation's Station: A History of Radio Station WLW" (unpublished Ph. D. dissertation, The Ohio State University, 1964), pp. 89–91.

214. Letter from Crosley to Ainsworth Gates Company, NA RG 173, March 18, 1925.

215. Letter from Tyrer to Faasen, NA RG 173, June 24, 1925.

216. Herbert Hoover, Interview in Oral History Collection of Columbia University, New York, November 14, 1960, p. 12.

217. Letter from Drake to Small, NA RG 173, May 23, 1925.

218. "Recommendations of the Fourth National Radio Conference," November 9–11, 1925 (Washington, D.C., U.S. Government Printing Office, 1925), pp. 1–9.

219. Benjamin, p. 234.

220. *New York Times*, November 11, 1925, p. 25.

221. *Ibid.*

222. Letter from Davis to Williams, NA RG 173, November 30, 1925.

223. "Recommendations of the Fourth Conference."

224. Letter from Carson to Rehnke, NA RG 40, December 31, 1925.

225. "Recommendations of the Fourth Conference."

226. *New York Times*, November 11, 1925, p. 5.

227. "Recommendations of the Fourth Conference."

228. *New York Times,* November, 27, 1925, p. 10.

229. "Radio Problems and Conference Recommendations—Address Broadcast from Washington, D.C.," HHPL, B-522A, November 12, 1925.

230. *Ibid.*

231. *Ibid.*

232. *Ibid.*

233. *Ibid.*

234. *Ibid.*

235. *Ibid.*

236. *Ibid.*

237. *Ibid.*

238. *Ibid.*

239. "Radio Control Policy," HHPL, vol. XXII, no. 5235, December 26, 1925.

240. Letter from Davis to Dr. Goldsmith, NA RG 40, July 2, 1925.

241. Lynville W. Jarvis, "Herbert C. Hoover: A Factor in Broadcast Legislation" (unpublished master's thesis, University of Alabama, 1963), p. 56.

242. *New York Times*, December 2, 1925, VII, p. 13.

243. Interview of C. C. Dill, Broadcast Pioneers History Project, July 21, 1964.

Chapter IV

1. J. H. Dellinger, from personal files, NA RG 167, January 6, 1928, p. 1.

2. *New York Times*, January 3, 1926, VIII, 13:5.

3. Dellinger papers, p. 13.

4. *Ibid.*, p. 14.

5. Hugh G. J. Aitken. "Allocating the Spectrum: The Origins of Radio Regulation," *Technology and Culture* (vol. 35, 1994), p. 709.

6. Report from Carson to Batcheller, NA RG 40, February 8, 1926.

7. *Radio Broadcast*, April 1927, pp. 555–556.

8. Letter from Terrell to Representative Ayers, NA RG 173, March 2, 1927.

9. Dellinger papers, p. 6.

10. *Ibid.*, p. 14.

11. *Ibid.*, p. 6 (see Chapter III, p. 82).

12. U.S. Congress, *Hearings on Appropriations, 1926*, p. 33.

13. *Ibid.*

14. Letter from McDonald to W. M. Dewey, NA RG 173, May 7, 1924.

15. The Zenith Radio Corporation also operated a portable radio station which was on a truck, licensed for a short time as WJAZ, then later WJAS.

16. Letter from Carson to Leslie, NA RG 173, April 4, 1924.

17. Letter from McDonald to Beane, NA RG 173, May 28, 1924.

18. *Ibid.*

19. Harold N. Cones and John H. Bryant, *Zenith Radio: The Early Years, 1919–1935* (Atglen, Pennsylvania: Schiffer Publishing, 1997).

20. Letter from Carson to Tomiseh, NA RG 173, April 7, 1924.

21. Letter from Beane to Carson, NA RG 173, April 19, 1924.

22. Letter from Davis to McDonald, NA RG 173, January 20, 1925.

23. Letter from McDonald to Davis, NA RG 173, January 27, 1925.

24. Letter from Carson to Beane, NA RG 173, March 21, 1925.

25. Telegram from Tyrer to McDonald, NA RG 173, June 12, 1925.

26. Telegram from Tyrer to McDonald, NA RG 173, June 12, 1925.

27. Telegram from McDonald to Terrell, June 15, 1925.

28. Telegram from Davis to McDonald, June 15, 1925.

29. Letter from McDonald to Davis, NA RG 173, June 26, 1925.

30. *Ibid.*

31. Letters to U.S. Playing Card Company and General Electric Company, NA RG 173, June 25, 1925.

32. Memorandum for Files, NA RG 173, July 13, 1925.

33. *Ibid.*

34. Letter from Martin P. Rice to Tyrer, NA RG 173, July 18, 1925.

35. Letter from Davis to Marks, NA RG 173, July 22, 1925.

36. Letter from Edwards to Terrell, NA RG 173, August 21, 1925.

37. Telegram from Drake to Zenith Corporation, NA RG 40, September 3, 1925.

38. Letter from Marks to Davis, NA RG 173, September 30, 1925.

39. *Ibid.*

40. Letter from McDonald to Davis, NA RG 173, November 12, 1925.

41. *Ibid.*

42. Handwritten note by Davis, NA RG 40, November 18, 1925.

43. Letter from MacCracken to Davis, NA RG 173, December 10, 1925.

44. Letter from Davis to MacCracken, NA RG 173, December 12, 1925.

45. Letter from Davis to Zenith Corporation, NA RG 173, December 17, 1925.

46. Memorandum from Beane, NA RG 40, December 19, 1925.

47. *Ibid.*

48. Handwritten note on Beane's letter to Carson, NA RG 173, December 22, 1925.

49. Telegrams from McDonald to Davis and Reply, NA RG 173, December 23, 1925.

50. Memorandum from Beane, NA RG 173, December 29, 1925.

51. *Ibid.*

52. Note on letter from Beane to Carson, NA RG 173, December 29, 1925.

53. Telegram from Davis to Rice, NA RG 60, December 31, 1925.

54. Letter from Davis to Attorney General, NA RG 60, January 12, 1926.

55. *Ibid.*

56. *Ibid.*

57. Telegram from Beane to Carson, NA RG 173, January 4, 1926.

58. Telegram from Davis to Beane, January 4, 1926.

59. Letter from Carson to Beane, NA RG 173, January 12, 1926.

60. Letter from Donovan to Olson, NA RG 60, January 14, 1926.

61. *Ibid.*

62. *New York Herald-Tribune*, NA RG 173, January 19, 1926.

63. Manuscript of speech, sent by Batcheller to Carson, NA RG 173, January 19, 1926.

64. Memorandum from Edwards to Carson, NA RG 173, January 12, 1926.

65. Letter from Department of Marine and Fisheries, Canada, to Carson, NA RG 173, January 19, 1926.

66. Telegram from Tyrer to Beane, NA RG 173, January 19, 1926.

67. "Statement on WJAZ," Department of Commerce, HHPL, 1-I/539, January 33, 1926.

68. Telegram from Carson to Olson, NA RG 173, February 13, 1926.

69. Letter from *St. Louis Globe-Democrat* to Davis, NA RG 173, February 17, 1926. Cones and Bryant, *Zenith Radio,* p. 43.

70. Press release of the Department of Commerce, NA RG 40, February 12, 1926.

71. Clipping from Department of Commerce Press File from *New York Herald-Tribune,* NA RG 173, February 16, 1926.

72. *Ibid.*

73. Clipping file, *New York Herald-Tribune,* NA RG 173, February 17, 1926.

74. *Ibid.*

75. Clippings from Press File, *Springfield Illinois Republican,* NA RG 173, February 24, 1926.

76. Letter 2276–NR to Supervisors, NA RG 173, March 13, 1926.

77. *U.S. vs. Zenith Radio Corporation,* Docket No. 14257, NA RG 173, April 14, 1926.

78. Speech by Irving Herriott, "The Real Facts As to the Status of Broadcasting Since the Federal Test Case Decision," presented over WJAZ, manuscript in NA RG 173, April 23, 1926.

79. Press release of the Department of Commerce, NA RG 173, April 16, 1926.

80. *New York Times,* April 18, 1926, 27:3.

81. "Zenith Radio Case Decision and Necessity for Legislation," Press release of Department of Commerce, April 20, 1926, HHPL, vol. XXIII, no. 572A.

82. Speech by Irving Herriott.

83. *Ibid.*

84. *Ibid.*

85. *Ibid.*

86. Letter from Herriott to Davis, NA RG 173, July 14, 1926.

87. Letter from Carson to Johnston, April 28, 1926.

88. Stephen B. Davis, *The Law of Radio Communication* (New York: McGraw-Hill Book Company, 1927), p. 44.

89. Donald R. LeDuc and Thomas A. McCain, "The Federal Radio Commission in Federal Court: Origins of Broadcast Regulatory Doctrines," *Journal of Broadcasting* (vol. 14, no. 4, Fall 1970), pp. 393–410.

90. Press release of the Department of Commerce, "The Opinion of the Attorney General on Radio," HHPL, 1-I/541, July 9, 1926. U.S. Department of Justice, *Federal Regulations of Radio Broadcasting,* opinions of the Attonrey General (vol. 35, 1926), p. 126.

91. *Ibid.*

92. *Ibid.*

93. *Ibid.*

94. *Ibid.*

95. *Ibid.*

96. *Ibid.*

97. *Ibid.*

98. U.S. Congress, *Hearings on Appropriations, 1926.*

99. Letter from Terrell to Inspectors, NA RG 40, January 11, 1926.

100. Reports of Complaints of Interference for 1926, NA RG 40.

101. Letter from Bryer to Edwards, NA RG 173, July 178, 1926.

102. *Ibid.*

103. Telegram from Northwest Radio Trade Association to Hoover, NA RG 173, July 13, 1926.

104. *Minneapolis Journal,* July 20, 1926, p. 1.

105. *Minneapolis Journal,* July 23, 1926, p. 1 (also in *New York Times,* July 21, 1926, 18:5).

106. *Ibid.*

107. 14 Fed. (2nd series) 166, 167, July 19, 1926.

108. *Minneapolis Journal*, July 23, 1926.

109. Letter from Hoover to Secretary of President, HHPL, 1-I/538, July 27, 1926.

110. Letter from Batcheller to *Radio Broadcast*, NA RG 173, August 11, 1926.

111. "The Broadcast Situation," *Radio News*, October 1926, p. 332.

112. *Radio Broadcast*, October 1926, p. 474.

113. Letter from Carson to Redfern, NA RG 173, September 16, 1926.

114. Elliot N. Sivowitch, "A History of Radio Spectrum Allocation in the United States, 1912–1926" (unpublished master's thesis, Syracuse University, 1954), p. 126.

115. Aitken, "Allocating the Spectrum: The Origins of Radio Regulation," p. 712.

116. Letter from Tyrer to Johnston, NA RG 40, December 18, 1926.

117. *Ibid.*

118. Alfred N. Goldsmith and Austin C. Lescarboura, *This Thing Called Broadcasting* (New York: Henry Holt and Company, 1930), p. 60.

119. Letter from Carson to Batcheller, NA RG 173, February 8, 1927.

120. Letter from Edwards to Carson, NA RG 173, January 12, 1926.

121. U.S. Department of Commerce Bureau of Navigation, *Radio Service Bulletin*, no. 106 (January 30, 1926), p. 23.

122. Dellinger papers, 1927.

123. Letter from Beane to Carson, NA RG 173, March 4, 1926.

124. Letter from Blackwell to Carson, NA RG 173, March 26, 1926.

125. Letter from Carson to Blackwell, NA RG 173, April 6, 1926.

126. Letter from Carson to O'Fallon, NA RG 173, June 5, 1926.

127. Letter from Tyrer to Pepper, NA RG 173, February 18, 1926.

128. *New York Times*, February 17, 1926, 3:5.

129. Lynville W. Jarvis, "Herbert C. Hoover: A Factor in Broadcast Legislation" (unpublished master's thesis, University of Alabama, 1963), pp. 57–58.

130. Statement of Herbert Hoover before the Committee on Merchant Marine and Fisheries, on H. R. 5589, HHPL, 1-I/J-29, January 6, 1926.

131. *New York Times*, February 28, 1926, 9:19.

132. Letter from Hoover to Sanders, NA RG 173, February 1, 1926.

133. *National Association of Broadcasters Bulletin*, NA RG 173, February 5, 1926.

134. Letter from Davis to Cooper, NA RG 173, March 8, 1926.

135. Melvin R. White, "History of Radio Regulation Affecting Radio Program Policy" (unpublished Ph.D. dissertation, University of Wisconsin, 1948), p. 109.

136. *Ibid.*, p. 110.

137. "Pirates of Air Before Senate Committee," press release of Zenith Corporation, NA RG 173, March 2, 1926.

138. *New York Times*, April 11, 1926, 9:21.

139. Letter from Hoover to Sanders, HHPL, 1-I/539, March 29, 1926.

140. Donald G. Godfrey and Val E. Limburg, "The Rogue Elephant of Radio Legislation: Senator William E. Borah," *Journalism Quarterly* (vol. 67, 1990), p. 215.

141. *Ibid.*, p. 223.

142. *St. Louis Globe-Democrat*, April 25, 1926, Sec. 5, pp. 1, 13; also the same opinion is expressed in Jarvis, p. 70.

143. "Speech of Irving Herriott," NA RG 173, April 23, 1926.

144. *New York Times*, April 19, 1926, p. 9.

145. "Zenith Radio Case Decision and Necessity for Legislation," press release of the Department of Commerce, NA RG 173, April 20, 1926.

146. Letter from McDonald to Rowbottom, NA RG 173, April 30, 1926.

147. *New York Times*, May 9, 1926, p. 14.

148. Letter from Davis to Peters, NA RG 173, May 3, 1926.

149. *National Association of Broadcasters Bulletin*, NA RG 173, May 5, 1926.

150. *Ibid.*

151. Jarvis, p. 76.

152. Duane Gene Straub, "The Role of Secretary of Commerce Herbert Hoover in the Development of Early Radio Regulation" (unpublished master's thesis, Michigan State University, 1964), p. 68.

153. *Memoirs*, vol. II, p. 142.

154. Straub, p. 68.

155. *New York Times*, September 12, 1926, 11:2.

156. *New York Times*, July 18, 1926, 7:10.

157. "Who Is to Control Broadcasting?" *Radio Broadcast*, October 1926, p. 572–574.

158. *Memoirs*, vol. II, p. 142.

159. Letter from Hoover to Sanders, HHPL, 1-I/538, July 27, 1926.

160. "Fourteen Years Without a Change in Radio Legislation," *Radio Broadcast*, September 1926, p. 372.

161. Letter from Hoover to Coolidge, HHPL, 1-I/241, November 20, 1926 (also cited as Coolidge speech in Davis, p. 54).

162. *New York Times*, November 13, 1926, 9:18.

163. S. J. Res. 125, 69th Congress, 1st Session, July 3, 1926.

164. Letter from Hoover to White, NA RG 173, December 8, 1926.

165. *New York Times*, January 16, 1927, 7:16.

166. *New York Times*, January 15, 1927, 4:3.

167. Clipping from unidentified newspaper in clipping file of Department of Commerce, HHPL, 1-I/538, December 21, 1926.

168. *Ibid.*

169. *Ibid.*

170. *New York Times*, January 23, 1927, 20:5.

171. *New York Times*, February 4, 1927, 1:4.

172. *New York Times*, February 6, 1927, 8:4.

173. *New York Times*, February 8, 1927, 6:1.

174. *New York Times*, February 13, 1927, 17:5.

175. *New York Times*, February 19, 1927, 1:3.

176. *Ibid.*

177. *New York Times*, February 24, 1927, 1:4.

178. Thomas W. Hazlett, "The Rationality of U.S. Regulation of the Broadcast Spectrum," *Journal of Law and Economics* (vol. 33, no. 1, April 1990), p. 175.

179. "Radio Situation on Completion of Legislation," press release of Department of Commerce, HHPL, B-706, February 24, 1927.

180. *Memoirs*, vol. II, p. 145.

181. Letter from Akerson to Shaforth, HHPL, 1-I/538, March 10, 1927.

182. *New York Times*, March 5, 1927, 2:5, 6.

183. "Radio Legislation Praised," press release of the Department of Commerce, HHPL, B-708, March 6, 1927.

184. U.S. Department of Commerce Bureau of Navigation, *Radio Service Bulletin*, no. 120 (March 31, 1927), p. 8.

185. Federal Radio Commission, *Annual Report of the Federal Radio Commission for Fiscal Year 1927*, Washington, D.C.: U.S. Government Printing Office, 1927, p. 10.

186. Laurence F. Schmeckebier, *The Federal Radio Commission: Its History, Activities and Organization* (Washington, D.C.: The Brookings Institution, 1932), p. 20.

187. *Ibid.*

188. *Ibid.*, p. 40.

189. *Ibid.*

190. Letter from Hoover to *Evening Express*, NA RG 40, January 28, 1928.

191. *New York Times*, March 16, 1928, 1:16.

192. "International Radio Telegraph Conference; Address at Opening Session," HHPL, B-777, October 4, 1927.

193. "International Radio Telegraph Conference; Address at Closing Plenary Session," HHPL, B-815, November 25, 1927 (apparently broadcast to public).

194. Dellinger papers, p. 17.

Chapter V

1. Thomas Streeter. "Selling the Air: Property and the Politics of US Commercial broadcasting," *Media, Culture & Society* (vol. 16, 1994), p. 99.

2. *Radio Act of 1927*, Section 4 (f). The Radio Act of 1927 may be found in Erik Barnouw, *A Tower in Babel: A History of Broadcasting in the United States to 1933*, p. 300; also in 44 Stat. 1162-1174; Public Law no. 632, 69th Congress, as reprinted in Udell, *Radio Laws of the United States*.

3. *Federal Radio Commission, 4th Annual Report* (1930), p. 54.

4. *G.E. v. Federal Radio Commission*, 31 F. 2d 630 (DC App. 1929); see also FCC Report no. G 98-10, June 17, 1998.

5. "Minutes of Open Meetings of the Department of Commerce Conference on Radio Telephony" (mimeographed), February 27, 1922, pp. 1–5. Wisconsin State Historical Library, Madison, Wisconsin.

6. Darrell Holt, "The Origin of 'Public Interest' in Broadcasting," *Educational Broadcasting Review*, October 1967, p. 17.

7. Letter from Hoover to White, HHPL 1-I/531, December 4, 1924.

8. U.S. Congress, House, *Hearings Before the Committee on Merchant Marine and Fisheries*, 68th Congress, 1st Session, March 11, 1924, pp. 8–11.

9. *Federal Radio Commission v. Nelson Bros.*, 289 US 266 (1933).

10. Daniel E. Garvey, "Secretary Hoover and the Quest for Broadcast Regulation," *Journalism History* (vol. 3, no. 3, Autumn 1976), p. 67.

11. Letter from Hoover to Ludwig Hesse, NA RG 173, March 23, 1921.

12. Letter from Hoover to Smithers, Chief Coordinator, HHPL 1-I/539, May 24, 1922.

13. "Radio Control Policy," HHPL, vol. XXII, no. 535, December 26, 1925.

14. Statement of Herbert Hoover before the Committee on Merchant Marine and Fisheries on H. R. 5489, HHPL, 1-I/J-29, January 6, 1926.

15. Letter from Hoover to Sanders, HHPL, 1-I/539, March 29, 1926.

16. *Ibid.*

17. Letter from Hoover to President Coolidge, HHPL, 1-I/241, November 20, 1926 (cited also as Collidge speech in Davis, p. 54).

18. Letter from Huston to Radio Inspectors, NA RG 40, January 11, 1922.

19. Letter from Dillon to Hoover, HHPL, 1-I/539, March 27, 1922.

20. Letter from Carson to Dillon, NA RG 173, October 26, 1922.

21. "Public Invited to Join in Unusual Radio Experiment," press release of the Department of Commerce, HHPL, 1-I/539, August 16, 1925.

22. *Radio Act of 1912*, Public Law no. 264, August 13, 1912, 62nd Congress, Section 4.

23. "Control of Radio Broadcasting," HHPL, vol. XV, no. 363, March 10, 1924.

24. "The Government's Duty Is to Keep the Ether Open and Free for All," interview with the *New York World*, HHPL, B-364, March 16, 1924.

25. Letter from Carson to Kolster, NA RG 173, April 18, 1922.

26. "The Government's Duty."

27. *Federal Radio Commission, 2nd Annual Report* (1928), p. 161.

28. *Great Lakes v. FRC* (D. 4900, 1928).

29. WCOT, *Federal Radio Commission, 2nd Annual Report* (1928), pp. 152–153.

30. *Duncan v. U.S.*, 48 F. 2d 128 (Cir. Ct. App. 9th, 1931).

31. *KFKB v. Federal Radio Commission*, 47 F. 2d 670 (DC App. 1931).

32. *Federal Radio Commission, 5th Annual Report* (1931), p. 78, and *Baker v. U.S.*, 115 F. 2d 533 (1940).

33. *Trinity Methodist Church, S. v. Federal Radio Commission*, 62 F. 2d 850 (DC App. 1932).

34. Letter from Hoover to Senator Kellogg, HHPL, 1-I/274, April 9, 1921.

35. Robert E. Cushman, *The Independent Regulatory Commissions* (New York: Oxford University Press, 1941), pp. 302–303.

36. U.S. Congress, *Hearings on Appropriations, 1927*, p. 40.

37. Cushman, p. 316.

38. Schmeckebier, *The Federal Radio Commission*, p. 20.

39. *New York Times*, April 17, 1927, VIII, 22:1.

40. Donald G. Godfrey and Val E. Limburg. *Historical Dictionary of American Radio* (Westport: Greenwood Press, 1998), p. 88.

41. Obituary notice, *Washington Evening Star*, March 24, 1965, Smithsonian Institution, Division of Electricity Library, Washington, D.C.

42. Cochrane, p. 289.

43. *Broadcasting*, July 6, 1942, p. 49.

44. U.S. Congress, Committee on Commerce, *Appointments to the Regulatory Agencies: The Federal Communications Commission and the Federal Trade Commission (1949–1974)* April 1976, p. 21.

45. Interview with George Sterling, November 15, 1968.

46. *Supra.*, p. 63.

47. U.S. Congress, Senate, Committee on Interstate Commerce, *Nomination of C. M. Jansky, Jr., and Arthur Batcheller as Members of the Federal Radio Commission*, February 18, 1929, p. 28.

48. C. M. Jansky, Jr., "Herbert Hoover's Contribution to Broadcasting," *Journal of Broadcasting* (vol. I, Summer 1956-57), pp. 244, 249.

49. Garvey, p. 85.

50. Alfred Balk, "In Radio's Past, a Hint of the Internet's Future," *New York Times*, August 16, 1998, Business section, p. 14.

51. Memorandum of RCA on First Radio Conference, HHPL, 1-I/539, April 17, 1922, p. 3.

52. Head, *Broadcasting in America*, p. 129.

53. Barnouw, *A Tower in Babel*, p. 178.

54. Schmeckebier, p. 6.

55. Archer, *History of Radio to 1926*, p. 249.

56. Walter B. Emery, *Broadcasting and Government: Responsibilities and Regulations* (East Lansing: Michigan State University Press, 1961), p. 20.

57. Head, p. 131.

58. Barnouw, pp. 195–199.

59. Head, p. 132.

60. Emery, p. 20.

61. Edgar E. Willis, "The History of Radio," *The Bulletin of the National Association of Secondary School Principals* (vol. 50, no. 312, October 1966), pp. 5, 6.

62. Donald R. Le Duc and Thomas A. McCain, "The Federal Radio Commission in Federal Court: Origins of Broadcast Regulatory Doctrines," *Journal of Broadcasting*, vol. 14, no. 4 (Fall 1970), p. 409.

63. U.S. Government Printing Office, *Hoover Commission Task Force on Regulatory Commission* (January 1949), p. 94.

64. *Broadcasting* (October 26, 1964), p. 80.

65. *Ibid.*

66. Hugh G. J. Aitken. "Allocating the Spectrum: The Origins of Radio Regulation," *Technology and Culture* (vol. 35, 1994), pp. 686–716.

67. Streeter. "Selling the Air," pp. 91–115.

BIBLIOGRAPHY

Books

Allen, Frederick Lewis. *Since Yesterday*. New York: Bantam Books, 1965.
_____. *The Big Change*. New York: Bantam Books, 1965.
_____. *Only Yesterday*. New York: Harper & Row, 1964.
Archer, Gleason Leonard. *History of Radio to 1926*. New York: American Historical Society, 1938.
Banning, William P. *Commercial Broadcasting Pioneer, the WEAF Experiment 1922–1926*. Cambridge: Harvard University Press, 1946.
Barnouw, Erik. *A Tower in Babel: A History of Broadcasting in the United States to 1933*. Volume I. New York: Oxford University Press, 1966.
Bernstein, Marver H. *Regulating Business by Independent Commission*. Princeton: Princeton University Press, 1966.
Brandes, Joseph. *Herbert Hoover and Economic Diplomacy*. Pittsburgh: University of Pittsburgh Press, 1962.
Chase, Francis, Jr. *Sound and Fury: An Informal History of Broadcasting*. New York: Harper & Row, 1942.
Cochrane, Rexmond C. *Measures for Progress: A History of the National Bureau of Standards*. Washington, D.C.: Department of Commerce, 1966.
Coons, John E. *Freedom and Responsibility in Broadcasting*. Evanston, Illinois: Northwestern University Press, 1961.
Cushman, Robert E. *The Independent Regulatory Commissions*. New York: Oxford University Press, 1941.
Davis, Stephen B. *The Law of Radio Communication*. New York: McGraw-Hill Book Company, 1927.
de Forest, Lee. *Father of Radio*. Chicago: Wilcox-Follett, 1950.

Douglas, Susan J. *Inventing American Broadcasting, 1899–1922*. Baltimore: The Johns Hopkins University Press, 1987.

Dunlap, Orrin E., Jr. *Radio and Television Almanac*. New York: Harper & Brothers, 1951.

Emery, Walter B. *Broadcasting and Government: Responsibilities and Regulations*. East Lansing: Michigan State University Press, 1961.

Field, Charles K. *The Story of Cheerio*. New York: Garden City Publishing Company, 1937.

Godfrey, Donald G., and Val E. Limburg. *Historical Dictionary of American Radio*. Westport: Greenwood Press, 1998.

Goldsmith, Alfred N., and Austin C. Lescarboura. *This Thing Called Broadcasting*. New York: Henry Holt, 1930.

Gross, Gerald C., and James M. Herring. *Telecommunications: Economics and Regulation*. New York: McGraw-Hill Book Company, 1936.

Head, Sydney W. *Broadcasting in America*. Boston: Houghton-Mifflin, 1956.

Hicks, John D. *The Republican Ascendancy, 1921–1933*. New York: Harper, 1960.

Hoover, Herbert C. *The Address Upon the American Road*. New York: D. Van Nostrand Company, 1922.

_____. *American Individualism*. Garden City: Doubleday, Doran and Company, 1922.

_____. *Memoirs; Volumes I and II*. New York: Macmillan, 1951–52.

Howeth, Linwood S. *History of Communications—Electronics in the United States Navy*. Washington, D.C.: U.S. Government Printing Office, 1963.

Irwin, Will. *Herbert Hoover: A Reminiscent Biography*. New York: The Century Company, 1928.

Jome, Hiram L. *Economics of the Radio Industry*. New York: A. W. Shaw Company, 1925.

Landry, Robert J. *This Fascinating Radio Business*. Indianapolis: Bobbs-Merrill Company, 1946.

Leighton, Isabel (ed.). *The Aspirin Age: 1919–1941*. New York: Simon and Schuster, 1949.

Lord, Walter. *A Night to Remember*. New York: Henry Holt, 1955.

Lyons, Eugene. *The Herbert Hoover Story*. Washington, D.C.: Human Events Press, 1959.

Maclaurin, W. Rupert. *Invention and Innovation in the Radio Industry*. New York: Macmillan, 1949.

Malin, James C. *The United States After the World War*. Boston: Ginn and Company, 1930.

Perry, John. *The Story of Standards*. New York: Funk and Wagnalls, 1955.

Schmeckebier, Laurence F. *The Federal Radio Commission: Its History, Activities and Organization*. Washington, D.C.: The Brookings Institution, 1932.

Schubert, Paul. *The Electric Word: The Rise of Radio*. New York: Macmillan, 1928.

Slate, Sam J., and Joe Cook. *It Sounds Impossible*. New York: Macmillan, 1963.

Slosson, Preston W. *The Great Crusade and After: 1914–1928*. New York: Macmillan, 1930.

Sterling, Christopher H., and John M. Kittross. *Stay Tuned: A Concise History of American Broadcasting*. Second edition. Belmont, California: Wadsworth Publishing, 1990.

Strauss, Lewis L. *Men and Decisions*. Garden City: Doubleday and Company, 1962.

Swanberg, W. A. *Citizen Hearst*. New York: Scribner & Sons, 1961.

Villard, Oswald Garrison. *Prophets: True and False*. New York: Alfred A. Knopf, 1928.

Weber, Gustavus A. *The Bureau of Standards: Its History, Activities, and Organization*. Baltimore: The Johns Hopkins University Press, 1925.

Wilbur, Ray L., and Arthur M. Hyde, *The Hoover Policies*. New York: C. Scribner's Sons, 1937.

Wolfe, Harold. *Herbert Hoover: Public Servant and Leader of the Loyal Opposition*. New York: Exposition Press, 1956.

Articles and Periodicals

Aitken, Hugh G. J. "Allocating the Spectrum: The Origins of Radio Regulation." *Technology and Culture* (Vol. 35, 1994).

Benjamin, Louise M. "In Search of the Sarnoff 'Radio Music Box' Memo." *Journal of Broadcasting and Electronic Media* (Vol. 37, No. 3, Summer 1993).

_____. "Working It Out Together: Radio Policy from Hoover to the Radio Act of 1927." *Journal of Broadcasting and Electronic Media* (Vol. 42, No. 2, Spring 1998).

Broadcasting. (1964–present).

Davis, Stephen B. "The Law of the Air." *The Radio Industry—The Story of Its Development* (London: A. W. Shaw Company, 1928).

Degler, Carl N. "The Ordeal of Herbert Hoover." Bobbs-Merrill reprint series, History, No. H-52; from *The Yale Review* (Vol. LII, No. 4, Summer 1963).

Garvey, Daniel E. "Secretary Hoover and the Quest for Broadcast Regulation." *Journalism History* (Vol. 3, No. 3, Autumn 1976).

Godfrey, Donald G., and Val E. Limburg. "The Rogue Elephant of Radio Legislation: Senator William E. Borah." *Journalism Quarterly* (Vol. 67, 1990).

Hazlett, Thomas W. "The Rationality of U.S. Regulation of the Broadcast Spectrum." *Journal of Law and Economics* (Vol. 33, No. 1, April 1990).

Holt, Darrell. "The Origin of 'Public Interest' in Broadcasting." *Educational Broadcasting Review* (October 1967).

Jansky, C. M., Jr. "Herbert Hoover's Contribution to Broadcasting." *Journal of Broadcasting* (Vol. I, Summer 1956-57).

Le Duc, Donald R., and Thomas A. McCain. "The Federal Radio Commission in Federal Court: Origins of Broadcast Regulatory Doctrines." *Journal of Broadcasting* (Vol. 14, No. 4, Fall 1970).

McChesney, Robert W. "The Battle for the U.S. Airwaves, 1928–1935." *Journal of Communication* (Vol. 40, No. 4, Autumn 1990).

_____. "Free Speech and Democracy! Louis G. Caldwell, the American Bar Association and the Debate Over the Free Speech Implications of Broadcast Regulation, 1928–1938." *The American Journal of Legal History* (Vol. 35, 1991).

National Magazine. "The Department of Commerce Considers Interference and Other Problems in Radio." (Vol. 52, March, 1924).

New York Times (1920–present).

Radio Broadcast (1920–1928).

Radio News (1921–1925).

Stashower, Daniel. "A Dreamer Who Made Us Fall in Love with the Future." *Smithsonian* (August 1990).

Streeter, Thomas. "Selling the Air: Property and the Politics of US Commercial broadcasting." *Media, Culture & Society* (Vol. 16, 1994).

Webster, E. M. "The Interdepartmental Radio Advisory Committee." Proceedings of the Institute of Radio Engineers (I.R.E.) (August 1945).

Willis, Edgar E. "The History of Radio." *The Bulletin of the National Association of Secondary School Principals* (Vol. 50, No. 312, October, 1966).

"Yankee Internationalist." *Time* (January 13, 1967).

Public Documents

Federal Communications Commission. *Authority of the Federal Communications Commission with Respect to the Programming of Radio and Television Stations.* FCC Mimeo No. 49935 (September 27, 1957).

Federal Communications Commission. Second Interim Report by the Office of Network Study. *Television Network Program Procurement, Part II.* Docket No. 12782 (1965).

Federal Radio Commission. *Annual Report of the Federal Radio Commission for Fiscal Year 1927* (1927).

Udell, Gilman G. *Radio Laws of the United States.* Washington, D.C.: U.S. Government Printing Office (1962).

U.S. Congress. Committee on Commerce. *Appointments to the Regulatory Agencies: The Federal Communications Commission and the Federal Trade Commission (1949–1974)* (April 1976).

U.S. Congress. House. Committee on the Merchant Marine and Fisheries. *Hearings on H. R. 11964: To Amend the Radio Act of 1912* (67th Congress, 4th Session, January 2–3, 1923).

U.S. Congress. House. *Hearings Before the Committee on the Merchant Marine and Fisheries, on H. R. 7357, to Regulate Radio Communications* (68th Congress, 1st Session, March 11–14, 1924).

U.S. Congress. House. Committee on the Merchant Marine and Fisheries. *Hearings on H. R. 5589: To Regulate Radio Communications* (69th Congress, 1st Session, January 6, 7, 14 and 15, 1926).

U.S. Congress. House. *Report of the Federal Trade Commission on the Radio Industry*. In response to House Resolution 548, 67th Congress, 4th Session. Submitted December 1, 1923.

U.S. Congress. House. Subcommittee of House Committee on Appropriations. *Hearings on Legislative, Executive, Judicial Appropriation Bill, 1922* (December 20, 1920).

U.S. Congress. House. Subcommittee of House Committee on Appropriations. *Miscellaneous Hearings on Appropriations, 1921* (April 22, 1921).

U.S. Congress. House. Subcommittee of House Committee on Appropriations. *Second Deficiency Appropriation Bill, 1925* (68th Congress, 2nd Session, February 10, 1925).

U.S. Congress. House. Subcommittee of House Committee on Appropriations. *Appropriations, Department of Commerce, 1927* (69th Congress, 1st Session, January 25, 1926).

U.S. Congress. House. Subcommittee of House Committee on Appropriations. *Appropriations, Department of Commerce, 1928* (1927).

U.S. Congress. Senate. *Hearings Before the Committee on Interstate Commerce* (71st Congress, 1st Session, May 24, 1929).

U.S. Congress. Senate. Committee on Interstate Commerce. *Nomination of C. M Jansky, Jr., and Arthur Batcheller as Members of the Federal Radio Commission* (February 18, 1929).

U.S. Department of Commerce. *Annual Reports of the Secretary of Commerce* (1921–1928).

U.S. Department of Commerce. *Historical Statistics of the United States: Colonial Times to 1957* (1961).

U.S. Department of Commerce. *Minutes of Open Meetings of the Department of Commerce Conference on Radio Telephony*. First National Radio Conference (February 27–28, 1922).

U.S. Department of Commerce. *Proceedings of the Third National Radio Conference* (October 6–10, 1924).

U.S. Department of Commerce. *Proceedings of the Fourth National Radio Conference and Recommendations for Regulation of Radio* (November 9–11, 1925).

U.S. Department of Commerce. *Radio Instruments and Measurements*. Circular 74, First printing (March 1918).

U.S. Department of Commerce. Bureau of Navigation. *Radio Service Bulletin* (1921–1927).

U.S. Department of Justice. *Radio Communication—Issuance of Licenses.* Opinions of the Attorney General (Vol. 29, November 22, 1912), pp. 579–583.

U.S. Department of Justice. *Federal Regulations of Radio Broadcasting.* Opinions of the Attorney General (Vol. 35, 1926).

U.S. Government Printing Office. *Official Register of the United States* (1926).

U.S. Government Printing Office. *Hoover Commission Task Force on Regulatory Commissions* (January 1949).

Unpublished Material

Fowler, Paul C. "The Formation of Public Policy for Commercial Broadcasting by the Federal Communications Commission." Unpublished Ph.D. dissertation. Indiana University (1956).

Harrison, Belle C. "The History of Radio in the U.S." Unpublished master's thesis. University of Southern California (1934).

Hettinger, Herman S. "The Use of Radio Broadcasting as an Advertiser in the United States." Unpublished Ph.D. dissertation. University of Chicago (1933).

Jarvis, Lynville W. "Herbert C. Hoover: A Factor in Broadcast Legislation." Unpublished master's thesis. University of Alabama (1963).

Killough, James A. "Federal Regulation of Radio and Television Broadcasting." Unpublished Ph.D. dissertation. University of Pennsylvania (1934).

Lichty, Lawrence W. "The Nation's Station: A History of Radio Station WLW." Unpublished Ph.D. dissertation. The Ohio State University (1964).

MacQuiney, Donald R. "Administrative Frequency Control." Unpublished Ph.D. dissertation. American University (1956).

Magruder, Jane N. "Development of the Concept of Public Interest as It Applies to Radio and Television Programming." Unpublished Ph.D. dissertation. The Ohio State University (1960).

McCandless, T. H. "Federal Control of Radio to 1933." Unpublished Ph.D. dissertation. University of Southern California (1945).

McMahon, Robert S. "Federal Regulation of the Radio Television Broadcast Industry in the United States, 1927–1959 with Special Reference to the Establishment and Operation of Workable Administration Standards." Unpublished Ph.D. dissertation. The Ohio State University (1960).

Nelson, Clair E. "The Image of Herbert Hoover as Reflected in the American Press." Unpublished Ph.D. dissertation. Stanford University (1956).

Olson, Paul R. "The Regulation of Radio Broadcasting in the United States." Unpublished Ph.D. dissertation. University of Iowa (1931).

Sivowitch, Elliot N. "A History of Radio Spectrum Allocation in the United States, 1912–1926." Unpublished master's thesis. Syracuse University (1954).

Straub, Duane G. "The Role of Secretary of Commerce Herbert Hoover in the Development of Early Radio Regulation." Unpublished master's thesis. Michigan State University (1964).

Weeks, Lewis E. "Order Out of Chaos: The Formative Years of American Broadcasting, 1920–1927." Unpublished Ph.D. dissertation. Michigan State University (1962).

White, Melvin R. "History of Radio Regulation Affecting Radio Program Policy." Unpublished Ph.D. dissertation. University of Wisconsin (1948).

Williford, Imogene. "The Development of Radio Regulation." Unpublished master's thesis. American University (1933).

Libraries

Herbert C. Hoover Presidential Library. West Branch, Iowa.

National Archives. Washington, D.C.

Smithsonian Institution. Division of Electricity. Washington, D.C.

Wisconsin State Historical Society. Mass Communications Division. Madison, Wisconsin.

Interviews

Broadcast Pioneers History Project. "Interview with Senator C. C. Dill" (July 21, 1964).

Kolster, Charles C. Telephone interview (May 25, 1968).

Oral History Project of Columbia University. New York. "Interview with Herbert C. Hoover" (November 14, 1950).

Sterling, George. Telephone interview (April 15, 1968).

Turner, George. Telephone interview (April 11, 1968).

Weeks, Lewis E. "Interview with Herbert C. Hoover" (November 3, 1961). Copy provided by Mr. Weeks.

Other Sources

History of Broadcasting and KDKA Radio. Pittsburgh: Westinghouse Public Relations Department, KDKA Radio (1966).

Letter from Herbert Hoover, Jr. (April 11, 1966).

INDEX

263